The **Two Faces** of **Political Apathy**

The **Two Faces** of **Political Apathy**

Tom DeLuca

**Temple University
Press**

Nothing is more practical
than a good theory.
—a homeless New Yorker

**To my parents and
my brother**

Temple University Press
Philadelphia 19122
Copyright © 1995 by Temple University
All rights reserved
Published 1995
Printed in the United States of America

⊗ The paper used in this book
meets the requirements
of the American National Standard
for Information Sciences—Permanence
of Paper for Printed Library Materials,
ANSI Z39.48-1984

Library of Congress Cataloging-in-Publication Data

DeLuca, Tom, 1946–
    The two faces of political apathy / Tom DeLuca.
        p.   cm.
    Includes bibliographical references and index.
    ISBN 1-56639-314-0 (case).—ISBN 1-56639-315-9 (paper)
    1. Political participation—United States.   2. Apathy—United
States.   3. Democracy—United States.   I. Title.
JK1764.D47   1995
324.6'3'0973—dc20   94-48181

Contents

Part III
Overcoming Apathy   171

Preface

Democracy. It is at the heart of American character, the drum major of American history. Yet, it is not discussed in any presidential election, never edges out the nightly murder report on the evening news, usually isn't part of parlor chatter, or barroom talk. It is the most important issue facing American politics today.

I write this book as a challenge, to myself, to the public, to political leaders, and to the profession of political science, to make democracy and the severe problems of nonparticipation central political issues today. That as democrats we challenge ourselves, citizens and thinkers, citizens as thinkers, to return to the root of democracy—and the root is *rule by the people*—by asking ourselves sharp questions:

What do we mean by democracy, how much are we really committed to it, what are we willing to do to bring it more fully about? Should we rule ourselves, or are we better off letting others—business leaders, experts, TV commentators, bankers, special interests—make the important decisions for us? As Americans, we have the freedom to ask these questions. As average Americans, we may not have the power to implement the answers we find.

I hope to make a small contribution to this discussion in three ways. First and foremost, this book is a critique of political analysis, how it has been applied to the problem of nonparticipation within democratic theory—indeed, whether nonparticipation has been considered a serious enough problem at all. Second, it suggests alternative theoretical and political directions that reveal nonparticipation to be a severe problem and important issue, and that clarify those things we need to think through, decisions we need to make, actions we need to take, to make American democracy come alive. And so, third, it makes a friendly but firm challenge to each of us, and to all of us as a people and a nation, to consider these issues, to ask some hard questions, to decide what we really think about democracy.

Political apathy is central to this work and to this challenge, for how we understand it foreshadows our decision, stalks it from ahead. Perhaps this is too academic a book, but that's not the subject's fault. For, in part, the book is addressed to the profession of political science, which for too long has too often encouraged the belief that half-hearted demi-democracy is all we can really expect—in the way we have explained nonparticipation in politics, by the way we have looked mainly to the appearance of apathy as sufficient explanation. As political scientists, we need to challenge ourselves.

But the question—Why do so few participate?—is not only for professionals. It is deeply political. It gets to the heart of the matter, peels down to the core. Thinking through an answer, hopefully with some professionalism, is a matter for all of us.

If people choose freely and in great numbers not to participate in politics, this is powerful evidence that the ideal of democracy needs to be tempered, is unrealistic, and out of character with human nature at this point in history. If too many people are apathetic, this seems to put the burden of proof on those who call for more participatory zeal and public interest in the face of natural indifference.

What if circumstances, practices, disadvantages, institutions, even beliefs we hold, compromise our democratic ideals and quietly conspire to render us passive? What if apathy is not freely chosen, the problem is not all us? What if what appears as apathy is really a political attitude of another kind? What if apathy has two faces?

Acknowledgments

All books are autobiographies and all lives have many authors. I want to thank my mother and father, Katherine and Thomas DeLuca, for teaching me a sense of justice, and my brother, Bob, for adding a sense of humor. I dedicate this book to them. I want to pay special thanks also to all my good friends, especially Cookie, Alan, Kathy, Norma, Robin, Jim, Mike, Carol, Margie, Jack, Jeff, Eliza, Joan, and Al for always standing by. And to my grandparents, who are always with me.

John Buell, a fine political theorist and good friend, has my gratitude for reading the manuscript and making excellent suggestions on how to improve it. His modest but clear voice speaks for a perceptive, encyclopedic mind that benefits all who listen.

An eminent theorist and fine teacher, Bill Connolly read a very early draft of this work and encouraged me to consider revising and publishing it. More important, he inspired me through his ideas, teaching, and charisma. He is always two steps ahead of me in theory (his real ambition is to do the same on the basketball court).

I want to thank Fordham University for granting me a summer fellowship in 1993, which enabled me to draft Part I of this work. I especially want to thank my colleagues in political science, Susan Beck, Ralph Meyer, Susan Berger, and Nicole Fermon; the dean of the college, Ed Bristow; the chair of social science, Barry Goldberg; and my colleague in anthropology, Stewart Guthrie, for their advice, counsel, support, and patience. John Roche, Ray Seidelman, Bob Higgins, Donald Chankin, and Peter Cocks read selective portions, and I benefited from their advice, as well as from Bruce Bernstein's consultation on statistics, and Hilde Jenssen's help with graphics. My office neighbors in the 921 "hood," Giuseppe, Lenny, and Susan, and my computer neighbors, Janis, Shapoor, and Mark, gave me support, loaned me office space, made way at the printer, or told me jokes. David Malcolm patiently helped make me semi-WordPerfect literate. Bob Wasserman encouraged me in a way I needed most, as did Lisa Freeman and David Roll. Brian and all my friends at "The Kettle" were always there for support, as were those at Rocco's, and Bleecker St. Pastry, especially Monica, Carmen, Katia, Joe, and Prudence. My old friends Tom, Peggy, and Karen helped out early on when writing was most difficult. Many years ago at Brooklyn College, David Abbott helped me believe I could learn something about politics.

Anne Mannion, my former division chair and present friend, has my very special thanks for always being there. Jerry Quinn, our dean, was tragically taken from us much too young, but he helped make this work possible by supporting my re-entry into academic work.

Doris Braendel, my editor, deserves hearty thanks for unflagging patience, good humor, and professionalism. David Bartlett and the staff of Temple University Press especially deserve mention for getting the job done and doing it well. Susan Joseph, Mary McDonald, and Barbara Hults also provided valuable technical assistance.

Finally, all my students at Fordham University, I want to thank you for being understanding, for caring, and giving me the benefit of your own political virtue and wisdom. And Kristine Dimitrova and Paul Wells have my special gratitude for putting their own work aside to help get me through.

These are the people that made this book possible.

⌑ Introduction

The Politics of Nonparticipation

The Virtues of Apathy

In their influential 1954 book, *Voting*, Bernard Berelson, Paul Lazarsfeld, and William McPhee made the startling claim that political apathy is good for democracy. How could "a mass democracy work," they ask, "if all the people were deeply involved in politics? Lack of interest by some people is not without its benefits."[1]

In the 1970s and 1980s, Samuel Huntington, the eminent former president of the American Political Science Association, articulated a modern elaboration of Berelson's claim. Although more self-conscious about the problematic nature of apathy within democracy, Huntington writes,

> the effective operation of a democratic political system usually requires some measure of apathy and noninvolvement on the part of some individuals and groups. . . . In itself, this marginality on the part of some groups is inherently undemocratic, but it has also been one of the factors which has enabled democracy to function effectively.[2]

George Will speaks more plainly in a 1983 essay in *Newsweek*. Using as evidence the fact that the Nazis were brought to power in 1933 in an election in which turnout hit nearly 89 percent, he argues that high rates of participation may actually indicate lack of stability. Low rates, therefore, may be explained by the health and maturity of a political order.[3]

In a 1990 essay for *Time* magazine, the journalist Charles Krauthammer calls low turnout "a leading indicator of contentment," reminding one of political scientist Heinz Eulau's comment, thirty-five years before, that apathy indicated the "politics of happiness."[4] Nonvoting, he suggests, makes "more room for the things that really count: science, art, religion, family and play."[5]

In the 1993 edition of their very influential textbook, *The Irony of Democracy*, Thomas Dye and Harmon Zeigler argue that "Democracy is government 'by the people,' but the survival of democracy rests on the shoulders of elites. This is the irony of democracy: Elites must govern wisely if government 'by the people' is to survive."[6] But because the "masses are authoritarian,

1

intolerant, anti-intellectual, nativistic, alienated, hateful, and violent," one important responsibility that falls to the "enlightened elite" is to protect democracy by formulating policies that—while "public-regarding"—do not stir the public out of its natural (and rational) political indifference.[7]

The conclusions of Berelson, Lazarsfeld, and McPhee, Huntington, Will, Krauthammer, Eulau, and Dye and Zeigler, strike an odd tone in the democratic ear, but they resonate cleanly within the outlook on democracy held historically by many political elites, including political theorists and writers. Nor should this be surprising.

The history of American democracy and political thought is, in part, a history of the fear of democracy. Indeed, as the concept *democracy* metamorphosed from a term of disapprobation to an imprimatur sought by all, some writers increasingly equated and confused democracy with a distilled conflation of republicanism and liberalism.

Historically, there has been a contest over the very meaning of democracy. Theoretically, the debate has been about what are the proper criteria for a democratic political system. Politically, the struggle has been over whom to include, how much political equality to countenance, how much and what kind of participation to allow, and most essentially, how much power to disperse.

One of its terrains is explaining nonparticipation in politics, a place where evidence is gathered and judgments are made as to whether a polity deserves to be called a *democracy*. This book is first of all an effort to uncover historical, philosophical, and political roots of nonparticipation in politics, as well as the way it has been explained. Second, it analyzes, compares, and critiques representative classic models through which nonparticipation has been and is explained. Finally, it suggests a way to approach the problems of nonparticipation and political apathy that also serves to overcome both.

Inequality and Democracy

Today almost all Americans would agree that until the enforcement of the Voting Rights Act of 1965, or the passage of the Nineteenth Amendment in 1920, the United States did not fully meet one basic criterion of democracy: the right of all adult citizens to participate in the political process. Just as Susan B. Anthony was arrested for trying to register to vote in Rochester, New York, 1872, Martin Luther King Jr. was arrested for trying to register voters in Selma, Alabama, in 1965. Each event, for its time, marked reasons why certain classes of Americans did not vote. But the reasons given from the top down differed sharply from those of the bottom up.

The nineteenth-century "gentleman" who opposed suffrage for women and the twentieth-century segregationist who opposed it for African-American men and women both would use rationales similar to those democratic

Athens used to refuse slaves, women, and people of non-Athenian birth (or *metics*) citizenship—the excluded did not meet the criteria of responsible adult citizens. For Anthony and King, these criteria themselves were based on sexist and racist attitudes, and consequently a stunted view of citizenship embodied in disenfranchising laws, institutions, and practices, all of which were incompatible with real democracy.

In a more subtle but equally compelling way, explanations of nonparticipation given by political scientists, journalists, and other students of politics over the past half-century have also had as a backdrop their own conceptions of what democracy means.

In the 1993 edition of his widely used text, *The American Polity*, Everett Carll Ladd reports, "Today there is also concern over the low and somewhat diminished level of voter turnout in the United States."[8] He states that "millions of Americans take their job of assessing candidates very seriously. It must be acknowledged, however, that other millions stand on the sidelines, deciding not to vote."[9] Although those who "stand on the sidelines," he implies, do so freely if irresponsibly, he continues that "people of high socioeconomic status generally vote at a much higher rate than those of low status," and that turnout is significantly lower in the United States than virtually all other democracies.[10] Now his conclusion:

> This is partly because the United States has so many elections that it is hard for any one to seem a special event. The low turnout is also partly a response to a system where political stresses have been relatively manageable. The perceived cost of not voting, in short, has not been nearly as high in the United States as in most other democracies.[11]

Not only doesn't he explain adequately why the "cost of not voting" should be lower here than in Europe and Japan, but why it should be lowest among our poorest citizens. Inexplicably, the class differentials that he reports don't find their way into his concluding summary.

In *Equality in America*, Sidney Verba and Gary R. Orren report that

> the United States ranks among the most open and participatory of modern democracies when it comes to politics and among the least egalitarian when it comes to economic matters. The nation embodies democratic polity and capitalist economy at their fullest![12]

In *The Politics of Rich and Poor*, Kevin Phillips also recounts that by "several measurements, the United States in the late twentieth century led all other major industrial countries in the gap dividing the upper fifth of the population from the lower—in the disparity between top and bottom." From the New Deal on, these gaps have not lessened and have been consistent and enduring features of the socioeconomic landscape. In fact, during the Reagan presidency, he suggests, the disparity grew even wider: in the years 1977 to

1988, those in the bottom 10 percent of family income lost an average of 14.8 percent (a loss of $609) in constant (1987) dollars, while the top 1 percent gained 49.8 percent (an annual increase for them of $134,513). Overall, the bottom 80 percent lost some ground. Looked at over time, he says, the average American was no better off than twenty-five years before, as after-tax real median family income, with some ups and downs, remained stagnant since 1973. By the middle of Reagan's second term, the top 1/2 percent of the population, Phillips argues, "had never been richer."[13]

In spite of wider gaps of income and wealth, Verba and Orren note, the United States ranks consistently at or near the bottom of western nations in using government to mitigate inequality, measured by social insurance coverage, public income maintenance as a percent of gross domestic product, percent of gross national product spent on Social Security, social transfers, and others. Regarding "the extent to which taxes reduce inequality," for example, "U.S. policy produces little redistribution, and the United States ranks near the bottom of the industrial nations." And though the United States adopted its Medicare and Medicaid programs in 1965, undemocratic Prussia committed itself to medical care in 1883 and "most other industrialized democracies had followed suit."

They find one major exception. The United States ranks first in per capita expenditure for education and first in the percentage of people that get a higher education—not surprising, they suggest, since the more educated people are, the more likely they are to participate. Therefore, while education is a "main channel for upward mobility," actually it turns out "it is a source of economic inequality rather than equality." Verba and Orren conclude, the United States is "a nation which tolerates, even celebrates, economic hierarchy."

But is it possible for a "democratic polity at its fullest" to reside, as Verba and Orren claim, in such an inegalitarian economic order, and one that does not address inequality effectively through democratically elected governments at that?

Who Doesn't Govern?

Comparing the United States to other democracies, Verba and Orren themselves report:

> Although the United States ranks first in the diffusion of political participation, having a much higher proportion of moderately active citizens than in comparable nations, it also ranks first or second in the correlation between participation and socioeconomic status. . . . In other words, there are proportionately fewer activists in other nations, but they represent a wider variety of income and educational levels. In the United States,

activists come disproportionately from the better educated and more affluent.[14]

Let's consider nonvoting. In his 1992 analysis, *The Disappearing American Voter*, Ruy Teixeira reports that, of twenty industrial democracies, the United States ranks nineteenth in voting turnout, about 53 percent in presidential years, well below eighteenth-ranking Japan at 68 percent, and number one Belgium at 94 percent, during comparable elections. Moreover, by 1988, turnout had declined to the lowest point since 1924, a drop of 13 percent since 1960.[15]

Within the United States, nonvoting is sharply skewed by education, occupation, class, age,[16] and to some degree by race and gender. While drops in turnout since 1960 were across all demographic groups, in 1988, 77.6 percent of people with college degrees or more reported voting, while only 36.7 percent of those with eight years of school or less did so; 75.7 percent of professional-technical workers voted, while 38.2 percent of laborers did; the highest sixth in income voted at a rate of 74.1 percent, while the lowest at 40.7 percent; whites at 61.8 percent, African-Americans at 52.1 percent, and Latinos (citizens only) at 48 percent.[17] According to M. Margaret Conway, while controlling for educational level and region reduces black-white turnout differentials, black citizens "are nevertheless less likely to vote than are white citizens of the same socioeconomic status." Lawrence Bobo and Franklin D. Gilliam Jr., however, "find that blacks generally participate at the same rate as whites" when socioeconomic status is controlled for.[18] Conway also suggests that while turnout disparities between men and women are narrowing—and largely disappear when age and level of education are held constant—they remain in the 5–10 percent range. Norman R. Luttbeg and Michael M. Gant report somewhat different findings: even without controlling for socioeconomic status, they claim, women actually now vote at a slightly higher rate than do men—2.1 percent higher, for example, in the 1992 presidential election.[19]

According to Frances Fox Piven and Richard Cloward, in Europe, economic class and education are not themselves significant determinants in voting turnout levels. Nor were they in the United States in the nineteenth century, when educational levels were lower while turnout of eligible voters, often reaching near 80 percent, soared way beyond what would become the best twentieth-century levels. While other "democracies have many people with low levels of education and income . . . nowhere are these demographic factors so dramatically associated with high rates of nonvoting as they are in the United States." Theories that focus on individual attributes, therefore, are "pernicious as well as wrong," they charge, preventing "popular understanding of institutional barriers to voting and falsely point the finger of blame at individuals." Legal and administrative barriers, party mobilizing strategies, party and candidate ideological appeals, all impinge less on the well-off and well-educated than they do on the poor and uneducated. . . . [P]eople with lower levels of education vote less in the United States because the political system tends to isolate them, and not because less education is an inherent impediment to voting. *Apathy and lack of political skill are a consequence, not a cause*, of the party structure and political culture. . . . The political system determines whether participation is predicated on class-related resources and attitudes.[20]

As Verba and Orren point out, while voting participation is extremely low, in one way America is actually more participatory than other democracies. Here, there are extensive networks of activist organizations; consequently those who participate may do so intensely and in a variety of ways. But activists differ in class and educational background from nonactivists, and there are various magnitudes of difference based on gender, race, and ethnicity, since women, African-Americans, and Latinos participate less. For example, Lawrence Bobo and Franklin D. Gilliam Jr. found on eight of fifteen measures of participation, including voting, donating money and working in campaigns, and contacting officials, a statistical difference between black and white sociopolitical participation.[21] For Latinos, the problem is compounded by language and/or recent immigration. For all three, there is the question of how they will be received should they try to influence political events for which white men are still overwhelmingly the gatekeepers, with these strata greatly underrepresented in elected offices.[22]

As Teixeira suggests, the "needs and interests" of "high-impact" activists—those who contact officials, are involved in community organizations, contribute to campaigns, and so on—"differ ever more sharply from those of the rest of the population." And what he calls "special interest" activity is on the rise, a form of participation that attempts "to influence public policy directly through extensive personal contacts and the dispensation of favors." That kind of participation needs to be democratically balanced. Teixeira concludes, "Widespread nonvoting makes it less likely that electoral participation by ordinary citizens will be that counterweight."[23]

Philip Green cautions, however, that "the great democratic revolutions of Eastern Europe" suggest that we need to look beyond the formal institutional processes of liberal democracies. Otherwise, we miss a critical face of democracy itself, in which people in their search for greater equality and more justice engage in direct action: "The great moments of *this* democratic process are strikes, demonstrations, marches, occupations, even funerals." Democracy, in his view, is better understood "as a series of moments: moments of popular insurgency and direct action, of unmediated politics." The "real history of democracy" is "the history of popular struggle,"[24] he concludes.

Two questions emerge. First, what is to count as legitimate democratic political participation? Second, does this question gain added legitimacy if important inequalities do exist within institutional political practices? This leads precisely to the moral question posed to democracy by the civil rights movement: How do we decide whether direct action or institutional political practices fall within the purview of what we want to consider democratic and/ or appropriate—most especially when the majority view is clearly represented and held to be immoral by a minority?

Taken together, these questions and these studies point to several important conclusions. First, American democracy is distinct in several ways from other democratic nations. Given the nature of political development, institutions, and electoral laws, socioeconomic class and educational disadvantages here have a major impact in depressing voting turnout. Second, for all people, regardless of class or education, it seems harder to get to the polls in the United States than in other democracies in spite of generally more positive attitudes here toward government. Third, there are relatively large numbers of politically active people here. Still, U.S. political participation and the setting of the political agenda has an oligarchical quality in which, like Europe and Japan, elites have disproportionate influence; but unlike them, the "democratic counterweight" of voting is lighter. Finally, in all settings, what type of political participation will truly reveal the popular will is itself a political question.

Explaining Nonparticipation

The investigation of nonparticipation, then, is an exploration of how power is implicated in the relationship between nonparticipants and their act of not participating. Does a person withdraw from politics voluntarily, freely consenting not to participate because he or she is simply not interested? Have unfair voter eligibility requirements disenfranchised a particular race? Do cumbersome registration requirements make withdrawal more likely by less educated citizens? Does either of the two main political parties represent concerns that speak to the needs of nonparticipants? If not, are there other political avenues open to them? What, in fact, is genuine political participation?

Are nonparticipants unable to articulate grievances as political issues because there are no political ideas, forums, or aggregating institutions to help give form to their deepest troubles? Do the present political structure and its elites socialize and perhaps manipulate nonparticipants into a posture of apathy?

Questions like these are the natural backdrop as we explain nonparticipation. They help us decide whether an agent freely chooses not to participate in politics, or whether there may be constraining factors, some of which the agent may not be aware. Explanations of nonparticipation, intentionally or not, sometimes suppress questions of interests, ethics, and political power. They cannot eliminate them.

Explanations of nonparticipation, in fact, are predicated on a collateral analysis of how power is distributed in society and on a particular understanding of power as a concept. But they are not just about power.

They really tell a story using a full array of concepts—apathy and power, freedom and political responsibility, what is real participation and what is fake, and in turn how each of these infuses and clarifies nonparticipation. And how this shapes our hopes for democracy. And this, our sense of what human interests really are. An explanation of nonparticipation tells a story about people, and one as well about the explainer.

The most central idea in the story I will try to tell is that of apathy. But by itself, apathy is not the most important one. It is more a clue about the others, about how free we are, how much power we really have, what we can fairly be held responsible for, whether we are being well served—by others or even by ourselves.

The Power of Ideas

What we mean by words has always been at the heart of politics. When politics takes the form of a contest, a good one, the debates are fueled by powerful ideas, not semantics. Each word is loaded. Yet there is also a conversation that makes the contest possible. To engage another on whether democracy really exists, how it can be enhanced, even what it means, requires more than a touch of common commitment and meaning. The contest is important precisely because it is over a shared ideal, an idea with drawing power for each and for those each cares about.

The same is true for competing political explanations. As we review how various schools explain nonparticipation, we'll repeatedly see partial agreements and partial contests over the meaning and application of key terms and, reflexively, skirmishes over allied ideas. Perhaps it seems surprising that a discussion of how to explain the facts of politics should involve such controversy. Aren't we talking about a *science* of politics?

If by science one means a view that there is a way to determine and analyze something called "facts" without reference to world views, paradigms of understanding, or values, then the answer is no. Even in the natural sciences, such a view cannot be sustained. Facts and values are different things, and the values one brings to inquiry, the suppositions one makes, the questions one asks, the tools one uses, can help determine what will count as a "fact," what a theory will see—and what it will hide, even from itself. All social scientific analysis privileges certain hunches, chooses certain methods, defines concepts in such a way, implies the direction it will take, ultimately sees the world in a certain way. And so while insisting on a meaningful distinction between facts and values, I reject the notion that one can sort them in a way that does not itself implicate one in making normative judgments.

Therefore, I also don't share the belief that explanation or even description is a kind of cloth that can be scrubbed free of embedded evaluative grit. Evaluation is a thread interwoven with explanation, both are in the cloth, and pulling at either weakens the fabric.

An essential corollary is that there are no value-neutral ways to define essential concepts in political explanation. They can't be scientifically "operationalized"—if by that is meant developing from the "real world" or logic itself criteria that fully stipulate their precise contours and when they are operative—in such a way that all fair-minded people will agree. Fair-minded people will disagree about the nature and shape of explanatory concepts, and they will disagree most emphatically when the concept is an important one. Although political analysis and explanation should be, and often are, more objective, more careful, more refined in technique than political rhetoric, they too fight over ideas.

So, following W. B. Gallie, I subscribe to the notion that important concepts are "essentially contested," there is debate over their meaning precisely because they are important to how we view life.[25] As we'll see, the terms *political participation, democracy, power, freedom, interests, equality, public, private, economic, political, citizenship,* and *apathy* itself are all contested among competing explanations of nonparticipation.

Proceeding through a range of theories, then, we will find debate over facts and values, over concepts, goals and dreams, and even over what the debate is really all about. Every one can't be pointed out, but the important ones will become clear.

There is also common ground. The different schools explaining nonparticipation disagree based on prior agreement that democracy is a valued way of political life. They agree enough to disagree, to try to show the illogic of their adversaries' position, to try to draw the same audience into each's position. Political wars are civil wars.·

The methodology presumed here accepts that objective inquiry at its best (or, if you like, most scientific) has at its heart the goal of demonstrating—with imperfectly shared ideas but within a common language—why one's interpretation of ideas, and ultimately one's construal of human interests, is the better one. It does not fault a theory for having different ideas, just for not having good ones. Far from arguing that all inquiry is relative, it considers that any efforts to plainly state the explanatory catch and the moral net of a theory are the hallmark of a responsible, objective science of politics. Theorists can't choose whether their theories imply certain notions of human interests. But they can choose to take responsibility for those notions implied by their theories.

Most critically, decisions about how to develop, choose, and deploy explanations of nonparticipation have direct methodological and indirect (but equally powerful) political implications. In stipulating one explanation, or a particular array of them, an analyst (1) projects a view about what contemporary American politics looks like and whether this is an acceptable or desirable state of affairs; (2) stipulates a range of what should count as political; (3) suggests a view of human nature, including anthropological assumptions about how much and what kind of participation is desirable for the individual and the society; (4) describes and evaluates contemporary nonparticipation against this view; (5) considers whether and when contemporary social structure, ideologies, and beliefs enable or inhibit free action, nurture or discipline differences; (6) implies at least one contrast model of political participation against which contemporary affairs are judged; (7) explains nonparticipation in a way that has implications for the decision whether to (and how to) design future strategies to increase participation, and for the evaluation of such decisions and designs; (8) ultimately offers an interpretation of the political world that, if taken seriously, becomes part of the political reality that it studies.

That these are entailed by each of the explanations of nonparticipation we'll look at is not a defect of any of them. It is inherent in theorizing. To the degree we respectfully entertain these inevitable consequences of theory, we enable a fuller examination and testing of our theories, and give them a chance to be as strong as theories can be within the human sciences.

Political Apathy

Political apathy itself, it turns out, is a contested concept, with competing claims as to its meaning and criteria of application. In democratic discourse, political apathy is an important appraisive concept, yet in accepting a particular set of criteria for its proper application, one goes some way toward accepting, even ratifying, a complementary democratic theory as well. Prior to the debate over particular interpretations of the concept, however, there is important shared meaning which makes the debate possible.

Because America takes pride in being democratic, and political democracy is generally thought incompatible with pervasive indifference, Americans generally agree that, all other things being equal, apathy should be discouraged. Within democratic discourse, widespread apathy is a clear signal that something is fundamentally wrong. As we'll see, writers as diverse as (elite) empirical democratic theorist Bernard Berelson and participatory democratic theorist Peter Bachrach recognize that political participation plays a special role within democracies, in contrast to traditional regimes or modern totalitarian ones. Even Berelson and his co-authors would acknowledge these presumptions, and agree that apathy in a democracy needs some justification. Indeed, they feel compelled to begin by explaining why present conditions in America differ sufficiently from the past or from "classical" models to warrant praising apathy today.

While Berelson and Bachrach share common reference points, they disagree profoundly over the meaning of democracy, the concept of apathy and its criteria of application, and the function the term should serve within a grammar of democracy. Their explanations of nonparticipation are radically different, and their explanatory dispute is partly a political one.

If important political concepts stand in a reflexive relationship with the political and social structures we sustain or develop and the way we understand these arrangements, then debate over the use of concepts carries political import. Consider what is involved in the type of conceptual reform Berelson and his colleagues attempt by altering the normal meaning that the term *apathy* has in ordinary usage as well as democratic discourse. William E. Connolly writes,

> To reform successfully a notion embedded in our political life that bears close conceptual ties to our basic ideas of responsibility is to infuse the norms of responsibility themselves more deeply into the political practices of modern society. Debates over the grammar appropriate to such concepts are at root debates over the extent to which such infusions are justified.[26]

When Berelson and Bachrach witness nonparticipation in politics, and especially when they both describe it as political apathy, their common reference points about democracy erode. Apathy, for Berelson, carries with it one set of responsibilities and reflects one set of norms, one version of political power; for Bachrach, quite another. Where Berelson focuses on the behavior of disparate but free individuals, Bachrach sees groups and classes of people subordinated to a disempowering political system. They are each looking at one of the two faces of apathy.

Power and the Two Faces of Apathy

Where the first face of apathy indicates individual responsibility for nonparticipation, the second shifts responsibility or attributes causal agency to other sources, perhaps elites, institutional practices, social structures, or even the organizing principles of a society. The first face is inherent in the idea of free choice—one becomes apathetic to some issue, but one could have made other choices that would not have led to apathy. The second face implies a condition under which one suffers—apathy is a state of mind or a political fate brought about by forces, structures, institutions, or elite manipulation over which one has little or no control, and perhaps little knowledge. Both suggest passivity. Both are rooted in ordinary language. Each assigns responsibility in radically different ways.

Part I of this book is an overview and analysis of the historical, philosophical, and methodological background to competing contemporary explanations of nonparticipation and of debates over the concept of apathy. Part

II organizes these explanations of nonparticipation into various schools of thought according to their attitude to the concept of power, and analyzes each in turn. To elucidate the characteristic points of view of each, I choose classic as well as representative thinkers. I do not claim to cover either each school or all of the work of each writer thoroughly. I do attempt to give fair exegeses.

Some years ago, Steven Lukes identified three dimensions of power, each of which has different implications for the facts seen, the theories developed, and the adopted view of the political world. The two faces of apathy are reflected differently in each of the three dimensions of power. The first face, within what I call the republican liberal school, investigates political power in a way that closely parallels Lukes's first dimension. The theorists of this school include Berelson and his co-authors, Huntington, an early Robert Dahl, and William Riker. They share certain fundamental assumptions of a modern brand of liberalism wedded to a peculiar notion of republicanism, downplay the importance of political participation and popular rule within democratic theory, have a similar understanding of what a science of politics is, and ground their conclusions in a common notion of how political power is properly conceived in inquiry. According to Lukes, the one-dimensional view of power

> involves a focus on *behaviour* in the making of *decisions* on *issues* over which there is an observable *conflict* of (subjective) *interests*, seen as express policy preferences, revealed by political participation.[27]

Because this school tends to view adopted political roles as freely arrived at, it downplays the ways in which other dimensions of power curtail political participation. In this view, if there is no cue of overt conflict over clearly articulated issues, political nonparticipation reflects the contentment or personal indifference of the apathetic citizen. It is here we find, prototypically, the first face of apathy—apathy issuing from free choices of consenting citizens who have the power to do otherwise.

The second school, what I call plain democratic theory, includes within it the work of E. E. Schattschneider and an early Peter Bachrach. This group is united by the belief that political participation is important to democracy, that people know what they need, but that the scope of politics, through the alternatives presented by political institutions, keeps issues that would satisfy certain needs off the political agenda. This school presents what I call a normal thesis of depoliticization as central to a full explanation of nonparticipation. It generally employs Lukes's second dimension of power:

> a *qualified critique* of the *behavioural focus* of the first view . . . it allows for consideration of the ways in which *decisions* are prevented from being taken on *potential issues* over which there is an observable *conflict* of (subjective)

interests, seen as embodied in express policy preferences and sub-political grievances.[28]

Tending to see nonparticipation as rejection of a political agenda that fails to meet nonparticipants' needs, this framework tends *not* to use the concept of apathy as an explanation. There is no corollary face of apathy.

Finally, the works of C. Wright Mills and Herbert Marcuse fall into what I call the radical democratic school of explaining nonparticipation. These authors have been specifically chosen because, although they were not political scientists, their accounts most clearly manifest the second face of apathy; indeed, they were probably two of the most politically influential exponents of it.

According to this view, power may corrupt participation not only by preventing subjectively felt needs from being represented politically, but by shaping the need structure itself. Moreover, power may restrain both participation and development of interests not just by ideological manipulation, but by the way in which the normal workings of institutions and society enable and facilitate certain kinds of thoughts and behaviors, and disable or impede others. Here the question is put most forcefully of whether even participation such as voting is actually democratic political participation at all. Lukes's third dimension of power, embedded within their work, involves

> a *thoroughgoing critique* of the *behavioural focus* of the first two views as too individualistic and allows for consideration of the many ways in which *potential issues* are kept out of politics, whether through the operation of social forces and institutional practices or through individuals' decisions. This, moreover, can occur in the absence of actual, observable conflict, which may have been successfully averted—though there remains here an implicit reference to potential conflict. This potential, however, may never in fact be actualised. What one may have here is a *latent conflict*, which consists in a contradiction between the interest of those exercising power and the *real interests* of those they exclude. These latter may not express or even be conscious of their interests, but . . . the identification of those interests ultimately always rests on empirically supportable and refutable hypotheses.[29]

It is in the radical democratic explanation, prototypically, that we find the second face of apathy employed extensively—apathy as a condition of consciousness, created by an exercise of power, that thoroughly restricts freedom. Marcuse's "one-dimensional man," and Mills's "cheerful robot" are paradigms. As we will see, however, none of the theorists, including those in the radical democratic mold equipped with the three-dimensional view of power, sufficiently consider the role of race and gender in depoliticization.

Organizing these explanatory frameworks according to their formal definitions of power, however, is not to suggest that the theorists considered do not range beyond their confines. In fact, not only do they but, whether or not they formally acknowledge these dimensions of power, they cannot help but do so. In investigating the reasons for a lack of social conflict, for example, an analyst cannot help but decide whether it reflects a (true) consensus based upon freely held values, or a (false) consensus based upon some form of ideational control.

This, of course, is not all there is to say about power,[30] and since Lukes has described power in this way, his view has been subject to a variety of critiques. But Lukes's breakdown is an excellent first design, particularly well suited to organize this study.

In Part III, I extend Lukes's conception of power to help refine explanations of nonparticipation and suggest strategies through which participation may be enhanced. I develop a thesis of complex depoliticization, including a notion I call *displacement of interpretation*, and suggest these are useful ways of understanding how power may keep people from fully participating in political life. I also suggest two related ideas: *Political subordination* indicates how the normal working of a polity may suppress political understanding from emerging, while *political mortification* specifies how "apathetic" individuals or groups participate in suppressing, killing off, deflecting, and ultimately denying themselves political interpretation of what appears to be their personal or collective fate.

Finally, after an analysis of the empirical explanations of nonparticipation and proposals for reform of Ruy Teixeira, Frances Fox Piven and Richard Cloward, and Walter Dean Burnham, and a comparison of the latest proposals for democratic renewal of the old adversaries Robert Dahl and Peter Bachrach, I end the work where it began—with some proposals for political reform, and a challenge in the form of questions to each of us.

My goal is that this work in some small way will help contribute to reinforcing the consensus around political democracy itself and its foundational idea, political equality. My hope is that this consensus may extend to working toward the ideal of *real* political equality—political equality in fact as well as principle or even law—a consubstantiation in which political equality actually means that each citizen has similar resources of political power, as well as the same liberties and rights. It is political democracy of this unfulfilled sort that really protects every individual and to which we should commit ourselves.

Part I

The Roots
of Apathy

In Part II, we will turn to an essential basis of arguments for and against change: the explanations of nonparticipation. In Part I, we first consider the historical and philosophical roots of these explanations and how they were shaped in the development of both American political life and a science of politics.

Because the liberal and the republican frameworks have been dominant in American politics as well as in the study of it, I will focus on their political, economic, philosophical, and historical underpinnings. In the beginning, we will see that arguments like those of Berelson, Huntington, Riker, and the early Dahl are grounded in such assumptions; in the end—reformulated in the modern context—they help engender the contemporary fear that mass industrialized society, mixed with frenzied citizen political action, could become the seedbed of modern totalitarianism. Understandably, like many political analysts who grew and wrote in the shadow of the post–World War II triumph of mass-based Communism, and others who traumatically were affected by the need for war to defeat populist-based Fascism, some of these thinkers became skeptical of the democratic virtues of twentieth-century "political man" and afraid of popular movements. Today, similar fears continue.

But the tack of Berelson and those who followed him, the unexamined anxiety that there might be, to use José Ortega y Gasset's phrase, a "revolt of the masses," is not really new. It is predicated on a fear of too much participation that dates back to the founding of the American republic—a time, in fact, when democracy was more scorned than prized.

Liberalism also had a radical edge. For in its attack on the privileges and constraints of traditional authority, it substituted the individual for the group, caste, or estate as the basic unit of social intercourse. Coupled with Protestant ideas that individuals unmediated by the church were capable of understanding God's word, grounded in early Christian ideas about the equality of the rich and poor in the eyes of God, liberalism held within it an incipient notion of radical political equality. If all men had natural rights, all men deserved to have those rights protected by and from the state, and therefore, each man deserved to have his interests represented in the state.

If "property," as both broadly and narrowly conceived by Locke, is preeminent among rights, but is endowed unequally among men, then those with property have more rights in need of protection and more interest in (and interests to be protected by and from) government than those without. Just as liberalism develops as a philosophical basis with which to pry ideas about rights, obligations, responsibilities, and privileges away from the existing stratification, it engenders a new theory of value, based on the talents of the emerging entrepreneurial classes, that justifies a new form of political inequality and theory of the proper role of the state. Liberalism becomes an important political and philosophical rationale for, and historical sidekick of, the emerging theory of free-market economics embodied most famously in Adam Smith's 1776 work, *The Wealth of Nations*.

In the effort to free markets and marketeers from the suffocation of feudalism, liberalism suppressed its radical edge of egalitarian individualism in favor of its private-property–based theory of individual worth, or what C. B. Macpherson calls a theory of "possessive individualism." In matters of state, liberalism becomes the philosophical basis for limited government. In matters of life, it grounds a civil society in which private property, broadly defined, becomes the mark for the theoretical delimitation of rights and judgments about merit which, increasingly, would themselves be practically ascertained by an accounting of property in the narrow sense. In this way, liberalism becomes transformed into a philosophical rationale not only for limited government and meritocracy, but also for the accumulation of capital.

Classical liberalism, and its complement of a civil society driven by laissez-faire economics, differs fundamentally from classical Greek democracy. Even the radical edge of liberalism, and the legitimacy it afforded political equality, and the Greek ideal of citizenship are profoundly different.

All classic conceptions of the polity, whether or not democratic, were based on civic virtue. In liberalism, politics and the state are things to be suffered in order to avoid the worse alternative of the state of nature. For the Greeks, a life in the politics of the city was the only way to lead a good life, one of deep fulfillment—*this* was the state of human nature. Individuals were citizens in the organic sense that they were part of the *polis* or city-state; they needed it, but more, they were of it—the city was essential to their identity.

Political life was the essence of life. Where liberalism sought government to protect the private life of the self-sufficient individual, Athenians defined as an "idiot" the purely private individual, "irresponsible because unconcerned with public affairs." This spirit is beautifully captured in the funeral speech of the Athenian democrat Pericles at the close of the Peloponnesian War, attributed to him by the Greek historian Thucydides, himself no real friend of democracy:

> Here each individual is interested not only in his own affairs but in the affairs of the state as well . . . we do not say that a man who takes no interest in politics is a man who minds his own business; we say that he has no business here at all.[3]

The Greeks did not conceive of a state distinct from civil society, and the thought of grounding the commonweal precisely on a rigid separation of the two was completely foreign to them.

Democracy in classical Greece also was thought of as a form of political class rule—rule by the people—to be contrasted with rule by an aristocracy of the rich. As Aristotle, at best a skeptic when it came to democracy, put it: "the real difference between democracy and oligarchy is poverty and wealth. Whenever men rule by reason of their wealth, whether they be few or many, that is an oligarchy, and where the poor rule, that is a democracy."[4] To ensure popular rule, democracy for the Greeks was what we sometimes today call direct democracy, or what James Madison derided as "pure democracy"; the citizens were the assembly, the coordinating committees, and the juries, and most offices were filled by lot, precisely to ensure democratic distribution of directly held power, and not by elections, then considered an aristocratic device.

From the beginning, the engine of democracy has been a kind of class struggle. In ancient Athens, democracy was born of a conflict between the "notables" and "the masses," resulting first in Solon's reforms of 594 B.C., and then Cleisthenes' more radical democratic changes in 504 B.C. Over the last two hundred years, democratic mass movements often combined the radical edge of liberalism with a liberal renovation of the ancient ideal of democracy, formulating ideas as to how excluded groups might be justly represented within the state and greatly expanding the scope of who should count as a citizen. Unsurprisingly, these were resisted at every turn: male property owners, in both Britain and America, trying to restrict the franchise to themselves; men in both countries preventing women from gaining suffrage; many whites in America violently preventing the franchise from being extended to African-Americans. Today, the moral foundation for legitimate government practically everywhere in the world rests on the idea that the people as a whole govern through their representatives. The triumph of this version of the democratic ideal is historically inconceivable without the struggle of ex-cluded classes.

After the fall of Athenian democracy in 322 B.C., the idea of democracy was largely submerged until the late 1700s, although democratic practices could be found interspersed within medieval institutions, Italian city-states, Leveller proposals, and quite independently, some have suggested, within some Native American and African tribal practices.[5] Given that history is written usually by those who win; given the radical potential of the Greek democratic ideal (despite Greek economic inequality, imperialist foreign pol-icy, and the exclusion of slaves, women, and foreign-born residents, or *metics*, from citizenship), especially in an unstable liberal posttraditional context; and given that much of what we know about Greek democracy we have been told by men either skeptical of or thoroughly hostile to it—Socrates (who was "implacably anti-democratic"), Plato, Aristotle, Thucydides, and Aris-tophanes (who often mocked it)—as interpreted by scholars also critical. It is not surprising that when democracy resurfaced, it did so with a decidedly negative connotation as rule by the mob. As Wordsworth confessed in 1794, really without irony, "I am one of that odious class of men called democrats."[6] The political theorist C. B. Macpherson wrote in 1966,

> Democracy used to be a bad word. Everybody who was anybody knew that democracy, in its original sense of rule by the people or government in accordance with the will of the bulk of the people, would be a bad thing—fatal to individual freedom and to all the graces of civilized living. That was the position taken by pretty nearly all men of intelligence from the earliest historical times down to about a hundred years ago. Then, within fifty years, democracy became a good thing. Its full acceptance into the ranks of respectability was apparent by the time of the First World War, a war which the Western allied leaders could proclaim was fought to make the world safe for democracy. Since then . . . everybody claims to have it.[7]

Indeed, until Tom Paine excoriated and ridiculed British constitutional monarchy in his extremely influential 1776 pamphlet *Common Sense*, most Americans didn't even think of themselves as republicans, for they believed themselves to be, and wanted to be treated as, citizens under the British con-stitution as well as subjects of the crown. Once the Revolutionary War settled the issue between constitutional monarchists and republicans, significant po-litical opinion in America was certainly not advertised as aristocratic nor yet labeled democratic. It was virtually all called republican.

An American Republic

Like the ancient idea of democracy, the notion of a republic—literally "for the good of the public"—was a word within the ancient Greek political vocabulary. For the Greeks, the inventors of politics as well as democracy, the pursuit of politics was essential to leading a moral life, whether the form was monarchic, aristocratic, oligarchic, or democratic. In Plato's *Republic*, civic virtue is no less important than in Pericles' funeral oration, however different the role each man expected the commoner to play. Through the undemocratic republic of ancient Rome, the pseudo-republic of the Roman Empire, the fall of Rome and with it the independent life of European towns, the development of city life in the Renaissance, particularly in Italian city-states, the ancient republican ideal persevered and then was revivified in the political writing of Niccolò Machiavelli.

For Machiavelli, witness of war and competition between Italian city-states, the preeminent moral question was how to secure liberty, for only under liberty were states able to enjoy "dominion or wealth." Liberty, however, required stability. Otherwise, in his view, the failures of ancient Greek democracy would be repeated.

Central to Machiavelli's politics, of course, was the use of power, externally and internally, to secure the city. However, this Italian thinker also believed that loyalty to the city, and to its use of power, required that civic virtue be inculcated in its citizens, primarily through the institutions of religion and law. But there were other ways. Showing his modern touch, Machiavelli's view was that sound constitutional design must recognize the self-interested and anarchic impulses in human nature, to include and balance them to prevent the arrogation of power by one group over others, and to encourage each to feel included in the decisions made. Loyalty could thereby be engendered. Recalling the success of the Roman republic, he advocated mixing monarchy, aristocracy, and democracy to achieve balance, avoid the characteristic pitfalls of each, and create a stable and inclusive form of government that, most important, would inculcate civic virtue in its people.

Viewed in terms of power, "reasons of state" subordinated individual interests. Viewed in terms of legitimacy, civic virtue tempered personal desires. Taken together, virtue allowed the unfettered application of the city's power, which itself created conditions for more virtue. Both power and virtue were required to underwrite liberty.

His writing is important to American political development because it articulates the first modern expression of what might be called the "civic humanist" or "classical republican" tradition. In trying to design a modern political theory for his day, Machiavelli embodied both the ancient relationship of the citizen to the *polis* and the modern science of using institutions to harness human nature for the good of the body politic. He may have been the father of a modern science of power, but he also was creating a "science of virtue."[8]

In so doing, he helped keep alive and reinvigorated the idea of republican civic virtue. Most designers of the American constitutional system, following

Machiavelli, had not given up on the idea, as their political progeny later would, that government did more than create the conditions to pursue private interests.[9] It could also promote the general interest and in so doing help produce a virtuous citizenry, so necessary to combat the two threats the founders viewed most dangerous to a republic: foreign political and economic domination or outright invasion; and domestic faction.

The American constitutional design developed through a debate between two camps within republicanism that grew quickly out of concentrated criticism of the original American constitution, the Articles of Confederation. The Articles embodied a traditional concept of a republic that was suspicious of centralized authority, believed (with Baron de Montesquieu) that republicanism could only thrive in small republics, and wanted power closer to the citizen, fearing aristocratic manipulation. Some of its critics, however, quietly applauded the prospect of an opportunity for elite power and were terrified by brewing economic discontent exemplified most famously by former Revolutionary War Army officer Daniel Shays's rebellion of Massachusetts debtor farmers. Some believed a stronger central government was needed in order to make states feel less vulnerable to foreign threat or Native American resistance. Others, like Alexander Hamilton, believed all these things and sought a more organized and truly national economy as the key to a solution. Together with a stronger federal government, more taxing power, more ability independent of individual states to raise an army and navy, he believed, the nation would be better able to endow itself with more wealth, prestige, and international power, protect itself better, and pay off the holders, including many speculators, of Revolutionary War debt, thereby establishing its fiscal bona fides.

The convention that was charged by the Continental Congress with only the task of amending the Articles developed instead (unconstitutionally) a brand-new Constitution, including greater centralization of power and integration of the states into the republic as a whole. Where in the Articles sovereignty resided in each of the states, under the new Constitution, it would theoretically reside in "We the people." In reality, significant power was shifted from the political units closer to the people—the states—to the national government. In the debate over whether to adopt this proposal, republicanism as vague ideology splintered into two main factions, one more traditional and sympathetic, at least, to the spirit of the Articles, the other a proponent of the new arrangement, believing only an extended republic could avoid the problems associated with popular rule as illustrated by the weak record of the Articles.

In one of the ideological coups of history, the newer band of republicans arrogated to themselves the name "Federalists," formerly an idea associated with decentralized government and still powerful in the popular republican imagination, leaving the more traditional republicans with the negative appellation of "Antifederalists." The effect was a nascent positive image in the popular mind for an emerging republican philosophy that more accurately might have been called nationalist, or as it sometimes was called, "continentalist." Neither, however, was democratic or aristocratic, and to the extent these proclivities existed in the major players involved, they were concealed by republican rhetoric.

The Science of Virtue

Any notion as to whether the new Constitution was designed to be a democratic document should be answered by a reading of the most important polemic in support of its adoption, James Madison's justifiably famous *Federalist* No. 10. In this brilliant tract of rhetoric and equally brilliant treatise in political theory, Madison makes clear that what he calls (curious to the modern ear) "majority faction" is the primary vulnerability of republican government. With the fatal defects, in his view, of Athenian democracy and what he calls "pure democracy" never far from mind, he writes,

> To secure the public good and private rights against the danger of such a faction, and at the same time to preserve the spirit and the form of popular government, is then the great object to which our inquiries are directed.

But what, we might ask, is the foundation idea of representative democracy if not "majority faction"? Taking apparent aim at what he calls the "pure democracy" of direct citizen governance, but his real target the specter of popular majorities democratically controlling representative government, Madison asserts that

> democracies have ever been spectacles of turbulence and contention; have ever been found incompatible with personal security or the rights of property; and have in general been as short in their lives as they have been violent in their deaths.

The spirit of faction is so deeply rooted in self-interested human nature, by Madison's account, that efforts to snuff it out likely would fail; but even if they could succeed, the price simply would be too great—it would mean the elimination of liberty itself.[10] He illustrates with a wonderful analogy:

> Liberty is to faction what air is to fire, an ailment without which it instantly expires. But it could not be a less folly to abolish liberty, which is essential to political life, because it nourishes faction than it would be to wish the annihilation of air, which is essential to animal life, because it imparts to fire its destructive agency.

The cure, he suggests, would be "worse than the disease."

The primary virtue of the new Constitution, therefore, would be to control the effects of faction. Madison's truly distinctive theoretical contribution, however, put him at odds with most republican thinking up to that time, including that of Montesquieu. For Madison saw republican principles most enhanced not in a nation-state of limited territory, but rather in one whose very size would mitigate the threat democracy poses for liberty:

> Extend the sphere and you take in a greater variety of parties and interests; you make it less probable that a majority of the whole will have a common motive to invade the rights of other citizens; or if such a common motive exists, it will be more difficult for all who feel it to discover their own strength and to act in unison with each other.[11]

Should a majority coalition be cobbled together out of the "great variety of interests, parties, and sects which it embraces," it would be of a higher quality, and not likely to oppress residual minorities, for it "could seldom take place on any other principles than those of justice and the general good." Less appreciated about Madison is that he believed this to be an important protection for majorities as well, and therefore for the very idea of republican government. If minorities could not plausibly claim they were likely to be oppressed by a majority, they would lose the "pretext" to displace republican by aristocratic government with "a will independent of the society itself."[12]

The other problem, of minority faction—powerful self-interested groups using government to promote their own interests, closer to the way we use the word *faction* today—was more tractable for Madison and dispatched quickly by him. Effective counter, he believed, would be found in applying the "republican principle, which enables the majority to defeat its sinister views by regular vote."[13]

An extended republic, of course, would broaden the authority of representatives, deepening the public's dependence on people whose electorate would become much larger than in a small republic. Madison applauded this prospect as broadening the pool in which virtuous men could be found and chosen to then mediate between the people's passions and the public's true interests. The larger the electorate, moreover, the less likely politicians would be able to practice the "vicious arts" of political manipulation, and the freer the electorate would be to make wise choices.

The American constitutional design, and Madison's defense of it, however, does follow Montesquieu's major dictum that "power should be a check to power" by creating institutions that will both separate functional powers and create discrete arenas in which all major interests can be represented, betting that the resulting clashes of interests will disperse power and thereby protect liberty. There could be no liberty, Montesquieu claimed, "were the same man or the same body, whether of the nobles or of the people, to exercise those three powers, that of enacting laws, that of executing public resolutions, and of trying the causes of individuals."[14] And it is only through a constitution, and not reliance on natural rights, natural law, social contracts, or heroic individuals, that the evils of concentrated power can be avoided and liberty be ensured.

Montesquieu's arguments deeply influenced the founders, and in the American Constitution become the separation of powers originally conceived to include a president elected by an elite electoral college, a Supreme Court appointed for life by him, an elite Senate chosen by members of the state legislatures, a House of Representatives chosen by those citizens granted the franchise by each of the states (then and for some years to come, restricted to white males with property). Madison himself was very afraid that without checks and balances and separation of powers, even after splitting the legislative function into two, the most democratic branch, the House of Representatives, would naturally dominate the government. John Adams put the point more bluntly, reflecting the belief of many founders that the preservation of liberty required institutional protection from democracy for the dominant social classes:

> The rich ought to have an effectual barrier in the constitution against being robbed, plundered, and murdered, as well as the poor; and this can never be without an independent Senate.[15]

An extended republic based on principles of federalism and separation of powers would have another important virtue:

> In the compound republic of America, the power surrendered by the people is first divided between two distinct governments, and then the portion allotted to each subdivided among distinct and separate departments. Hence a double security arises to the rights of the people. The different governments will control each other, at the same time that each will be controlled by itself.[16]

Reflecting touches of Hobbes's understanding of human nature but rejecting Hobbes's authoritarian solution, Madison turns, in *Federalist* No. 51, to the following "expedient" to maintain "in practice partition of power[s]":

> the great security against a gradual concentration of the several powers in the same department, consists in giving to those who administer each department the necessary constitutional means and personal motives to resist encroachments of the others. . . . Ambition must be made to counteract ambition. The interest of the man must be connected with the constitutional rights of the place. It may be a reflection on human nature that such devices should be necessary to control the abuses of government. But what is government itself but the greatest of all reflections on human nature? If men were angels, no government would be necessary. If angels were to govern men, neither external nor internal controls on government would be necessary. In framing a government which is to be administered

by men over men, the great difficulty lies in this: you must first enable the government to control the governed; and in the next place oblige it to control itself. A dependence on the people is, no doubt, the primary control on the government; but experience has taught mankind the necessity of auxiliary precautions. . . . [In this way] the private interest of every individual may be a sentinel over the public rights.[17]

The Antifederalists, having lost the initiative to those intent on a radical redrawing of the confederation, were left to act as dissenters challenging Madison's design. In addition to arguing for a Bill of Rights, not included in the original Constitution, they also believed too much power was being concentrated in the central government and, given the large size of districts and proposed terms of office, representatives would become too distant from the citizenry. Also skeptical about human nature, the Antifederalists nevertheless placed more faith in the "genius of the people" than they did in that of elites. An Antifederalist and an aristocrat with some "democratical" tendencies, Richard Henry Lee defended what he believed to be true republican and federalist principles in his "Letter from the Federal Farmer."

A virtuous people make just laws, and good laws tend to preserve unchanged a virtuous people. A virtuous and happy people by laws uncongenial to their characters, may easily be gradually changed into servile and depraved creatures. Where the people, or their representatives, make the laws, it is probable they will generally be fitted to the national character and circumstances, unless the representation be partial, and the imperfect substitute of the people. However, the people may be electors, if the representation be so formed as to give one or more of the natural classes of men in the society an undue ascendancy over the others, it is imperfect; the former will gradually become masters, and the latter slaves.[18]

More in the classical republican tradition, the Antifederalists agreed with Montesquieu, as "Agrippa" put it, "no extensive empire can be governed upon republican principles, and that such a government will degenerate to a despotism, unless it be made up of a confederacy of smaller states, each having the full powers of internal regulation." The "idea of an uncompounded republick, on an average one thousand miles in length, and eight hundred in breadth, and containing six millions of white inhabitants all reduced to the same standards of morals, of habits, and of laws, is itself an absurdity, and," he adds, sharply disagreeing with Madison's reading of history, "contrary to the whole experience of mankind."[19] For his part, Richard Henry Lee refused to serve as a delegate to the Constitutional Convention and opposed ratification because of the omission of a "bill of rights" and the restrictions on representation, objecting most strenuously to the proposed limit of sixty-five representatives (and not to exceed one to every thirty thousand) as being far too few, elected too infrequently, and therefore a violation of republican principles:

> a full and equal representation is that which possesses the same interests, feelings, opinions and views the people themselves would were they all assembled—a fair representation, therefore, should be so regulated, that every order of men in the community, according to the common course of elections, can have a share in it. . . . the representation must be considerably numerous.[20]

And where Madison swiftly dispatched the problem of minority faction with the "republican principle" of majority rule and focused his argument on individual ambition and, of course, "majority faction," it was precisely minority faction that Lee saw as the primary threat to republican government.

> I mean the constant liability of a small number of representatives to private combinations; *the tyranny of the one, or the licentiousness of the multitude, are, in my mind, but small evils, compared with the factions of the few.*[21]

As if to confirm Lee's fears, John Adams wrote that the Constitution was "calculated," in his view, "to increase the influence, power, and wealth of those who already have it," and that ratification would be "a grand point gained in favor of the aristocratic party."[22]

With the major exception of winning agreement to later adopt a bill of rights, the Antifederalists lost the argument. Nevertheless, the founding of the nation and adoption of the Constitution was accomplished through dialogue between Federalists and Antifederalists and, as Herbert J. Storing reminds us, the Antifederalists also should be counted among the founders.[23] It was they who defended traditional republican principles and forced the Federalists to think through their ideas and arguments with an eye to the political repercussions. But it was Madison's plan that was implemented, one that he believed could provide "a republican remedy for the diseases most incident to republican government,"[24] striking the best political bargain with human nature.

The adoption of the new American Constitution created the institutional framework within which Alexander Hamilton could pursue his vision of an economically and militarily secure American nation,[25] including the establishment of the Bank of the United States, the federal funding of national Revolutionary War debts and of state debts, a national revenue system, and a strong army and navy. Oriented toward manufacture and trade, Hamilton's proposals challenged the Antifederalist belief that republican principles could best be actuated in a confederation of states in which virtue was based in the agrarian life of the independent farmer.

Like Thomas Jefferson, Madison became suspicious of Hamilton's tendency to equate virtue with individual self-interest, and worried that however inevitable commercialization might be, it could lead to a corruption of republican values. Indeed, Madison finally broke with Hamilton over the very aggressive commercial and fiscal policies he pursued as Secretary of the Treasury in President George Washington's cabinet. Madison argues, in a series of essays in the *National Gazette*, that these policies were antirepublican and could lead to tyranny (Jefferson helped found this newspaper to rebut Federalist attacks on the republican principles articulated by Tom Paine in his 1792 *Rights of Man*, including his defense of the French Revolution). Except in these essays, unlike in *Federalist* No. 10 and No. 51, Madison grounds his defense of republicanism in the virtue of the citizenry rather than in institutional forms, and later in 1793, he would argue that a too strong federal executive could lead to imperialistic usurpation of power. By 1798, Madison was collaborating with Jefferson on the Kentucky and Virginia Resolutions, opposing the Alien and Sedition Act's repression of opponents of the Federalist party, and espousing the republican principles of the "spirit of '98," including the idea that the states could interpose their interpretation of the Constitution to block federal laws.

The French Revolution deepened the divide between the two camps of republicanism, with the Federalists becoming disenchanted and then hostile to it, and the Jeffersonians, soon to be known as Republicans, defending it. Support for the ideas of the French Revolution began to take on a "democratic" form, even while Federalists denounced such support as being "democratical" or Jacobin. And the term *democracy* was used in a favorable light by the Republican press beginning in 1794, glorifying popular sovereignty and criticizing elitist Federalist policies. Democratic-Republican societies began to sprout up around the country. While attacks by the Federalist press, the XYZ affair, and the Alien and Sedition Act of 1798 successfully undermined these societies, as Russell Hanson suggests, along with Jeffersonian-Republicans they:

> succeeded in neutralizing [for the idea of democracy] the more odious connotations of "mob rule" through their counter-educational efforts, and their "responsible" opposition to Federalist policies. They also initiated the process by which the rhetorical links between democracy and the ideas of popular sovereignty and political equality were forged. . . . This trend toward the popularization of democracy proceeded by fits and starts into the nineteenth century, eventually culminating in the Democratic Party of "Old Hickory," Andrew Jackson.[26]

Democracy, a term of derogation since its overthrow in Athens in 322 B.C., was on the way back to being a prized ideal. But it was now ensconced in a state of liberal Federalist republican design, which was to have implications for the scope and type of participation available. For while the Federalist strategy of denouncing "democracy" was ultimately, in Hanson's words, "self-defeating, given the decline of deferential politics and the hierarchical society on which it was based," its constitutional design, including its Burkean view of representation, succeeded in blunting citizen political action which, after the experience under the Articles, was exactly what the Federalists hoped it would do. Hanson suggests this had the unintended consequence of hastening "the decline of civic virtue" among the citizenry, a problem Madison belatedly saw, and tried ineffectually to remedy in order to counter, as Hanson puts it, the "enervating effects of representation over an extended sphere."[27] The deed was done. Hanson concludes,

> In limiting popular participation to the selection of leaders, the Federalists consigned the population to a state of civic lethargy, in which citizens failed to develop a sense of moral and political responsibility that, according to classical republican theory, accompanied civic involvement. . . . And they failed to learn to love liberty, i.e. to love and pursue the public good in politics. Thus, the Federalists' "realistic" assessment of the decline in virtue in America turned out to be a "gigantic self-fulfilling prophecy" once it found institutional expression in Constitutional arrangements that made scant provision for civic involvement.[28]

Hanson is right to point out the enervating and self-fulfilling consequences of the Constitution, but it may be the case that civic virtue appears to have declined more than it actually has. Repeatedly in American history, citizens have argued for a more inclusive and democratic notion of an American republic, sometimes forcing a broadening of participatory opportunities, sometimes failing and withdrawing. What seems to be decline may reflect continuing practical limitations in opportunities, only some constitutionally based, as much as it does actual civic lethargy.

However much the Constitution made citizen involvement difficult, and however little this is understood to this day, it became an independent source of legitimacy for the political order, creating loyalty for and pride in the nation. Civic virtue, after all, is not necessarily the kind that participatory democrats would care to embrace. From Hanson's perspective, the real problem seems to be that the Constitution created not only a decline but also the wrong kind of civic virtue—commitment to an elite-dominated republic.

It is also important to look at the kind of political activity the Constitution *did* encourage. Creating a system with many niches in which "minorities rule," as Robert Dahl calls it, facilitated the eventual development and institutionalization of extensive lobbying networks; these, in turn, helped create that particularly American characteristic of concentrated vigorous participation by an upper echelon of politically active citizens, with virtually no participation whatsoever by about half.

In order to fully comprehend the impact of the founding on political participation, we need to look beyond the political structure itself. As powerful as Madison's design in blunting popular rule was Hamilton's economic nationalism. A singular achievement of Madison's work was that it was a fairly sound vehicle through which Hamiltonian economic nationalism could be exercised. None of this was foreordained, of course, and many political battles, perhaps most famously for a national bank, had still to be engaged in and won.

An extended compound republic, separation of powers, and checks and balances were important in deflecting major conflict (and in limiting the prospects of would-be tyrants). But an economic system—within a congenial legal framework that protected the creation, accumulation, and concentration of wealth, and speculation and investment with it—helped build the foundation for inequality that would manifest itself politically and become, arguably, the most important check on majority faction. Their ultimate political rift is paradoxical because Madison's politics and Hamilton's economics worked hand-in-glove to mute participation and republican civic virtue.

The Madison–Hamiltonian system, however, was fated to mature in a political culture with an egalitarian ethos, nurtured by what seemed a limitless frontier and the belief that liberty and, in Jefferson's account, democracy depended on owning and working one's land. The "Jacksonian revolution" eliminated property rights for voting, thus accomplishing universal white male suffrage in the United States by the 1830s, well before anywhere in Europe (excepting the dramatic political equality of men during the all too brief period of democracy during the French Revolution). Political equality and egalitarian individualism would later become important ideals in arguments that denial of the vote to women and African-Americans violated fundamental American principles. Thus American national and economic power grew at the same time that, in politics at least, the nation underwent selective democratization, creating a fundamental historical tension between concentrated wealth and claims of individuals to have a right to protect their own well-being.

Jefferson believed that constitutions and governments should be changed as needed by the people. As president, however, he did not seriously move to alter the structure of government or the Hamiltonian institutions designed to develop the national economy. Nevertheless, there was an important difference between Jefferson's liberal democratic egalitarianism and Hamilton's liberal yet aristocratic nationalism. This tension was creative in the sense that it allowed men to participate up to a point in the political system, affording them an outlet for simmering discontents, especially late in the nineteenth century under the pressures of industrialization and the end of the frontier. When the danger of populism and unionism made this tension seem unmanageable, efforts were again made to redefine the meaning of democracy and equality in a liberal republic.

 **Chapter 2**

Love and Fear of Equality

American cultural and political commitments to republicanism and to Lockean individualism betrayed, virtually from the beginning, an ambivalent attitude toward equality. On the one hand, the Declaration of Independence proclaimed:

> We hold these truths to be self-evident, that all Men are created equal, that they are endowed by their Creator with certain unalienable Rights, that among these are Life, Liberty, and the Pursuit of Happiness—That to secure these Rights, Governments are instituted among Men, deriving their just Powers from the Consent of the Governed.

Yet, the American Constitution was soon designed precisely to make it difficult for a "majority faction" to use the levers of government to augment its political power, thus equalizing the life chances of the less privileged. Unlike some modern thinkers who fear equality of condition could blur prized individuality, Madison believed that because of inherent inequality in faculties, the interests between men could be harmonized only with great difficulty if at all. Extending Locke's labor theory of value, he claimed it is from the "diversity in the faculties of men, from which the rights of property originate" and the responsibility of government ensues:

> The protection of these faculties is the first object of government. From the protection of different and unequal faculties of acquiring property, the possession of different degrees and kinds of property immediately results; and from the influence of these on the sentiments and views of the respective proprietors ensues a division of the society into different interests and parties.[1]

Thus Madison argues for an extended republic, one which will disperse the interests that inevitably develop, especially around claims to property:

> A rage for paper money, for an abolition of debts, for an equal division of property, or for any other improper or wicked project, will be less apt to pervade the whole body of the Union than a particular member of it, in the

same proportion as such a malady is more likely to taint a particular county or district than an entire State.[2]

Equality broadly conceived is probably impossible and certainly undesirable in Madison's account. But seeking such fool's gold ends up in political disorder and worse—oppression by a majority or, in reaction to it, tyranny by an elite.

Is *political* equality possible or desirable? "Theoretic politicians" who have championed "pure democracy," he complains, "have erroneously supposed that by reducing mankind to a perfect equality in their political rights, they would, at the same time, be perfectly equalized and assimilated in their possessions, their opinions, and their passions."[3] Political equality, therefore, cannot cure the factious human nature that always has and always will subvert democracy, but the belief that it can sustains an illusory quest that can only result in disorder and injustice.

In fact, Madison expected inequality to worsen and wealth to become more concentrated as commerce replaced agrarian society and surplus labor increased. Under such circumstances, political equality was especially undesirable. If "the majority shall be without landed or other equivalent property and without the means or hope of acquiring it," Madison later asks,

> what is to secure the rights of property against the danger from an equality and universality of suffrage, vesting complete power over property in hands without a share in it: not to speak of a danger in the mean time from a dependence of an increasing number on the wealth of a few?[4]

His primary answer had been, of course, the American Constitution. Given legitimacy by the claim "all men are created equal," the American republic was constructed, in part, to contain the domino of political equality.

Those concerns with political equality that did exist at the time were circumscribed, limited to the universe of white males. Abigail Adams wrote her husband, John, during the discussion on adoption of the Declaration of Independence, "I desire you would Remember the Ladies. . . . Remember all Men would be tyrants if they could. If particular care and attention is not paid to the Ladies we are determined to foment a Rebellion, and will not hold ourselves bound by any Laws in which we have no voice, or Representation."[5] His reply is emblematic, and while the language is dated, the sentiment is clear to most women today: "Depend upon it, We know better than to repeal our Masculine systems. Altho they are in full Force, you know they are little more than Theory. We dare not exert our Power in its full Latitude. We are obliged to go fair, and softly, and in Practice you know We are the subjects. We have only the Name of Masters, and rather than give up this, which would compleatly subject Us to the Despotism of the Peticoat, I hope General Washington, and all our brave Heroes would fight."[6]

If women simply were not seriously considered, to the extent African-American men were, their rights were subordinated to attitudes of racism and what was considered the imperative of harmonious nation-building. In spite of serious concerns over slavery harbored by the two men who would lead the two main political parties soon to develop—John Adams the Federalist, and Thomas Jefferson (himself a slave holder) the Republican—the constitutional compromise enshrined slavery in the nation's fundamental law: the slave trade would be allowed until 1808; slaves (although this word is not used) would be counted as three-fifths a person for purposes of taxation and representation; and fugitive slaves would have to be returned to their masters.

The attitude of many of the founders toward the equality of white men in general, and their political equality in particular, must in the end be judged to have been highly ambivalent. For in the civic republican tradition, it was widely realized that, as Robert Bellah puts it, "power follows wealth; and for that reason a rough equality of property was assumed to be one of the prerequisites of a democratic republic."[7] Surely this belief is partly responsible for Jefferson's model of a democratic society based on the independent yeoman farmer, whose property would ground not only his character but also his power, and the passionate commitment to equality of influential people like Tom Paine. Likewise, the belief that private property roots political power is surely a cornerstone upon which John Locke based his liberal philosophy, and a premier practical reason he believed equally passionately in the right of private property.

The reasons for ambivalence toward equality are perhaps most insightfully discussed in the political theory of a Frenchman, Alexis de Tocqueville, in his writings on America. While Tocqueville believed equality to be necessary for democracy, his deeper commitment was to liberty, and his classic 1835 work, *Democracy in America*, is in part an effort to reconcile liberty with democracy. Robert Dahl attributes to Tocqueville four propositions at the heart of his argument: first, equality is increasing; second, liberty is of supreme importance; third, concentrated power "spells the death of liberty";[8] fourth, in democratic countries the majority can rule despotically: "The rights of every people are confined within the limits of what is just. . . . If it be admitted that a man, possessing absolute power, may misuse that power by wronging his adversaries, why should a majority not be liable to the same approach?"

Five years later, in his second volume, Tocqueville discusses a new "type of oppression which threatens democracies," so new in world history that "old words as 'despotism' and 'tyranny' do not fit. The thing is new."

> I see an innumerable multitude of men, alike and equal, constantly circling around in pursuit of the petty and banal pleasures with which they glut their souls. Each one of them, withdrawn into himself, is almost unaware of the fate of the rest. Mankind, for him, consists in his children and his personal

friends. As for the rest of his fellow citizens, they are near enough, but he does not notice them. He touches them but feels nothing. He exists in and for himself, and though he still may have a family, one can at least say that he has not got a fatherland.

Over this kind of men stands an immense, protective power which is alone responsible for securing their enjoyment and watching over their fate. That power is absolute, thoughtful of detail, orderly, provident, and gentle. . . .

Thus it daily makes the exercise of free choice less useful and rarer, restricts the activity of free will within a narrower compass, and little by little robs each citizen of the proper use of his own faculties. Equality has prepared men for all this, predisposing them to endure it and often even regard it as beneficial. . . .

It does not break men's will, but softens, bends, and guides it; it seldom enjoins, but often inhibits, action; it does not destroy anything, but prevents much being born; it is not at all tyrannical, but it hinders, restrains, enervates, stifles, and stultifies so much that in the end each nation is no more than a flock of timid and hardworking animals with the government as its shepherd.[9]

However, Dahl argues, while Tocqueville concludes that democratic equality makes the destruction of liberty likely, it does not make it inevitable. Under certain conditions the two could be reconciled: first, a diffusion of "physical prosperity"; second, a dispersal of power and social function among independent associations standing between the individual and the state and society; third, laws, especially a constitutional division of power embodied in separation of powers, federalism (and further decentralization also to local political authorities), and decentralized judicial power; fourth, and most important, the mores of the people, their "habits of the heart," the civic virtue that makes them good democratic citizens.[10] Tocqueville outlines many of the essential themes that characterize the American debate over liberty, democracy, and equality, from the founding to the present.

In displaying an appreciation of the central importance of groups and associations as institutional mediators between the individual, society, and the state, Tocqueville also seems to prefigure an essential element of later pluralist democratic theory. But there is a qualitative difference. Pluralists tend to see such groupings as supplanting the individual as the basic unit of democracy, and their basic role as representing the members' interests. Tocqueville saw voluntary associations as rescuing individuals from isolation and, through participation in them, developing their interests as well as a sense of political identity necessary for civic virtue. For Tocqueville, such associations fostered and depended on participation, while for many pluralists, interest groups often substitute for it. Indeed, Tocqueville saw apathy as a symptom of the breakdown of pluralist political culture. Unlike pluralists who (as we will see) view apathy as a resource for political stability, he believed that in mass society it would lead to the dissolution of consensus.[11]

Tocqueville was also concerned about industrial development and commercialization, and even how they might threaten equality and, consequently, economic and political liberty. His fear of an atomized society, therefore, was not only caused by the passion for equality. For, as Robert Bellah suggests, while he "appreciated the commercial and entrepreneurial spirit [of America] . . . [he] saw it as having ambiguous and problematic implications for the future of American freedom." Observing what Bellah calls "utilitarian individualism," he feared people would lose themselves in private economic pursuits, in the "calm and considered feeling" of individualism, thereby undermining their own ability to function as democratic citizens:

> there are more and more people who, though neither rich nor powerful enough to have much hold over others, have gained or kept enough wealth and enough understanding to look after their own needs. Such folk owe no man anything and hardly expect anything from anybody. They form the habit of thinking of themselves in isolation and imagine that their whole destiny is in their hands. . . . Each man is forever thrown back on himself alone, and there is danger that he may be shut up in the solitude of his own heart.

Such isolation causes people to "forget their ancestors," their descendants, and their fellow citizens, and is the sort of social arrangement that is encouraged by and can end in despotism. The antidote, Tocqueville argued, can be found in the American mores of the day, especially in the biblical and republican traditions of civic responsibility: "Citizens who are bound to take part in public affairs must turn from the private interests and occasionally take a look at something other than themselves." Religion and democratic participation provide the practices through which people can expand their worldview beyond narrow self-interest, in which intelligent opinions are forged and tested, and public responsibility learned. The vehicle for such practices is the associational life found in intermediate and mediating civic organizations. Light years away from the pluralist notion of interest groups as aggregations of self-interest, these associations are the cornerstone of civic virtue. As Bellah puts it,

> Associational life, in Tocqueville's thinking, is the best bulwark against the condition he feared most: the mass society of mutually antagonistic individuals, easy prey to despotism. These intermediate structures check, pressure, and restrain the tendencies of centralized government to assume more and more administrative control.[12]

Tocqueville's concerns regarding excessive individualism were well founded. As the nineteenth century came to a close, laissez-faire came to dominate economic and political thought, complemented by Social Darwinism as public philosophy, clearly articulated by men like William Graham Sumner. These developments pushed American thought further away from civic republican tradition and helped recast the meaning of equality, liberalism, and democracy for Americans. Built on shaky analogies with the natural sciences, Social Darwinism also could plausibly be derived from important principles of liberalism and laissez-faire, especially where they focus on individual merit and limited government, and not be too far removed from aspects of Locke's labor theory of value and Adam Smith's free market. But Social Darwinism carried these to extremes, discarding any notion of civic virtue or social responsibility recognizable to the classical liberal tradition, as well as any idea of basing judgments about the public good in moral, spiritual, communitarian, or religious terms, while utterly dispensing with the presumption that individual worth might be grounded in natural rights. Its doctrine was unvarnished: The good of the community as a whole is assured when each is free to pursue his talents unrestricted by government and unfettered by extraneous claims, through government or other institutions, of rights owed to the less well established. In his 1884 book, *What Social Classes Owe to Each Other*, Sumner wrote:

> There is a beautiful notion afloat in our literature and in the minds of our people that men are born to certain "natural rights."
> If there were such things as natural rights, the question would arise, Against whom are they good? . . . The common assertion is . . . that society is bound to obtain and secure them for the persons interested. Society, however, is only the persons interested plus some other persons; and as the persons interested have by the hypothesis failed to win the rights, we come to this, that natural rights are the claims which certain persons have by prerogative against some other persons. . . .
> This theory . . . comes to mean that if any man finds himself uncomfortable in this world, it must be somebody else's fault, and that somebody is bound to come and make him comfortable. Now, the people who are most uncomfortable in this world . . . are those who have neglected their duties, and consequently have failed to get their rights. The people who can be called upon to serve the uncomfortable must be those who have done their duty, as the world goes, tolerably well. Consequently the doctrine . . . turns out to be in practice only a scheme for making injustice prevail in human society by reversing the distribution of rewards and punishments between those who have done their duty and those who have not.[13]

The good of society as a whole (to the extent a theory that considers society merely a collection of individual "persons" admits of such a notion) is assured simply by allowing unfettered competition, which itself becomes the basis for civilized living. Without any conception of structural disadvantages, by racial, social, economic, or gender position, and with little or no compassion for those who couldn't compete, Social Darwinists believed the fittest should and would survive, allowing the nation to reap the benefits of their talents. Presumably the weak or lazy would eventually disappear. Both consequences would contribute to the good of society.

Unlike the civic republican tradition, Jefferson's democracy, or even Locke's liberalism, citizenship and political independence based on property are not seen as valued for themselves. Property no longer functions to turn mere inhabitants into virtuous citizens, and equality becomes a radical, intensely competitive, and extremely harsh version of equality of opportunity, with no admission of disabling disadvantage. Good citizenship, therefore, is no longer embodied in a good and valued member of the community. It is an epiphenomenal attribute of economically successful people.

Democracy becomes not a way of life, as for the Greeks, nor a way independent farmers, who sustain themselves and their society by the sweat of their brow, can protect and advance their interests, as for Jefferson, but a system in which the "liberties" of the successful are protected and their rewards left unmolested. The idea of self-interest itself is reduced to raw acquisitiveness, devoid of any thought that looking out for the good of others might be understood as being in one's enlightened self-interest.

In the hands of Social Darwinists, private property becomes the linchpin of an argument against using government to redress any economic grievances, and most forcefully against democratically using it to redistribute power and wealth, or to reorder life chances. Using government in these ways, Sumner complained, was "jobbery" plain and simple, the "vice" of "plutocracy" under which it "corrupts a democratic and republican form of government."[14]

This belief represented the strong version of a subtle shift in the meaning of democracy away from any notion of rule by a class of the poor, or even by a majority, or as a way of life imbued with civic virtue, to a liberal system of electoral plebiscites focused on preventing the interference with rights, prominent among them the right of property. Notions of political and economic equality, at the same time, became equated with the right to compete in politics and economics. Whether one has the resources to compete effectively was not often considered. Louis Hartz is right when he claims Social Darwinism ended in the "capture of the American democrat by the Whigs."[15]

But Social Darwinism could take root partly because of the success of Madison's extended republic and Hamilton's economic nationalism, however distasteful that fact might have been to Madison, and perhaps even to Hamilton. While a majority could form more quickly and easily in small republics, in an extended republic it would be reduced to the status of a minority interest or a group. If a majority of the propertyless somehow managed to form quickly and dominate the legislature of a state, it would still have to dominate the governorship. If it dominated both, it would still have to dominate the other states and the United States government. At the national level, even after controlling the House of Representatives, the most democratic branch of government, it would still need to win over the Senate, the presidency, and a Court, thanks in part to Hamilton, appointed for life.

The design would work so well that later scholars would forget it was conceived to deny equality of opportunity for most to participate fully in political life, and was sustained by growing economic inequality. Because class conflict as a political response fared poorly in American history, group con-flict took on the appearance of the essence of human nature in politics itself.

Living today, Madison, and especially Hamilton, would be proud of their handiwork. Neither would be fooled so easily. They would clearly understand E. E. Schattschneider when he said, "the flaw in the pluralist heaven is that the heavenly chorus sings with a strong upper class accent."[16] They would know that lurking beneath the appearance of dominant explanations of non-participation as founded in mass apathy was some careful planning that made it seem so. Madison at least would be uneasy at the extent of inequality and apparent apathy, and perhaps the power of the national government, but he would also gain satisfaction from the nation's prosperity and growth and its avoidance of his twin fears of elite tyranny and democratic anarchy. Both men would read the years since the adoption of their ideas as a time in which the liberal right of property had been defended from the republican danger of full political equality and too vigorous political participation. They had succeeded in giving their posterity "a republican remedy for the diseases most incident to republican government." With formidable assistance from history, their plan worked.

▣ Chapter 3

American Political Development

The basic contours of American political and economic development are familiar to us. America was born as the stepchild of the accidental "discovery" of two continents unknown to Europeans, colonized through war and extermination by imperial rivals and with slavery, and populated by people of true grit, willing to endure countless hardships, persevere and sometimes dish out cruelty, to gain wealth or freedom or at least a new chance in life. Settled and dominated by the English victors in the colonial wars, America saw itself as part of the British crown, and Americans saw themselves as British citizens. Reluctant republicans, most in the minority who would eventually throw off constitutional monarchy for thoroughgoing republicanism only did so when they felt they never would be treated as full British subjects. Inhabiting a limitless continent rich with natural resources, inconveniently populated by those most regarded as "savages," free from the corruption of Europe but full of European Enlightenment ideas about liberty, property, rationality, science, and enterprise free of feudal obstructions, they came to believe themselves exceptional.

Making the first modern revolution when their colonial progenitors stifled their liberty, interfered with their business, or simply made them pay what they considered to be too much in taxes, penning one then another "first" written constitution later emulated throughout the world, they viewed themselves as the "first new nation." Like ancient Athens, their society included a slave economy. When they set out to design a republic that would protect liberty, however, the historical example they avoided was not slavery but the excesses, as they saw it, of Athens's one hundred fifty years of "pure democracy." Under a rapidly expanding economy, endowed by a seemingly limitless frontier of "free" land, with an infinite supply of European surplus labor, Madison's "extended republic" soon became Manifest Destiny, and that, as the frontier ended, an "open door" to the markets of the rest of the world. In a little more than a hundred years, the American republic had become a dominant world power.

Within this epic of rise to power and influence, however, there are countless shorter stories of political and economic struggle, of the many losers who gave way to those who won. And one fundamental story is how American political and economic developments were able to, if not stop, then contain the impulse of democracy, of majority faction, of mass movements, of widespread political participation—and how these political and economic dramas in the history of depoliticization would be forgotten as so many modern writers rushed to explain nonparticipation as mass apathy. Once again, I believe, the story begins with the collaboration, both intended and unintended, between James Madison and Alexander Hamilton.

The intended working relationship centered on their successful joint effort to have the Constitution ratified. In so doing, they wrote into fundamental law many institutional checks, not only on concentrated power and tyranny, but on the formation of democratic mass movements.

While Madison effectively carried the ball in this effort, it may have been Hamilton who better understood the possibilities the new structure afforded, as well as what it would take to move the design from theory into evolving practices capable of withstanding the realities of politics. For Hamilton saw the document not just constructing a neat balance between state and federal powers, and between institutions, but creating the opportunity to build a truly national political and economic system out of what he took to be the embarrassing confusion of the Articles of Confederation. Madison was not insensitive to this concern. Indeed, in *Federalist* No. 42, he points to a major defect of the Articles—the inability of the Continental Congress to regulate commerce between the states and with foreign nations.[1]

And the power of this new system would undergird, and make effective, the institutional design helping it build the legitimacy to guide the American future. What appeared as careful balance to Madison was seen by Hamilton as potential to create the kind of system in practice, had he the political reach, he would have written directly into the document in the first place.

Hamilton's argument at the Constitutional Convention that Congress should have "the power to pass all laws which they shall judge necessary to the common defense and general welfare of the Union" was rejected in favor of the implied power to "make all Laws which shall be necessary and proper" to carry out what became Congress's specifically enumerated and ostensibly limited powers.[2] The presidency was not as powerful as he would have liked (Jefferson was later to accuse him of monarchist tendencies); however, through George Washington he could make it powerful. The Supreme Court was not explicitly given the power of judicial review, but the justices' life tenure, which he argued strongly for in his *Federalist* No. 78,[3] would enable it to expand its power through early Federalist domination of appointments and what became the brilliant guidance of Chief Justice John Marshall. Most famously it did so in the 1803 case of *Marbury v. Madison*, granting itself the prerogative of judicial review against the objections of President Thomas Jefferson. It soon fortified the constitutional rights of property against governmental interference through its reading of the contract clause in the 1810 case of *Fletcher v. Peck*. Then in 1819, through *McCulloch v. Maryland*, it underscored the supremacy of the national government and strengthened its ability to guide the political economy, declaring the National Bank constitutional, while declaring unconstitutional a state's effort to tax it. And in 1824, with *Gibbons v. Ogden*, the Court again augmented federal economic power by giving an early broad interpretation of the meaning of "interstate commerce" and Congress's authority over it. Although there would be important retrenchments in the Court's view, a central role in "regulating" commerce would become the federal government's most essential constitutional rationale for its role as overseer of the national economy.

The federal powers were enumerated, and technically those not stated were left by the Bill of Rights to the states or the people. But the powers were supreme, broad, and could be so construed as Hamilton did in the fight to establish a national bank, successfully convincing President Washington of its constitutionality and laying the groundwork for the famous opinion by Chief Justice Marshall in the *McCulloch* case, delivered long after Hamilton was shot dead by Aaron Burr in their famous duel. Where Madison got the design he wanted, Hamilton saw a flawed plan but one that was the best he could hope for and one he could work with. He did so very effectively, in some respects too effectively to suit Madison's tastes.

How this all evolved over the next two hundred years is a rich story of political, economic, and constitutional development to which a brief summary would only do injustice. The plan did not always work as intended. Political parties immediately formed, creating the dreaded specter of institutionalized faction. But even here, parties and the two-party system that historically developed have helped forge compromises without aggregating effective majority factions, a result that undoubtedly should have pleased Madison. Later leaders of government and business would use their power to pursue political and economic development in ways to suit their interests and philosophies, and these too would become part of the evolving structure.

For forty extremely formative years in the late nineteenth and early twentieth centuries, during the heyday of American industrial capitalism, the Supreme Court would read into the Fourteenth Amendment, where no such words could be found, a "liberty of contract" under which it would declare unconstitutional many efforts by states (and some by the federal government) to regulate business—even on issues of health, safety, and general welfare, normally state prerogatives. Long before it would be deployed against racial injustice, this "Civil War Amendment" was used to protect large scale private property against democratic interference.[4] At the same time, the Court was narrowly construing the reach of the commerce clause, making it more difficult for the federal government to regulate business. This one-two legal counterpunch provided an important defense against populist, then progressive, then New Deal public sentiment clamoring for government protection.

This conservative judicial activism in the Court was not anticipated by Hamilton as such, but the life tenure of justices, coupled with the power of judicial review, allowed the Court wide latitude to block the will of democratic majorities, in state legislatures, and, especially during the Great Depression, in the Congress and presidency. While such judgments blunted the power of the national as well as state government, something that might have concerned Hamilton, the effect was to provide political space and a legal rationale for a national corporate economy to develop relatively free from the constraints of popular control.[5] And as capital was accumulated, invested, and reinvested, private political and economic power was amassed that could dominate national and then international politics, set the terms of political agendas, and control majority factions here and sometimes even abroad. When this power was used during the Depression in ways that seemed contrary to both the survival of free enterprise and the public good, the Constitution could be interpreted creatively, through the commerce clause, now to expand the central government's authority. Backed by public support, a popular president had a way to challenge the Court's reading of the Constitution, the constitutional reach (through Congress) to threaten the Court with expansion, the right to appoint sympathetic justices when vacancies occurred, and ultimately enough power to prevail in its decisions on his programs.

Madison might smile to see his checks and balances work, but Hamilton would realize that, looked at over time, both of his central objectives had been accomplished: a vibrant, powerful, private national economy, and a strong central government to nurture, guide, and help it along. The powerful would be free to do their job, while those with little power could gain some as long as they didn't interfere too much. With the threat of majority faction checked, private interests and passions could be dissolved into the real goal: a flexible national political and economic system based on free enterprise. And the power of this system would be instrumental in giving authority to the Constitution that originally sketched its parameters. American history is full of similar stories of the constitutional design working itself out in real time in ways that, if not always, often would have pleased Hamilton.

One episode that is striking both in its importance in American political and economic development and in the history of American political participation is the formation of the "system of 1896."[6] Where presidential electoral turnout in the nineteenth century from the 1840s on averaged over 77 percent of the eligible electorate, after 1896, turnout dropped until it reached modern lows of 49.3 percent in 1920, and 48.9 percent in 1924.[7] While there have been up-and-down twentieth-century variations, turnout has never approached these nineteenth-century levels, making this election a watershed in the history of depoliticization. It is worth considering how such depoliticization was accomplished and what role the Madison-Hamilton structure of American political development played. E. E. Schattschneider, a student of American politics with a sharp understanding of Madison, argues: "The most powerful instrument for the control of conflict is conflict itself." In his view, the ultimate policy and "grand strategy" of politics "deals with public policy concerning conflict," and, in the first instance, it is concerned with the very structure of institutions: "The function of institutions is to channel conflict; institutions do not treat all forms of conflict impartially." For Schattschneider, drawing particular political lines of conflict suppresses other potential lines of conflict, thereby working to the disadvantage of those whose interests the subordinated conflicts might represent. Thus, for Schattschneider, "the definition of the alternatives is the supreme instrument of power," and the design and working of institutions a primary mode of definition.[8] Ineluctably, in his account, conflict lines have a bias favoring some against others.

Conflict also has a *scope*, by which he means the degree to which people either remain an audience to an argument or become participants:

> Every change in the scope of conflict has a bias; it is partisan in its nature.
> That is, it must be assumed that every change in the number of participants
> is about something, that the newcomers have sympathies or antipathies that
> make it possible to involve them.

Madison, he argues, "understood something about the relation of scope to the outcome of conflict," illustrated most famously in his argument for an extended republic in *Federalist* No. 10.[9] If an extended republic could displace the kinds of fundamental conflicts that might pit a majority of citizens against a minority—for example, by avoiding basic economic class issues—it could limit both the range of issues considered and the scope of participants who would take interest in and thereby help determine the nature of the conflict. If the bias of conflict could be shaped in this way, the political agenda could be kept under some control. Indeed, in 1896, the pressures of industrialization came close to, but ultimately failed at, dividing the American electorate by economic class as cross-cutting cleavages of ethnicity, region, and religion played a key role in dispersing class conflict. For Schattschneider, the depoliticizing effects of the "system of 1896" is the primary historical example of Madison's genius.

The third political party system in the United States ended in 1896 with the decisive defeat of populism. A sharp, long-term decline in voting followed. As an era, it had been marked first by the Civil War and Reconstruction, then post-Reconstruction abandonment of the South by the Republicans and its domination by elite southern Democrats, and throughout this "gilded age" of industrial development by intense political and economic conflicts. According to Kevin Phillips, such heyday periods of capitalist expansion include the following characteristics: conservative politics; reduced role for government; difficult times for labor; large-scale economic and corporate restructuring (in this period, the rise of the great corporations, the organization of the first trusts, and a merger and consolidation wave); tax reduction; deflation (the depressions of 1873 and 1893); a two-tier economy with difficult times for agriculture and mining, and good times for industry and finance; concentration of wealth; increased debt and speculation; and a speculative implosion (the depression of 1893).[10]

The second party system, lasting roughly from 1828 and the ascendancy of Jackson's Democratic party into the late 1850s, was also characterized by high voter turnout and what has been described by Richard Jensen as "militarist," highly disciplined parties and intense political mobilization. With universal white male suffrage accomplished by the 1830s, and a turnout of eligible voters reaching 80 percent by 1840, others recall this period as a "golden era" of American democracy. In an 1831 description Americans today would find foreign to their mood, Tocqueville comments:

> It is hard to explain the place filled by political concerns in the life of an American. To take a hand in the government of society and to talk about it is his most important business and, so to say, the only pleasure he knows.[11]

Yet, as Piven and Cloward perceptively argue, the politics of this period did not challenge elites because political mobilization was dominated by what they call "tribalism" (intense ethnic, religious, and sectional partisanship) and "clientelism" (citizen links to parties based on patronage). The rapid industrialization and concentration of economic resources following the Civil War, however, created conditions for new conflict by displacing the ethno-religious, sectional, and patronage-based party fights that had carried over from the second party system and been intensified by the deep scars of the Civil War. If the discontents of the growing urban industrial working class, including its teeming scores of new Catholic immigrants, could prompt them to find common ground with western populist Protestant farmers, and if both could make common cause with white and African-American southern agrarian workers, then the third party system might realign into a fourth in which the political agenda would be dominated by a conflict bias mirroring sharp economic cleavages. This, of course, is precisely what failed in the historic election of 1896.

From the Civil War on, pressures within the economic system helped propel a number of political protest movements, often based in agricultural regions. These included midwestern Granges battling over high rates for rail transport that was their only link to markets, high grain storage rates, and crushing debt to bankers; southern Farmers' Alliances engaged in similar struggles; and northern unions fighting over working conditions and pay, especially in railroad and steel industries. Electoral efforts developed at the state and national level. Some won significant local, state, and congressional victories. Prominent national efforts included the Greenback-Labor, farmer-worker coalition in 1876, and the evolution of the Farmers' Alliances into the People's party by 1892, winning 8.5 percent of the vote for its presidential candidate, James B. Weaver.

In 1896, the People's party endorsed the Democratic presidential candidate, William Jennings Bryan, with his fiery populist oratory to oppose the Republicans and William McKinley. The lines of political conflict seemed finally to be issue-oriented, and drawn around fundamental issues at that. Having thrown off the conservative domination by President Grover Cleveland's industrial and financial supporters, and backed by the Populists, the Democrats appeared to be giving themselves national reach beyond section, religion, or even party loyalty. They seemed ready to become the "majority faction."

The decisive defeat of populism in 1896 can be attributed to a number of factors, including conservative mobilization through industrial associations and alliances in the period leading up to it, the formation of private armies to break strikes, and massive organizational and virtually unlimited financial backing for McKinley. The ability of capital to concentrate itself within a Hamiltonian national economy dominated by finance and industry gave it the resources to defend itself politically.

The extended nature of the republic was also decisive and race remained critical. Farmers wanted to get away from the gold standard and hard currency that kept prices low and interest rates high, thus devastating farming regions while benefiting financiers who held bonds from the Civil War. In the South, white and African-American farmers were forced into sharecropping and tenancy. With little enthusiasm for Bryan and thoroughly frightened by populism (which had captured eight southern state legislatures in 1890), southern Democratic elites concentrated on strengthening their regional control, using race-baiting to split populist whites and blacks, ultimately disenfranchising almost all blacks as well as many poor whites. Reviving Civil War and Reconstruction animosities, southern elites effectively drove a wedge between southern and western populists,[12] while northern Republican elites were reminding workers of the price they had paid in blood in the Civil War.[13] Catholic urban workers were suspicious of western Protestant populists, who called not only for greater government regulation of business, something unions and working men and women supported, but also for limiting or ending immigration, motivated in part by ethnic and religious prejudice. Bryan's evangelical oratory didn't help.

Finally, Bryan's program, while deeply troubling to economic elites within Democratic ranks and splitting eastern financial interests from "silverites," was in fact tepid, focusing on the demand for silver currency as a way to inflate the economy (and support growing silver mining interests in the

West) while avoiding tougher issues like democratic control of the nation's money system, an important Greenback and Populist demand. It had little appeal to urban industrial workers in a depression economy. Indeed, a good argument could be made that their short-term interests lay with eastern financiers, who intended to propel economic growth (thereby creating jobs) through protective tariffs and "sound money," and with industrialists themselves, who would command industrial development even if its rewards would be malapportioned. It had none of the visionary appeal of populist critiques of industrial capitalism and calls for economic cooperation. In fact, Richard Hofstadter argues that the choice of Bryan and association with his program were fatal to the Populist party.

In addition, the Knights of Labor was weakening and refrained from alliance; the growing American Federation of Labor believed in a political, craft-oriented unionism. And the Democratic party remained saddled with the fact that under Grover Cleveland, a Democrat, the nation had plunged into depression three years earlier.[14]

At precisely that point of political and economic development where, under intense pressures of industrialization, many European nations would build "modern" political party systems based on fundamental social and economic interests, American political development seemed to stop. It produced, by Schattschneider's account, "one of the most sharply sectional political divisions in American history," allowing two minorities to dominate: in the North, business-Republicans (having decisively defeated the radical agrarian movement within their own party); and in the South, conservatives in the now "Solid-South" Democratic party (having split southern from western populists, and poor whites from blacks). Schattschneider writes,

> The establishment of the alignment of 1896 is perhaps the best example in American history of the successful substitution of one conflict for another. The radicals were defeated because the conflict they sought to exploit was subordinated to an inconsistent cleavage which split the radical movement, isolated the southern and western radicals from each other and overwhelmed both wings in one-party sectional alignments. On the other hand, the conservatives won power because they were able to impose on the country the conflict which divided the people the way they wanted them to be divided.[15]

Madison's constitutional design and Hamilton's nationalism were essential to this objective, as were the power and skill with which the conservatives divided and defeated their adversaries. The Populists were up against enormous and growing industrial and financial power. And they were up against powerful ethnic and racial prejudices, including their own. But the mistakes the reformers made were also important. In one respect, they were too traditional for the changing times, looking too much to an agrarian past and too little to the industrial future that was, for good and ill, changing the face of America. Their program was not only watered down and then outflanked; it failed to address the needs of the emerging, often urban and immigrant people who worked in industry, and the essential issue of how to organize production itself. Some had ideas and proposals, but these were not central and were no match for the reality of growing industrial capitalism.

The election of 1896 is only part of the story of twentieth-century depoliticization. Scholars disagree whether developing political and economic power (what Walter Dean Burnham calls "systemic forces" making possible "such a remarkable solution to the problem of adjusting mass politics to the exigencies of industrialism") was itself thoroughly decisive, or whether of primary importance was the political space the election created in which to change the "rules of the game" in ways that restricted participation and, therefore, allowed this power to thrive. These included devices to disenfranchise blacks and poor whites: poll taxes, long residency requirements, discriminatory literacy tests, and extra-legal means of intimidation, including lynchings for blacks. Various reforms weakened party-voter linkages and loyalty, such as the Australian ballot and Progressive Era reforms of direct primary election of party nominees, direct election of senators, the initiative and referendum process, and nonpartisan elections. Personal voter registration made voting more costly in time, energy, and knowledge, and allowed for manipulation. Discriminatory registration practices and malapportioned state legislatures were used to weaken the voting power of immigrants. Some argue even the Nineteenth Amendment, however laudable, was supported by some to dilute Catholic votes, with American Protestant women more likely to exercise the franchise than recent immigrants steeped in conservative ethnic and Catholic mores.

Whatever the causes, the consequence of the "system of 1896" was to initiate a fourth party system during which the Republicans largely dominated national politics for the next three decades—reaching its conservative zenith during the "Roaring Twenties" and the elections of Presidents Harding, Coolidge, and Hoover. To be sure, this process itself was intensely political, with challenges—including at the ballot box—from progressives (in 1912 splitting the Republican party), and socialists that sometimes yielded reforms and other times won repression, as with the anti-radical Palmer raids after World War I. Some reforms had ambiguous consequences. If the direct primary was democratic because it took power from party bosses, it also weakened the one institution best geared to mobilize the common citizen—the political party. If the Federal Reserve Act gave the government greater power over the banking system, it also integrated private bankers into the decision-making structure of the federal government.

If the conservative prototype of the age was Calvin Coolidge, its progressive spirit was best captured by one of Theodore Roosevelt's mentors, Herbert

Croly, who tried to synthesize Jefferson's concern for democratic equality of rights with Hamilton's for economic liberty and nationalism. Croly's writing contains within it not only foundational ideas of the progressive tradition, but ideas in harmony with both Franklin Roosevelt's New Deal and Lyndon Johnson's Great Society calling for a broad national consensus. His work is an effort to discredit traditional liberal economic thinking, to question the adequacy of Jeffersonian democracy in the modern age, and to show how, with modifications, Hamilton's political economy could be given a human face. It embodies the shift in liberal thought from enterprise free of government involvement, to the modern liberal idea that a positive state will need to intervene in economic affairs to protect the public interest and ensure the integrity of the private enterprise system itself, as well as "a morally and socially desirable distribution of wealth."

Unlike Sumner, he understood that rabid competition could actually destroy the social fabric of the nation. While even democracy must "recognize political, economic, and social discriminations," he argued, "it must also manage to withdraw its consent whenever these discriminations show any tendency to excessive endurance. The essential wholeness of the community depends absolutely on the ceaseless creation of a political, economic, and social aristocracy and their equally incessant replacement."[16] For the sake of efficiency and effectiveness, elites would rule. But they would be elites dedicated to the commonweal and monitored by a democratic public ready to withdraw consent if they failed:

> It must cease to be a democracy of indiscriminate individualism, and become one of selected individuals who are obliged constantly to justify their selection; and its members must be united not by a sense of joint irresponsibility, but by a sense of joint responsibility for the success of their political and social ideal. They must become, that is, a democracy devoted to the welfare of the whole people by means of a conscious labor of individual and social improvement; and that is precisely the sort of democracy which demands for its realization the aid of the Hamiltonian nationalistic organization and principle.[17]

Yet even the Progressive era had profoundly depoliticizing effects that are with us to the present day. Its reform impulse was sometimes rooted in a desire for a more egalitarian, more democratic form of governance. But it was equally one attempting to increase stabilization and administrative control, often over an unruly, unpredictable mass politics. Imbued with a spirit of science and with the idea that nature was something to be controlled and bent to one's will (even conservationists were attempting to properly administer nature), it tried through reform to break the back of what it saw as corrupting partisan political nature. Business was influenced by Frederick Winslow Taylor's "scientific management," which fractured craftsmanship into discrete work units, allowed closer supervision and more control of the work process, and created less skilled workers, who became more dispensable. Greater productivity would be based upon more "efficiency," but efficiency of this sort itself depended on harder work and less resistance. As Kenneth Dolbeare argues, wide popularity of Taylorism, in manufacturing, mining and transportation industries, and in the press, "illustrates not only the extent to which the whole country was in thrall to science and managerialism, but also the profoundly political way its effects shaped work life, social mobility, self-understanding, and ways of thinking in the society."[18]

Culturally reflecting the values and image of the successful business enterprise, the progressive reform impulse tried especially to bring political order to what appeared as the chaos of the ethnic, urban political culture. Allied with the advent of modern mass journalism, also seeing itself as above the political fray, reformers often sought apolitical solutions to what were often intensely political problems. Burnham concludes,

> most if not all of these fundamental changes in the "rules of the game" were in effect devices of political stabilization and control, with strongly conservative latent consequences if not overt justification, and with an overwhelming antipartisan bias.[19]

With the establishment of the "system of 1896," voter turnout plummeted, most drastically in the South but severely throughout the nation. From an average of 77.7 percent from 1840 to 1900, it declined to a low of 48.9 percent in the 1924 presidential election,[20] while two-party competition dropped precipitously as well. Voting participation became sharply skewed by class as the requirements to vote became far more demanding, while the dominant political agenda constrained the range of interests and issues represented. In Schattschneider's terms, "the system of 1896" altered the scope of conflict, seriously restricting who was likely to—indeed, who could—get into the game. Voter turnout jumped to 56.9 percent in 1928 and edged up early in the fifth party system (beginning with the realigning 1932 election), until it reached 62.5 percent in 1940. Class skewing in voter participation mitigated as political conflicts were more distinctly drawn in economic terms. Clearly, the New Deal reversed some of the conservative trends of the era it replaced, stripping down the ideology of laissez-faire, increasing the dignity, political importance, and ultimately the security of working people, and for a time modestly widening the scope of conflict. But it did not challenge elite control in the South; it depended on it.[21] And it sought not to replace elite domination of the corporate economy housed in the Northeast. Its goal was to control it and make it act responsibly.

The New Deal was more of an instinct than a clear plan, however, usually driven by political necessities of coalition building and administered in an experimental fashion through the alphabet soup of agencies the "brain trusters" set up. It was an impulse driven by the short-run goals of getting out of the Depression and winning elections. To the extent it was ideological, it was so in the sense of trying to create an administrative state beyond partisan politics—of finding technical solutions to political problems. In the short run, the New Deal was intensely political, surrounded by class conflict. In the long run, it sought consensus on how best to scientifically manage a modern society in the interest of the only class, as Russell Hanson puts it, that really fit its ideology—a universal class of consumers.[22]

The conservatives were reeling from alleged responsibility for the Great Depression. Nevertheless, they attacked Roosevelt relentlessly for stirring up class conflict and undermining the American way of life, and worse. He attacked them with equal relish as "plutocrats" indifferent to the needs of the American people: "They are unanimous in their hate for me," he remarked, "and I welcome their hatred." There was also a challenge from the socialist left but, in an important respect, Roosevelt cut the political ground out from under it by taking up modified liberal versions of its demands for Social Security and workers' rights. Severely repressed during and after World War I, including beatings, deportations, jailings and lynchings, it really was just resurfacing as the Depression hit, and its response was not unified and would grow less so.[23] Lack of unity made it hard to get a clear message out, and each left faction was contending not only with Roosevelt, but Huey Long and Father Coughlin, among other brands of 1930s populists, the organizing drives of trade unions, in particular the creation of the Congress of Industrial Organizations, and each other. And some of the message that did get out was antithetical to American political identity, focusing too much on central planning and dismissing too lightly democratic institutions, even speaking in a language that seemed removed, foreign, and repressive. At the same time, American political views had been kept within bounds unfavorable to the left by the earlier repression of socialists and syndicalists.

In the end, some on the left made mistakes opposite to those of the populists. If the populists' reaction to industrialization was too much a "heartland" America looking to the past, the reaction of socialists and others on the left either was, or was easily caricatured as, not "American" enough and too far into a hazy utopian future, neglecting the central role in America of the individual, of property the individual earned, of democratic (sometimes derided as "bourgeois") political institutions, and of pragmatism. Just at those historical watersheds when industrial corporate development and concentration of power was eroding the social and economic foundation of important American identities—the economically independent and self-sufficient person—first populism and then socialism failed to supply an effective alternative. In the end, Hanson concludes, "the most conspicuous failure of the thirties was the inability of the left to capitalize on the Depression." And the

defeat especially of the democratically oriented left, he believes, had a profound impact on the contours of the debate on the idea of democracy itself:

> No longer would competing interpretations be rooted in moral traditions
> recalling an age of innocence long since past, nor would they anticipate
> movement toward the Just Society. From the New Deal on, American
> conceptions of democracy came to be associated with a particular kind of
> government, one whose primary responsibility was to serve the material
> interests of a consumer community.[24]

The New Deal, then, laid the groundwork and provided an implicit philosophical rationale for the modern administrative state, without really com-
posing a political critique of the system it was trying to reform. It attempted
pragmatically to put politics and governance on a rational footing. In so
doing, it saw no need and made little effort to shape the American party
system to conform to fundamental industrial fault lines—except when politically expedient, as in its alliance with some unions. In the South, it stood by
the party's coalition with some of the most reactionary elites in the nation.

The Roosevelt legacy of political administration and pragmatic politics
was a stabilizing force in American political life for the next fifty years.
Through conservative and liberal administrations it was refined, scaled back,
or advanced, but not effectively questioned. While voter participation declined after 1940, it edged up again in the 1950s, reaching a post-populism
high of 65.4 percent in the intensely competitive 1960 election. But this was
an election about how best to administer the state, with Kennedy and Nixon
disagreeing mostly at the margins.

It was not until 1980 and the successful conservative candidacy of Ronald
Reagan that the depoliticizing ideology of the administrative state was seriously challenged. Reagan argued that the administrative state, as such, had
political consequences, that running the nation's political system indeed was
as much about ideology as competence. And this challenge endeavored to
free business from the restraints of what he viewed as politically motivated
bureaucratic administration, however much expertise might be claimed as the
rationale. Regulation and administration were political, he argued, and bad
for business, and therefore, bad for the common good. Under the veneer of
administration, he claimed, was an intensely liberal ideology, with which he
relentlessly battered the sitting president, Jimmy Carter, who was hardly an
economic liberal but certainly was a technocrat.

President Reagan's two winning elections, in 1980 and 1984, and later
George Bush's win in 1988, were made possible by a number of disparate
factors. One of these was the constricted nature of the political universe, itself
facilitated by the trend dating back to the beginning of the century, and
accelerating from the 1960s, of the weakening of the political parties as insti-

tutions capable of aggregating the interests of a mass public. Following 1960, voter participation again edged downward and the economic rift widened between the "party of non-voters" and the "party of voters," shaving away part of the Democrats' natural constituency of poorer voters. Indeed, Burnham argues, the rightward Reagan revolution in public policy was made possible by an election that was *not*, itself, based upon a clear ideological shift to the right. It was one, however, in which low turnout allowed the future president to win a "landslide" victory with only one out of four votes of eligible voters.[25] By 1988 turnout had dipped further, to a post-1924 low of 52.8 percent, and then increased about 4 points in the unusually interesting (or peculiar) three-way race of 1992.[26]

Another kind of diversity had come to dominate the political scene, as Thomas and Mary Edsall suggest, divisions based on race, rights, taxes, and values. Just as sectional, ethnic, and religious conflicts helped bury the populist dream in 1896, liberal hopes of uniting the ethnically, racially, and economically marginalized with the working and middle classes were dashed as the New Deal coalition tore itself apart over issues like busing, Vietnam, women's rights, and which groups were pulling their economic weight, and who should pay the bill for those who weren't. Just as politics, by 1960, had become more national in scope, in Schattschneider's terms, these conflicts helped prevent more basic cleavages from surfacing. Without a fundamental economic crisis with a palpable cause, and without a philosophy capable of offering a critique of discontents that was at once accessible, comprehensible, and beyond the immediate social issues of the day, liberalism was thrown on the defensive and remains there still.

The Madison-Hamilton collaboration in designing the American republic seems to have succeeded. By creating an extended republic within which interest groups could thrive in any number of institutional niches in government, the constitutional design, fortified by a strong national economy, encouraged more manageable group conflict and discouraged class politics. Viewing American society as fundamentally class based, a division emanating from human nature, and believing this to be the critical threat republican government posed for itself, Madison sought a "republican remedy." But it was not, and never was intended to be, a democratic remedy. Political equality was sacrificed on the altar of realistic republicanism in order to avoid the worse alternatives of tyranny, chaos, or both. With the monumental exception of the failure of the system to prevent fundamental sectional, economic, and social conflicts between the North and South from exploding into civil war, American political history shows it to be a design that worked very well as intended.

The "system of 1896" illustrates how an extended republic could thwart majority faction. But more recent politics around social issues also exemplify this virtue of Madison's design. For if an extended liberal republic is more likely to house pluralism, a diversity of needs and interests, it is also likely to frustrate the development of common ground. And if fundamental common ground cannot be found and articulated in a plausible, realistic political strategy, groups are likely to retreat to pressing their own specific interests, priorities, or values, eschewing the idea that they are worth sacrificing for some long-range, more essential political or economic hope. As the populists of 1896 and the liberals of the 1980s and 1990s found out, an encompassing program in the interests of a majority is very difficult to come by. But without one, sectional, interest group, racial, religious, ideational cleavages, and value differences relegate potential majorities factions to minority status.

In the end, Madison's real genius notwithstanding, Hamilton may have proved more prescient. For he understood that by creating a strong unified economy, nurtured by a powerful, provident national government, the "rights of property" would not simply be protected against the depredations of majorities but would dominate. One political result that, in some measure, may be attributed to this domination is the low voter turnout and intense class differentials in electoral participation, after 1896, that have remained enduring features of the twentieth-century American political system.

Yet, as study of the problem of nonparticipation in politics took off particularly in the 1950s and 1960s, these fundamental institutional, constitutional, and economic concerns were often sublimated in myriad discussions of political apathy. Why did so few people participate in politics? Why did so few vote?

Too often in studies of these questions, the class skewing of nonparticipation was simply overlooked or, to the degree it was considered, was viewed as beneficial for the political system because lower-class voters were ill informed—or, worse, were perhaps authoritarian in temperament. If writers like Daniel Bell and Seymour Martin Lipset were right, following Max Weber, there was an "end of ideology," meaning that fundamental political conflicts had been mitigated in advanced industrial society. Conflicts that remained, including some residual class disputes between political parties, were around the edges of the unifying questions of how best to channel and administer differences through the state. If a wide consensus on values was emerging across class and participatory-nonparticipatory lines alike, then nonparticipation and its class character were becoming less important as political or moral issues. Within the profession of political science, a rationale was developing through which to address the problem of "mass apathy" without tackling the historical, institutional, political, ideological, and economic causes of nonparticipation.

 **Chapter 4**

The Science of Liberal Politics

One irony of American intellectual history is that the depoliticizing "self-fulfilling prophecy"[1] embedded in the American Constitution helped lay the groundwork for another within the dominant republican liberal explanation of nonparticipation. If the amount of participation existing in a democracy is presumed that amount optimal for democratic success, and if the constitutional design is assumed to be a democratic blueprint par excellence, an intellectual lethargy is created regarding any need to increase participation, and depoliticization is furthered. This sealed hermeneutic, however, awaited developments in liberal democratic theory that would stress liberalism at the expense of democracy and, in the study of politics, that would try to take the politics out of political science.

Seeing politics as a "science" goes back at least to Aristotle. The drafters of the American Constitution believed themselves to be practitioners of a "science of virtue"[2] that could, through smart and realistic constitutional design, even use the baser instincts of human nature to fashion virtuous citizens.

As success in and esteem for the natural sciences progressed in the eighteenth and nineteenth centuries, political thinkers began looking to them as a guide. One foundation of this developing science of politics is the utilitarian conception of human motivation, behavior, and nature. To comprehend why humans do what they do, how they conceive and pursue their interests, and under what conditions they will make political obligations and act on them, one must understand that people are primarily motivated by the seeking of pleasure and the avoidance of pain. To the degree the study of politics understands this, utilitarians believe, it can avoid the trap of philosophical rationalizations and become a science of politics.

Unlike many of their twentieth-century followers, acknowledged and unacknowledged, the most important utilitarian thinkers, such as James Mill and Jeremy Bentham, did not seek to separate the science of politics from the question of political virtue. Their purpose was to put political design on a firm scientific footing in order to achieve the public good: the most pleasure and the least pain, and the greatest happiness for the greatest number.

According to C. B. Macpherson, it is Mill and Bentham who successfully inject the idea of democracy into the amalgam of republican liberal thought that precedes them. For if the governors and governed alike are motivated by self-interested pleasure, the need arises to protect the citizenry and the public good from the self-interested depredations of the rulers, as well as from each other. Following English liberalism, this generally requires a restricted state that acts as an umpire between competing interests. But it also requires frequent elections, through which the populace can hold the umpires accountable. Thus Mill and Bentham devised a justification for greater democracy within liberalism—what has been called liberal democracy.

The political project of the utilitarians, as liberals, was to create a political order that would allow people freely to achieve the most pleasure they could from the one place pleasure really is derivable—pursuit of their private interests. Unsurprisingly perhaps, the motivations for making choices that lead to happiness—pleasure and pain—are surely the psychological specifications of profit and loss, the motivations for the accumulation of capital, which then creates economic progress.

While the utilitarians advocated a minimal state, however, they were ready to support those interventions by the state that would enhance the private utility upon which the public good ultimately depended. Utilitarianism, in this way, committed itself to defending private property, creating an administrative apparatus to manage people who threaten the liberal framework, and even using the state, if electorally sanctioned, to intervene in the private economy when the market failed the public good. Within utilitarianism developed essential rationales for the welfare state, a modern consumer society in which individuals see themselves and are appealed to as beings with a limitless appetite for pleasure, and an ideal of democracy that does not seek to develop individuals, as Rousseau thought, and certainly not one that sees itself intrinsic to the good life, as Pericles might have suggested, but as a means to the end of the greatest happiness for the greatest number.

Calling this the "founding model of democracy for a modern industrial society," and labeling it "protective democracy," Macpherson finds within it

> no enthusiasm for democracy, no idea that it could be a morally
> transformative force; it is nothing but a logical requirement for the
> governance of inherently self-interested conflicting individuals who are
> assumed to be infinite desirers of their own private benefits. . . . Responsible
> government, even to the extent of responsibility to a democratic electorate,
> was needed for the protection of individuals and the promotion of the Gross
> National Product, and for nothing more.[3]

The utilitarian conception of human interests and the state does accomplish objectives important to the development of empirical democratic theory in the 1950s. Like utilitarianism itself, empirical democratic theory was an effort to take the "soul stuff" (as Arthur Bentley called it in the early 1900s) out of the study of politics.

Utilitarianism served this project well, helping solve the problem of whether there were basic units that could be measured, and what they might be. If political behavior is best explained as individual calculations of pleasure and pain, and one presumes individual or group preferences, tendencies, and behaviors can be measured in a value-neutral way, then such preferences, tendencies, and behaviors become the molecular units of knowledge—just like atoms, neutrons, and electrons for the physical sciences.[4] And utilitarianism continues to serve well. In contemporary rational choice and social choice theory, political behavior is understood as the discrete choices of the individual actor (or of groups as compilations of individuals), as Anthony Downs puts it, "who moves toward his goals in a way which, to the best of his knowledge, uses the least possible input of scarce resources per unit of valued output."[5]

Utilitarianism bequeaths to the "science of politics" a theory of human motivation that appears both measurable and uncomplicated by constructs impossible to study. As a theory of how to study motivation, it also goes well with the techniques championed by behavioralists, such as survey opinion research and statistical analysis, and with rational-choice theorist calculations of individual utility. Finally, in its limited theory of "protective democracy," utilitarians focused on the vote as the one legitimate arena where political behavior should and did express itself, again an object eminently quantifiable, however restricted in its gauge of democracy as a viable political form. Therefore, while the new science of politics believed itself to be getting rid of the confusions of philosophy, it was grounded in the philosophy of utilitarianism, as well as the complementary epistemology of positivism.[6]

Emphasizing these continuities and affinities is not simply to equate utilitarianism and empirical political science, or to suggest empirical political science has been monolithic. Much empirical political science, particularly what became known as pluralism, following first Bentley (or what was perceived to be his work[7]) and later David Truman, substituted the interest group for the individual as the basic unit of study. More important group theorists such as Bentley, elite theorists such as Charles Beard, early practitioners of scientific politics such as Charles Merriam, institutional political scientists such as Woodrow Wilson, and the school of *reform* Social Darwinism important to progressive early twentieth-century thought—like early utilitarians but unlike later empirical theorists—intended to generate knowledge that could be put in the service of improving American democracy. For some, this meant engaging in advocacy; for others, it meant developing plans to fashion the state into a tool to protect all interests in society from an elite of wealth; for others yet, informing the citizenry and elites about how the processes of government and politics really work so they could better perform their respective functions. Whether it was through a developing welfare state, or civic or elite education, as with the utilitarians, science was to provide the objective data with which to intervene intelligently and rationally in political affairs. And while most would agree that an objective political science required holding one's values in abeyance in order to accurately understand the facts of a situation, few would dispute that the purpose of locating and assorting these facts was to improve upon the cherished value of a democracy not yet fully realized. This was soon to change with the behavioral revolution in political science.

Alongside early reformist political science, but before behavioralism, emerged what has been called the elite theory of democracy. This theory is based on a sense of pessimism within modern liberalism about how much democracy is really possible and, indeed, desirable in a modern political world dominated by a need for increasing size in organization and inevitable bureaucratization. It resonates with the kinds of analyses of large-scale organization undertaken by writers like Robert Michels, Vilfredo Pareto, Gaetano Mosca, and Maurice Duverger, and is best captured in the extremely influential work of the sociologist Max Weber and the economist Joseph Schumpeter. It predates the fear of mass politics embodied in the writings of men like Seymour Martin Lipset but formulates a way of redefining democracy that suits their objectives and mood.

Weber's pessimism results from his critiques of both classical liberalism and socialism and the implications of these for democratic theory. Against socialism, Weber perceptively argues that bureaucratic domination is not a particular attribute of class society, but rather a feature of all modern organization. The state both predates capitalism and is essential for the organization of all modern political life, and therefore is not an epiphenomenal superstructure of capitalism. The state would not and should not "wither away." The Leninist fantasy of "smashing the state" provided, instead, ideological cover for a new form of bureaucratic domination, this time located in the proletariat's political party that, without the offsetting influences of private institutions, would if anything be more oppressive. Joseph Stalin proved him prescient.

Although in the liberal tradition—he supported a private economy, parliamentary government, and viewed political parties as essential—Weber believed that increasing bureaucratization and rationalization of decision making were inevitable and desirable attributes of modern organizations of all types, including the state, private enterprise organizations, political parties, and thereby, of modern society itself. Expertise, technical competency, and rationality become the essential ingredients of continuing a social order that proves itself by its efficient production and distribution of the conveniences of modern life. He writes, "The decisive reason for the advance of bureaucratic organization has always been its purely *technical* superiority over any other form of organization."[8]

Against classical liberalism, Weber maintained that the legitimacy of modern organizations in general, and the state in particular, was based on its ability rationally to order society, and not on natural law or a social contract, and, against conservatives, certainly not on religion or tradition. As Seymour Martin Lipset points out, Weber saw a shift from emphasis on *Wertrationalität* (substantive rationality) "involving orientations toward ultimate values" to *Zweckrationalität* (functional rationality, geared to efficiency), making his work an important source within political sociology of the "end of ideology" school with which Lipset is identified. In "Science as a Vocation," Weber writes that suffering "the fate of an epoch which has eaten of the tree of knowledge" and reaping the rewards of technical mastery, one also undergoes "disenchantment," without "worldviews" or a common morality upon which to base political and social life. Consequently, "which of the warring gods we should serve" is decided by *personal* values. Law is transformed from a code of moral action to a system of rules facilitating the predictability of behavior and the rationality and efficiency of organizational production of all kinds. Grounded in this way, liberalism needs a procedure to facilitate individual value competition, minimize unnecessary bureaucratic or political domination, and promote efficiency. The procedure is democracy, now redefined as competition between qualified elites.

In the inevitable web of bureaucracy, with a premium on expertise, the ideal of the independent citizen becomes an unrealistic dream, while leadership and political party organization become paramount. Paradoxically for Weber, a mass-based citizenry's demand for goods and services requires efficiency, predictability, and organization. Because the competence of leadership could not be merely assumed, political accountability required a democratic electorate entrusted with the role of making changes when needed. Accountability of this sort could prevent the domination of important public arenas of decision making by private interests, something Weber feared, while classical or liberal democracy could not. But, he cautions in "Politics as a Vocation," political organization is

> necessarily managed by men interested in the management of politics. . . . It is unimaginable how in large associations elections could function at all without this managerial pattern. In practice this means the division of the citizens with a right to vote into politically active and politically passive elements.[9]

With mass political apathy a given, and the need for and development of large-scale organization inevitable, it is desirable for modern society to create a power structure based on talent but subject to elections as plebiscites to check elite power and examine its competence. As David Held points out, for Weber, democracy becomes a marketplace to determine "the most competent in the competitive struggle for votes and power," to select leaders and legitimate governing institutions.

Prefiguring influential contemporary writers like Samuel Huntington, Weber suggests that increased size and bureaucratization stem from both national and international sources:

> It is obvious that technically the large modern state is absolutely dependent upon a bureaucratic basis. The larger the state, and the more it is a greater power, the more unconditionally is this the case . . . the greater the zones of friction with the outside and the more urgent the needs for administrative unity at home become, the more this character is inevitably and gradually giving way formally to the bureaucratic structure.[10]

In seeking "balance between might and right, power and law, expert government and popular sovereignty," Weber believes the weight of modernity comes down on the side of power and expertise. Where classical direct democracy could only operate in isolated small institutions, now classical liberal democracy also was being transcended because of a need for accountable elite democracy. And the major contrast model of his era, socialism, was founded on a profound misunderstanding of the nature of power and modern organization.

Joseph Schumpeter also constructed an elite theory of democracy that was to have an important effect on the republican liberal explanation of nonparticipation. Schumpeter believed that increasing centralization of power and bureaucratic authority in modern society would render all private and public social organization, including capitalism, subject to technical management, ceding control of the economy from the market to bureaucratic planning. Unlike Weber, he equated such planning with socialism, which he thought inevitable, but unlike Karl Marx, socialism for him was a *technical* solution to how best organize a modern economy and polity, and had nothing to do with issues of class.

Schumpeter tried to show that "classical" conceptions of democracy needed to be displaced by his realistic formulation. For to hold on to classical ideas such as "popular sovereignty" would be to misapprehend a political reality in which consensus is, in fact, highly manipulable, in which leaders will in any case dominate, and in which, therefore, the people really have little say. Following Weber, he believed the public to be highly emotional (making them susceptible to manipulation), irrational, ignorant, and apathetic except in matters that directly concerned them; and, unlike John Dewey, he believed them extremely limited in the degree to which they could be educated for solid democratic citizenship.

He also thought the idea of a "common good" to be a dangerous illusion because, in increasingly pluralistic modern societies, people not only have different wants but different "ultimate values" not subject to rational examination or reconciliation. As Held suggests, like Weber, he alerts us to the new totalitarian dangers of technological society. If one assumes, as they did, that the modern vocation of politics is to privilege expert solutions, then forcing a rational consensus on wants and values where none can exist is politically dangerous precisely because the losers can then be viewed as irrational, and politics could be defined as an arena without limit, invading all aspects of public and private life.

To develop his political theory, Schumpeter looked at existing democracies, primarily the United States and Great Britain. Unsurprisingly, he came to the conclusion that democracy itself should be defined by the criteria these societies, which he presumed to be as fully democratic as possible, seemed to embody.

Thus, in *Capitalism, Socialism, and Democracy*, he comes to his famous conclusion that democracy as it exists in the real world is not a way of political life, but a method of governing, through which competing elites vie for power by trying to win the votes of citizens. Oppression can be prevented by registering popular preferences while conferring legitimacy on chosen elites to lead. Justice has no intrinsic relation to democratic governance as such. Once the people register their wishes, the people should get out of the way of their chosen leaders and let them do what they alone are best qualified to do—rule:

> in reality they neither raise nor decide issues but that the issues that shape
> their fate are normally raised and decided for them. . . . democracy does not
> mean and cannot mean that the people actually rule in any obvious sense
> of the terms "people" and "rule." Democracy means only that the people
> have the opportunity of accepting or refusing the men who are to rule
> them.[11]

Bringing democratic theory around in "full circle," as Held points out, Schumpeter asks that "lovers of democracy" accept the wisdom of his theory of "competitive elitism" and get rid of "make-believe" assumptions of the "classical doctrine," in particular their romance about the role of the "people."[12] Held concludes,

> Like Weber, Schumpeter did not examine the vicious circles of non-
> participation, although even he acknowledged that without scope for
> political initiative people are likely to become apathetic even in the face of
> all the information needed for active involvement. . . . Effective
> participation depends both upon political will *and* upon having the actual
> capacity (the resources and skills) to pursue different courses of action.[13]

This lacuna in his thought would be emulated by many of the most prominent democratic theorists who followed. Even more than he, however, they would claim a scientific status for their conclusions based on what became known as the behavioral revolution in political science.

The behavioral revolution in the science of politics traces its beginning to the early twentieth century, first clearly articulated in the work of Charles Merriam in the 1920s and 1930s, and in the 1940s by his student and colleague Harold Lasswell. It reached its apex in the 1950s and 1960s, when it came to dominate the discipline. Then, as the post-war political consensus fractured, it was subject to a sustained and partially successful counterattack by those who believed values should not be exorcised from political study, and those who argued that, in any case, they could not be. And worse, if they could not, behavioralism actually might be an ideological cover for certain value constellations, hidden from itself and others by a scientific veneer.

Albert Somit and Joseph Tanenhaus, in their 1967 *The Development of American Political Science*, suggest the "behavioral creed" is defined by the following characteristics: a science capable of prediction and explanation; one therefore that focuses on rooting out regularities, analyzing them, and developing a body of political knowledge, rather than engaging in descriptive study; theory focused on the development of hypotheses that can be tested by empirical data, that is "operationalized"; empirical data gathering that is based on observable phenomena that can be quantified and subjected to mathematical analysis, thereby allowing for the "discovery and precise statement of relationships and regularities"; focus on "pure" research rather than trying to solve social problems; a strict separation of facts and values, of empirical investigation and normative evaluation, in order to achieve objectivity, and because the "truth or falsity of values (democracy, equality, and freedom, etc.) cannot be established scientifically and are beyond the scope of legitimate inquiry."[14]

Based on an overly narrow view of science, and by extension social science, as a radically inductive process, behavioralists sought to cobble together empirically verifiable hypotheses in order to build political explanations of increasing power and generality. Their research was oriented to the observable behavior of people—the real phenomena of politics through which the epiphenomena of governmental institutional activity could be properly understood.

Post–World War II behavioralism constituted both a decisive break with the reformist political goals of its most important forefathers, men like Merriam and Lasswell, and a continuity and embellishment of their scientific concerns and methods. The science of behavioralism was thrust forward by pathbreaking advances in the tools of analysis, particularly in survey research methodology, sophistication of statistical analysis, and the computer revolution, which allowed enormous amounts of data to be assembled, stored, and speedily analyzed. These developments were facilitated in the 1950s and 1960s by substantial financial support from foundations and government; the decisions of many social scientists, who had labored during World War II in government, to find sinecures in universities, often in newly established university research centers; and the rapid growth of universities themselves and their increasingly behaviorally oriented political science departments.

While advances in behavioral science were generated by sincere intellectual development and real technological breakthroughs, they also were driven by the institutional, governmental, and foundation support given to the dominant political imperative of the post-war period: the consolidation, centralization, and strengthening of the powers of the state to enhance America's political, economic, and military power in the post-colonial world of the Cold War, instability, and Communist challenge. Gone was the optimism of progressive reform and New Deal activism that had animated earlier scientists of politics. It was a new era in which faith in the progressive embellishment of democracy gave way to a fear of the masses, driven by abhorrence of what the mass movements of Fascism and Communism had wrought, rigidified by the stifling anti-intellectual atmosphere of McCarthyism, and validated by the new science of survey research that demonstrated the impossibility of creating democratic citizens on the "classical model" out of beings who seemed indifferent to and ignorant about politics and authoritarian in temperament. Rejecting the assumptions of mentors like Merriam and Lasswell as overly optimistic, and perhaps downright naïve, and their science as methodologically suspect, the new behavioralists chose, as Ray Seidelman and Edward Harpham point out, "to transform political science into a pure science of the political process" rather than seek for it "a political role . . . in reviving democratic accountability through civic education and modern social and economic planning. . . ."

The political consequences of the difference between pre- and post-war behavioralism were striking. Pre-war behavioralists viewed empirical and normative theory as mutually reinforcing, "that the discoveries of a behaviorally oriented political science ultimately would provide the raw materials out of which reformers would construct a democratized American State." Political reform and behavioralism went hand in glove. For the post-war generation, however, "premature attempts" to tie knowledge to political action would both fail and "undermine the foundations" of scientific knowledge. Empirical and normative theory, therefore, were thought to be separate and distinct:

> Far from being a tool for building and democratizing American political
> institutions, empirical theory was used to consolidate behavioralists'
> understanding and appreciation of democracy as it existed in the real
> world.[15]

Assuming the existing American political system to be the best possible form of democracy, given the realities of a modern, complex society in a dangerous and hostile world, and enmeshed in its vision of itself as an emerging science, post-war behavioralism became inherently incapable of offering evaluation, critique, or proposals for change. With practitioners overlooking the historical roots of nonparticipation, too many simply took quick snap-shots with questionnaires, reported on the political "apathy" they discovered, and reinforced the tendency sometimes to "forget" history by not teaching it properly in the first place. In so doing, perhaps unwittingly, they encouraged us to forget that we too are historical agents, capable of action, success, and defeat, and that "forgetting," never knowing of this kind, produces apathy.[16]

Without a close reading of history there also was a tendency to create straw people out of the contrast models that existed all along. As Carole Pateman points out, Joseph Schumpeter and his followers created the idea of one "classical" theory of democracy, which they then proceeded to criticize. From the Athenian democrats to the Antifederalists, to Jean-Jacques Rousseau, Mary Wollstonecraft, John Stuart Mill, and later the populists, socialists, and theorists of participatory, nonadversary, and direct democracy, alternative ways of thinking about democracy and paths for history were too easily discounted, if they were considered at all. Madison might be right about human nature and the majority, but so might be Richard Henry Lee's more optimistic and democratic Antifederalist account. That the nation survived and grew does not demonstrate that it could not have done so in a more equitable, even more prosperous fashion, had greater democracy been instituted at its founding, or practiced thereafter in response to social movements calling for it. Without subjecting their own assumptions to the discipline of historical and theoretical contrast models, empirical democratic theorists weakened their own scientific enterprise.

Liberalism and republicanism, really, had been brought around full cycle by modern empirical democratic theory. Where earlier republican thought was critical of democracy, it was so based on its reading of history. If its fear was that republican political forms tend to degenerate, its hope, as J. G. A. Pocock points out, was that within history "Machiavellian moments" and actors could be found to create history for the better.[17] If individual citizens didn't always possess civic virtue, perhaps the system as a whole could, and this was the goal to which Madison devoted himself. For him, the task was to create the history of a republic that could endure the new environment of liberalism, which, as he knew intuitively, would itself erode the sense of civic virtue necessary for republican success.

As liberalism became pessimistic in this century, a new kind of republicanism became optimistic, now calling itself empirical democratic theory and claiming that the best possible solutions to the problem of governance had been achieved in an imperfect, rapidly becoming post-industrial world. Liberalism and republicanism became conflated, losing the sense of progress and correctibility of human affairs of one, and sense of basic values of the other. Forgetting the core value of civic virtue in early democratic and republican thought, empirical democratic theorists tried to squeeze questions of virtue out of political science. With questions of value thus suppressed, civic virtue became reduced to what Theodore Lowi calls "interest group liberalism," and the public interest to whatever the pluralist system produces from what Charles Lindblom once referred favorably to as its "science of muddling through."

Most practitioners of political behavioral science would spend the 1950s and 1960s celebrating the virtues of what they generally called American pluralism—real-world democracy at its zenith—even as evidence was piling up, from civil rights, student, and antiwar protests, that there was clear room for improvement. To the extent they had political influence, they shielded the system and its elites from timely awareness of brewing troubles. Intellectually, they blinded their science to the facts about to explode in its face.

Part II

Explanations of
Nonparticipation

In the heyday of behavioral political science, in the 1950s and for much of the 1960s, an underlying assumption was that a post-war consensus had been reached on political values. Industrial development and technological advances, it seemed, had solved the problem of whether enough goods and services would be available, and there appeared to be broad agreement that the going political and economic system was making inroads to distribute them more equitably. All major political players also seemed to agree that government now had a permanent place as watchdog of the economy.

This apparent fundamental consensus was viewed by some as indicating what Daniel Bell and others called an "end of ideology." Politics now seemed not to be, and seemed to need not be, organized around fundamental economic conflicts represented in earlier eras—for example, in basic struggles between capital and labor, free enterprise and socialism. In the eyes of most Americans, the fundamental conflict in the world was between the model of America's free institutions on the one hand, and on the other, world Communism directed by the Soviet Union. Any conflicts remaining at home seemed to pale in comparison.

Of course, this is a picture of America taken from the inside out—a picture of the self-image many Americans had, and were encouraged to have by dominant institutions of politics, government, corporate America, and the mass media. To be sure, there were those who dissented from this rosy assessment. In 1956, C. Wright Mills warned of a "power elite" dominating American economic, political, and military institutions. In some of his most interesting writing, he argued that troubles were brewing beneath a façade of quiescence and apparent contentment, still merely troubles because they had not yet been articulated into coherent political issues. By 1961, Dwight Eisenhower himself would warn of the development of a "military-industrial complex." By 1962, poverty would be rediscovered in America with the publication of Michael Harrington's landmark volume, *The Other America*. Undoubtedly, the "end of ideology" thesis seemed plausible because the McCarthy era stifled critical discussion. The fact there was indeed a Communist conspiracy with international roots overwhelmed the idea that under the Constitution, acts of treason aside, those few Americans who chose to might have a right to embrace the ideals it claimed to embody. Added to Communist thrusts in Europe and Asia was the nationalist challenge, as the "Third

73

World" fought to overthrow colonialism, increasing the premium on American stability.

With the war against fascism won and that against Communism underway, it's not surprising that in America this was an era of celebrating American political institutions. This was clearly reflected in mainstream discourse within political science in general, and in particular, in discussions of the role of political participation in American life and of the causes and consequences of nonparticipation.

Therefore, when Bernard Berelson, Paul Lazarsfeld, and William McPhee reported in 1954 in their influential work, *Voting*, that political apathy was functional for a successful democratic polity, it was against the backdrop of comparing America to two sets of competitors—defunct Nazis and ascendant Communists, both of which were clearly undemocratic—and the idea that a broad consensus on values existed in an established democratic nation in an otherwise unsettled world. If broad consensus existed, then it would be reasonable to assume, as Berelson and his co-authors did, that apathy reflected at worst acquiescence, and at best consent to the political system as it then existed. And it seemed reasonable to assume also that America, given the available contrast models, was indeed a democratic polity par excellence. If survey research indicated that nonvoters tended to be uninformed, uninterested, and authoritarian in temperament, and if their breezy hands-off approach to the political system was based on their fundamental consent, so much the better for their disposition to abstain.

All this, of course, was to change with the turbulent 1960s as civil rights demonstrations, white backlash, the Vietnam war, urban riots, black power, criticism of western colonialism, student protests, black and white students shot by Guardsmen, cultural revolution, and feminism not only fractured the post-war consensus on America's role in the world, but deeply questioned American institutions, values, national self-esteem, and power.

This was not what John Kennedy had in mind in 1960 when he exhorted America to get moving again, although his call was an effort to shake up the complacency and apathy he too discerned in the 1950s. When Students for a Democratic Society, in 1962, issued their famous Port Huron Statement, they did intend to shake America up, but even they were primarily trying to get the country to see that it was not meeting the standards of its own creed, as its institutions seemed now not to be fulfilling America's ideals of equality, freedom, justice, and especially democracy.

All of these movements and pleas served to put great strain on the American political system. The depth of the wrenching is well represented by the fact that in 1968 it was the Democratic National Convention, the convention that would nominate old-time liberal Hubert Humphrey—vice president in the administration that had promoted the Civil Rights Acts of 1964 and 1968, the Voting Rights Act of 1965, the constitutional amendment outlawing poll taxes, the War on Poverty, Model Cities, Medicare, and Medicaid (and sent 500,000 troops to Vietnam)—that was the target of a major antiwar protest, countered by a police riot under the guidance of a Democratic mayor.

It is also not surprising, therefore, that by the 1970s some analysts seemed to long for a time when political participation would abate and political apathy would help cushion the system once again. By 1975, a report for the Trilateral Commission would even warn that too many demands by citizens upon a democracy could serve to undermine democracy itself. Too much participation could be too much of a good thing. Now more apathy seemed to be needed because there was too much dissensus.

By the 1980s, however, a conservative revolt successfully challenged for the first time the assumption emblazoned by the New Deal, New Frontier, and Great Society—and not fundamentally challenged by interlopers Eisenhower, Nixon, or Ford: that rights ensured by government would continuously expand. As fiscal constraints in the 1970s and 1980s put pressure on the tax base and eroded political support for government programs, as conservative ideology about the role of government became respectable again, demands on the system did not disappear, certainly, but they did abate. But as political participation measured by voter turnout reached post–1920s lows, with barely 50 percent of the eligible electorate voting in 1988, concern increased once again that political apathy could be a source of stagnation in American politics, in some sense coming full cycle from the 1950s. Except now, apathy was seen as more likely stemming from political alienation than contentment.

In Part II, we will explore how mainstream political scientists and their major critics have understood nonparticipation and political apathy, by analyzing the work of representative and classic thinkers. First, we consider the republican liberal explanation of nonparticipation and the central role the concept of political apathy plays within it. We will look at a variety of authors writing at different times, coming to somewhat different conclusions but sharing similar background assumptions of republican and liberal political thought, dismissing other important classical liberal and republican assumptions, and embodying very similar notions of what constitutes a science of politics. They all fall within Lukes's one-dimensional view of power as discussed in the Introduction. These commonalities are more important than the differences, and their mode of analysis as a whole has implications for their explanations of nonparticipation, as well as, if we were to be influenced by it, those we would today cast to understand the political world.

The story begins with the behavioral analysis, with elite implications, of Bernard Berelson, Paul Lazarsfeld, and William McPhee, and the elite technocratic theory of Samuel Huntington. It then moves to the extremely influential classic statement of pluralist analysis by Robert Dahl. Finally, it concludes with the liberal rational and social choice theory of William Riker, and the starkly antiparticipatory implications it has for democratic theory.

At the end of chapter 7, I engage in a brief critique of the limits of the positivist idea of social science for a science of politics properly construed.

We then turn to major critics of the republican liberal school, in particular the plain democratic theory of E. E. Schattschneider, his arguments about the restricted bias of conflict, and how this is extended in the work of Peter Bachrach. Both share Lukes's two-dimensional view of power.

Next, we look at the radical democratic theory of C. Wright Mills and Herbert Marcuse, to see if their explanations of nonparticipation can enhance our own. Both fall into Lukes's third dimension of power. Finally, we look at some reasons the issues of gender and race were inadequately, if at all, incorporated into this classic debate.

Part II is organized as exposition, comparison, and critique of three fundamentally different sets of explanations of nonparticipation. Through it, I hope to set the stage for an explanation in Part III of current nonparticipation and apathy that points to ideas for democratic renewal.

◰ Chapter 5

The Virtues of Apathy

In their 1954 book, *Voting*, Bernard Berelson, Paul Lazarsfeld, and William McPhee offer an explanation of nonparticipation that helped set the terms of debate for much theory that was to follow. Berelson and his co-authors wanted to explain an anomaly they found in American society between widespread nonparticipation in politics, and the smooth functioning of a democratic polity:

> *Individual voters* today seem unable to satisfy the requirements of a democratic system of government outlined by political theorists. But the *system of democracy* does meet certain requirements of a going political organization. The individual members may not meet all the standards, but the whole nevertheless survives and grows.[1]

Drawing essentially the same portrait of "classical" democratic theory as being out of touch with modern life as Joseph Schumpeter had, they claimed it failed to account for several essential facts of contemporary "democratic practice," revealed by survey research. Here is the dilemma. Individual citizens often fail to meet the requirements of the "classical concept of meaningful participation," showing little interest, discrimination, or knowledge, with even many of those taking the trouble to vote doing so neither out of principle nor with full rationality. At the same time, we have in operation a successful democratic system of governance.

Fortunately, in Elmira, New York, the town Berelson and his co-authors studied, there was a functional division of political labor, with citizens spreading themselves along a spectrum from "sociable man," indifferent to public affairs, nonpartisan, flexible, to "political man," to "ideological man," absorbed in public affairs, highly partisan, and rigid.[2] Political and social pluralism, where political lines are meaningful "but are not identical with the lines of social groupings," mitigate against the formation of fundamental political cleavages.[3] And the political division of labor, "as repugnant as it may be in some respects to our individualist tradition—is serving us well today in mass politics."[4] While democratic political systems may require "incompatible properties" that in reality can't be found in each citizen or institution—such as involvement and indifference, stability and flexibility, consensus and cleavage, individualism and collectivism—"they can (and do) reside in a heterogeneous electorate" as a whole. Democratic systems can compensate for the fact that each citizen does not possess a perfect balance of qualities of ideal democratic citizenship if the system itself as a whole is in balance. A democratic system in harmonious balance is exactly what they find.

The Uses of Apathy

Eighteenth- and nineteenth-century democratic theory, they conclude, should be revised to accommodate twentieth-century facts, and this could be successfully accomplished without compromising democratic ideals. Indeed, these facts of modern democratic life are actually conducive to the survival of democracy, for how, they ask, could "a mass democracy work if all the people were deeply involved in politics?"

> The apathetic segment of America probably has helped to hold the system together and cushioned the shock of disagreement, adjustment and change. But that is not to say that we can stand apathy without limit.[5]

Having established, first, that modern democratic society could not stand the shock of widespread participation, and second, that we are now to look at the system as a whole for the balance of democratic attributes formerly sought by classical theory in the individual, Berelson, Lazarsfeld, and McPhee feel free to revise "classical" theories of democracy. From a democratic point of view, political apathy is functional and, indeed, essential to the functioning of a modern democratic polity. Their explanation of nonparticipation is tantamount to their explication of apathy, represented as follows:

> X (a person) is apathetic with respect to Y (politics) if he or she is content with and/or uninterested in present political decisions or arrangements. X freely chooses not to vote or participate in electoral activity.[6]

While this explanation of nonparticipation and the peculiar function it assigns the concept of apathy are gravely flawed, they do have one important virtue. Unlike those radical critics of American democracy who would explain away all nonparticipation as political alienation (and those who would explain away most participation simply as false consciousness), Berelson, Lazarsfeld, and McPhee's use of the concept maintains an essential link of responsibility between the nonparticipant and the act of not participating. Integral to the way *apathy* is used in ordinary language as well as within democratic discourse is precisely this function of helping locate responsibility for nonparticipation. By their account, freely choosing not to participate, apathetics are responsible for their own withdrawal.[7]

The problems begin in their reordering of the moral point of the term within their broader revision of democratic theory. If the notion that informed and involved people governing themselves, whether directly or through representatives, is basic to democracy, then claiming that political apathy or nonparticipation is a desirable attribute of modern democracy constitutes a redrawing of democratic theory with radical implications. *Political apathy*, a term that formerly served to warn about the malfunctioning of a democratic polity, is reconstituted as a virtue.

Under what circumstances is it legitimate to revise the critical grammar of any political language? Is their revision justified?

The connection they draw between responsibility and action is especially important within democratic discourse, where there is a prima facie case in favor of participation. All things being equal, widespread nonparticipation and political apathy are frowned upon, and the burden is on those who would insist that a polity with these characteristics is democratic to explain these facts in a way that justifies this claim. Berelson and his co-authors understand this, attempt to address it, and, I believe, fail.

Should one succeed in establishing that nonparticipation results from personal apathy, one can exclude as causes a disenfranchising political, educational, economic, or social system. One is then freer to argue that a nonparticipatory polity with extensive apathy is nevertheless a democratic polity. Instead, they seem to assume that America is a modern, industrialized, mass democracy par excellence, therefore its practices, however much they may deviate from the norms of "classical democratic theory," become the new standards for democracy. Viewed through the lens of "realistic theory," if these practices, including those that generate apathy, promote the stability of this democratic system, it follows they should be positively appraised and included in the repertoire of practices we consider democratic. Their argument is captured well by Carole Pateman:

> high levels of participation and interest are required from a minority of citizens only and, moreover, the apathy and disinterest of the majority play a valuable role in maintaining the stability of the system as a whole. Thus we arrive at the argument that *the amount of participation that actually obtains is just about the amount that is required for a stable system of democracy.*[8]

If the norms with which we judge contemporary affairs are drawn from the outer appearance of dominant practices, how are we to know if anything is amiss within or beneath these practices? By disposing of the critical dimension that had warned of threats to a particular political discourse's essential ideals, we at best lose some ability to analyze these practices from the point of view of that ideal, and at worst, through the back door, redefine that ideal in ways antithetical to a core element within its original intent:

> the voters least admirable when measured against individual requirements contribute most when measured against the aggregate requirement for

flexibility. . . . They may be the least partisan or interested voters, but they perform a valuable function for the entire system.[9]

Trapped by their view that the American polity is the functional equivalent of modern democracy itself, Berelson, Lazarsfeld, and McPhee in effect ask us to use the concept of apathy in the following peculiar way when explaining nonparticipation: "Giovanna didn't vote in the referendum because she is apathetic about the environment. Thank God for people like her, for without them our democracy couldn't stand the disruption of people making policy choices for themselves. If there were more people like her, our democracy would run even more smoothly."

Many arguments have been leveled at this thinking, particularly during the so-called pluralist-antipluralist debates of the 1960s and 1970s. Two are directly pertinent here. First, Berelson and his co-authors assume that participation has no intrinsic importance or developmental merit, and dismiss the value attached to participation historically by a diverse array of democratic theorists. Second, assuming that nonparticipation is motivated by indifference or contentment, in the above example they would see Giovanna's political apathy as adversely affecting neither her wants nor her capacities to understand and defend what is in her interest. Yet it is certainly reasonable to wonder whether what appears on the surface as her political apathy, once analyzed, instead turns out to be her rejection of a system that does not meet her needs. Over time, her political alienation might indeed take on the outward appearance of indifference and apathy. But by misdescribing rejection of political activity as apathy motivated by contentment, Berelson and his colleagues may also miss the deeper significance of what turns out to be, in fact, her principled *political act*, perversely changing it into a silent vote of approval.

Conceptual deficiencies further promote these problems. While there is a connection between apathy and contentment—a content person over time may become lulled into apathy—in order to remain content, one also has a need to maintain a sharply delineated conceptual distance between them. Consider that a politically content person may become lulled into apathy after deciding that withdrawing from political activity will not seriously jeopardize his or her future wants or needs, and thereby future contentment. But apathy indicates a letting down of the guard on these judgments, a weakening of will and discipline regarding them, making it more likely that contentment may be jeopardized in the future. Moreover, many of the criteria they suggest are hallmarks of modern democracy amount to little more than balancing opposing tendencies—involvement and indifference, for example—and certainly could be construed as qualities necessary for almost any successful political system.

Berelson, Lazarsfeld, and McPhee also write as if apathy can only be used to describe a grouping of disparate individuals all of whom coincidentally share the characteristic of apathy—that is, they are not really a group at all. Undoubtedly one sense of apathy relates to individual responsibility, but another begins to shift responsibility away from the person. It is clear what we mean when we say, "John is apathetic about the environment," but what if we say, "The poor are apathetic about the environment," or more generally talk about "the apathetic masses"? In the latter, the signal from language is that there may be something about being poor or in a mass that promotes this posture, shifting responsibility from the individual. While we might decide that the responsibility still lies with the group in question, we tacitly recognize that other factors, beyond *the* character of *an* individual, may play a role. Used exclusively with regard to individuals, the term loses a constituent critical component.

To the degree we use the term in vague reference to "politics" and not to specific issues or problem areas, we may also weaken its precision and critical vantage. To the extent apathy is issue specific, we then want to know why this issue motivates persons in this way, and hold open the possibility there also may exist a hidden range of other issues that would motivate interest and active participation. What is it about a class of people, poor people in Brooklyn, New York, and what is it about a specific issue constellation, perhaps the rain forests in Brazil, that might promote their apathy with reference to it?

Berelson and his co-authors also confuse the grammar of motivation (apathy) with that of action (nonparticipation). Although they suggest that participants are often indifferent, they virtually equate nonparticipation with apathy. Yet it is perfectly possible that Giovanna's refusal to vote in a referendum is based not in apathy but deep commitment.

In the end, the account of Berelson, Lazarsfeld, and McPhee has a clear ideological ring to it, one with the perverse political consequence of blaming our most disadvantaged citizens for their own disenfranchisement. Evidence has existed for some time that reveals a close connection between nonparticipation in political and organizational activity and low socioeconomic status, especially low educational levels. Indeed, in their 1944 work, *The People's Choice*, written with Hazel Gaudet, Lazarsfeld and Berelson report, "People on the lower SES levels are less likely to belong to any organizations than people on high . . . levels."[10] In *Voting*, the authors report that

> Nonvoting is related to persistent social conditions having little to do with the candidates or the issues of the moment. For example, because Democrats are on the average less well educated and less involved with dominant groups in the society than Republicans, they vote less on election day.[11]

Yet, the focus on apathy and indifference only obscures the importance of facts like these. For unless they are willing to suggest that our more disadvantaged citizens are pressured into these postures, dropping their view that the primary cause of nonparticipation is individual apathy, they are asking us to make the counterintuitive assumption that people are content to withdraw from a political system that patently harms their interests. And even were they to focus more seriously on social conditions and the psychological atti- tudes they produce, they would still not really be giving a satisfactory *explana- tion* of nonvoting, because in the institutional and political context of virtu- ally all European countries, socioeconomic class is not nearly as closely tied with nonvoting as it is here.[12] Should the disenfranchised read and take in explanations of their behavior focused on individual apathy, they will tend to blame themselves for their nonparticipation, and fail to analyze precisely those relations of political power that inhibit their own participation.

Elite Technocratic Theory

If the problematic that Berelson, Lazarsfeld, and McPhee were responding to in the 1950s was how to reconcile the existence of apathy with democratic society, in the 1970s and 1980s, Samuel Huntington took this task one step further, arguing that the frenzied participation of the 1960s and 1970s was actually weakening that same democratic society. Where Berelson and his co-authors considered too much participation in America as a hypothetical concern, Huntington addressed it as a problem of crisis proportions. Standing behind both is the transparent fear that too much democracy on the "classical model" could lead to chaos, or worse.

Writing in 1975 in a report for the Trilateral Commission, Huntington argues that our political system has become "overloaded" principally by en- larging the role of the welfare state beyond what it can reasonably be expected to accomplish. By overextending certain functions of government, we disable its authority, preventing it from accomplishing its essential tasks. With for- merly marginal groups now occupying their rightful place in the system, from a democratic point of view, excessive participation is not only no longer nec- essary, it may actually destroy democracy. "Less marginality on the part of some groups," he reports, "then needs to be replaced by more self-restraint on the part of all groups" because however worthwhile a value, "there are also potentially desirable limits to the indefinite extension of political democ- racy."[13] Democracy, he suggests, is "not necessarily optimized when it is maxi- mized," and concludes it "will have a longer life if it has a more balanced existence." Huntington predicts that what he calls a period of "creedal pas- sion," political action promoted by democratic beliefs, will turn back to one of "creedal passivity." He adds, "Prescriptively, the implication is that those developments ought to take place in order to avoid the deleterious conse- quences of the surge and to restore balance between vitality and governability in the democratic system."

Arguing that we err decisively in exaggerating the degree to which authority for our political system should issue from democratic participation, Huntington suggests new sources of legitimacy—in particular, expertise, seniority, experience, and special talents. Substituting reliance on expertise for participation, we lessen system demands, increase efficiency, allow the system to function under less duress, and thereby restore authority to a now more effective system, given greater legitimacy through a technological rationale.

The primary threat he sees to democracy, then, is from democratic ideals themselves: "the effective operation of a democratic political system usually requires some measure of apathy and noninvolvement on the part of some individuals and groups."[14]

In *American Politics: The Promise of Disharmony* (1981), Huntington extends this line of attack, criticizing consensus, pluralist, and class-conflict theorists for overemphasizing the role of material factors in political history and understating the power of values and moral passions. Restating within a cyclical theory of American political development his view that a rift between ideals and facts and/or institutions is a major motor of history, Huntington now suggests there exists a primary "American form of cognitive dissonance—a peculiarly 'American dilemma' " between the American ideas of "liberty, equality, individualism, democracy and the rule of law under a constitution" and existing American institutions, and in particular, between the ideal of equality and the fact of an inegalitarian society.

In order to be themselves, Americans must believe in the American creed, but the more they believe in the creed, the more "against themselves" they become. Because of this contest between ideals and institutions, he writes, "the legitimacy of American government varies inversely with belief in American political ideals."[15]

The gap between ideals and practices propels political history through a cycle with four moments. Periods of "creedal passion," characterized by moralistic reform attempting to eliminate the gap, are followed by cynical times during which people, incapable of infinite moral indignation, surrender to the feeling that the gap can't be eliminated. "Creedal passivity" then follows, an era of complacency characterized by "a dulling of perceptual clarity," of ignoring the gap and the discomfort it creates, but an era in which "cognitive dissonance lurks uneasily beneath the surface of conscience but is not sufficiently commanding to trouble people seriously."[16] Because the American creed is a fundamental component of the identity of Americans, however, their conscience seeks further resolution, engendering a period of hypocrisy during which they falsely affirm that the creed is fully practiced. Commitment to the values remains, though, eventually exploding the myth of fulfillment in another period of moral indignation—of "creedal passion"—completing the cycle.

Four periods of "creedal passion" have occurred during which Americans have tried to return to "first principles." The American Revolution, the Jack-

sonian period, the Progressive era, and the 1960s and 1970s were all characterized by distinctive political cleavage, major reform efforts, political and
social realignment, and intense involvement. Since they occur roughly every
sixty years, the next period, Huntington expects, will be in the decade of the
2010s.

During periods of creedal passion, the disharmony between American
ideals and practices erupts into a "moral intensity" without which the system
"could not change and hence avoid stagnation and decay."[17] Long-term stability depends upon these periods of adjustment. However, the institutions
whose power is necessary for the continuation of the society and its ideals
comes under assault. Due to this dual nature, Huntington concludes, a
"creedal passion period is American politics' finest—and most dangerous—
hour."[18]

Up to this point, Huntington's argument seems an interesting descriptive
analysis of American political development, and a step away from his Trilateral Commission call for apathy; he now seems to view the complacency stage
as only one of a necessary, broader historical dialectic. There is, however, a
parallel argument.

The character of reform in the twentieth century is different in critical
respects from earlier periods. In the nineteenth century, the realization of
American ideals fostered progress, successfully directed as they were at the
breakdown of traditional economic and political institutions. Reform in this
century has been less successful, with the exception of civil rights for African-
Americans, because now it involves more "a restoration of the past" than the
realization of the future.[19] Progress (ideals) and history (development) today
work increasingly, at cross-purposes:

> [a] sophisticated economy and active involvement in world affairs seem
> likely to create stronger needs for hierarchy, bureaucracy, centralization of
> power, expertise, big government specifically, big organizations generally. In
> some way or another, society will respond to these needs, while still
> attempting to realize the values of the American Creed to which they are
> so contradictory. If history is against progress, for how long will progress
> resist history?[20]

Huntington's fear is that because belief in progress toward American ideals is resilient, the system could get stuck oscillating between cynicism and
moralism, further depleting the authority under strain from the 1960s and
1970s. Continued weakening of authority could then generate demands for
authoritarian structures more capable of providing functional needs. He fears
democracy's self-destruction. His hope, however, is for the "cycle of response"
to stabilize:

> Americans could acquire a greater understanding of their case of cognitive
> dissonance and through this understanding come to live with their dilemma

on somewhat easier terms than they have in the past, in due course evolving a more complex but also more coherent and constant response to this problem.[21]

In order for American institutions to achieve post-industrial economic and political development, while acting forcefully in the international arena to protect us from foreign enemies, they must retain lost authority. The oscillation between moralism and cynicism must be broken. But with what?

We were just coming off a round of democratic surge. While American ideals succeeded in advancing civil rights, Huntington suggests, in other areas they were in conflict with the imperatives of modern economic and political development, weakening the authority of our institutions while being unable to change the massive, hierarchical, and bureaucratic character of them. Unrealistic activism would not make our society more democratic; it has the weight of historical institutional development and, therefore, system needs against it. But it could weaken our ability to survive as a modern democratic polity.

If the institutions cannot be changed without disastrous results, then it is our orientation to our ideals that must change. Huntington's overtly stated solution is to call for resisting extremes "in *any one of these responses*" to the gap between ideals and institutions (ideals versus institutions, or "IvI").[22]

Earlier in this work, his aim was more precise:

> The responses of cynicism, complacency, and hypocrisy to natural problems of cognitive dissonance do not have major direct consequences for the stability and continuity of the political system. . . . None of these responses challenge the continuing existence of the IvI gap.[23]

It is moralism, then, the cycle of reform and participation, of "creedal passion," that really threatens the gap by trying to bring practices into line with principles. How can excess here be mitigated? In calling for a more complex attitude toward the existence of the gap, Huntington implicitly suggests an acceptance of the discontinuity in ways that undermine the "creedal passion" phase and justify that of "creedal passivity," nudging us back into another passive era.

If internalized, this attitude would render complacency not just a moment within a cycle of American history, but a characteristic attitude toward the ideals themselves, narrowing the divide between institutions and ideals and, in the process, reflexively reconstituting the ideals themselves. The overt call is for a healthy and permanent dose of moderation. The tacit call is for more apathy.

In the end, Huntington's analysis of the role of political participation, and the use he urges implicitly for the concept of apathy in the explanation of nonparticipation, have essentially the same characteristic weakness and ideological predispositions found in *Voting*. For both, the essential point remains that modernity requires political democracy to shed outdated ways of thinking, accept that democracy as a political form has gone about as far as it can realistically go, and see the virtues and uses of apathy.

Huntington's analysis, however, is at once more sophisticated and more elusive. His theory of political development, something absent in *Voting*, is certainly worth considering. One need not accept along with it all of his conclusions and their implications for democratic theory.

It also is an important advance over *Voting* for two other reasons. First, Huntington acknowledges that a serious problem exists for his theory of democracy since it "requires some measure of apathy and noninvolvement on the part of some individuals and groups" that is "inherently undemocratic."[24] However Huntington may try to paper over this uncomfortable conclusion, to his credit he acknowledges it; and his praise for apathy remains somewhat faint, however necessary he believes it to be. Second, while Huntington urges us into another round of passivity and undoubtedly hopes we could accurately explain it as political apathy, he admits of other explanations. Hypocrisy and cynicism as well as apathy could result in decreased political participation.

Huntington's argument is extremely significant today. When we reconstruct and place it in its proper ideological frame, it serves as a modern road map for future strategies of depoliticization.

In the current era of fiscal restraints on all levels of government, accepted broadly across the mainstream political spectrum, Huntington's proposal for the role apathy can play to mitigate the problem of overload on government has serious implications. If his call for circumscribed and modulated demands on government were successful, his plea would result in less political involvement, lower levels of material rewards through political action, more satisfaction, and more complacency by, among others, those still disadvantaged. For Huntington, lower levels of political participation would indicate a more mature attitude toward democratic ideals in a complex modern world. Once levels of slackened participation were attained—in his cyclical theory of history, in other scholarship that emulates it, and in the discourse of participants and nonparticipants influenced by these—they would likely be explained as increased apathy, functional for democracy.

Like the account outlined in *Voting*, it would indicate a major redrawing of the contours of democratic theory—so much so, I would argue, that it loses plausibility as a theory of democracy, and is better characterized as modern republican liberalism with a very peculiar notion of civic virtue. And however much Huntington may want to reorder the moral point of the idea of political apathy, ordinary language will prove resilient, encouraging apathetics to point the finger of blame at themselves.

In an era in which the major existing democracies in Europe, North

America, and elsewhere are moving toward looser borders and freer trade as a way to increase profitability and make more efficient the international division of labor, they may also weaken the ability of national political movements to hold on to those political and economic concessions they have won within the nation-state. If the global market successfully erodes the ability of popular majorities to protect their short-term interests, causing defeat and despair, how would analysts be likely to explain this depoliticizing effect once the furor dies down? With the concept of political apathy now dressed as Huntington dresses it—as a mature attitude of modern democracy?

Furthermore, recall that Huntington asks that we seek to replace lost authority in democratic ideals with authority nurtured by a vision of technocracy. Technocratic roles themselves will prove only a weak legitimation, able to answer for us the question of how we do something and perhaps who should do it, but constitutionally incapable of answering satisfactorily the question "why?"

Huntington, however, is a technocratic theorist with a difference. In practice, people are asked to follow the technocratic dictates of modern economic and political development. At the same time, in theory they are asked to hold on to their beliefs, albeit in newly mature democratic ideals, as the creative motor of social change. But in adjusting the ideals, we reduce demands upon—thereby lending authority to—those very institutions that would manage our affairs most successfully if we also oblige by adopting the technocratic roles they assign to us. Perhaps intuitively understanding that anemic technocratic roles provide a weak legitimation for depoliticizing strategies, Huntington succeeds in injecting into them a healthy dose of abstract belief in, but complacency toward the practice of, democratic values. In Huntington's hands, democracy becomes a tool technocracy uses to legitimize less democracy.

Samuel Huntington, then, presents a sophisticated version of a simple point made by Berelson and his colleagues almost thirty years before. For the institutions of modern society to follow their natural course of development, they must be free from a future explosion between nineteenth-century ideals and twenty-first-century economic and political power. His distinct contribution is to make depoliticized technocratic roles seem attractive to us by whispering in our ears that if we adopt them we also become realistic democrats.

In so doing, he provides an incipient explanation of nonparticipation particularly suitable to the austerity of modern reindustrialization and postindustrialization, and the political requirements of a global market. Declaring the major problems of democratic rights solved, and cast in these terms, his explanation helps justify—and, if internalized, helps foster—the depoliticized roles he wants us to adopt, roles necessary for the reindustrialist's, postindustrialist's, and global marketeer's projects. The "promise of disharmony," now advanced from his Trilateral Commission report into a full-blown theory of American political development, still dissolves into a wish for apathy.

▣ Chapter 6

Apolitical Man

If there has been a dominant overall framework within the study of American politics over the last forty years, it would have to be what has been called pluralism. In the 1950s and 1960s, pluralists dominated the discipline and, since the 1960s, have been engaged in a debate with critics from the left, who charge they overlook fundamental inequalities of power and resources in American politics. Perhaps pluralists are best understood as philosophical liberals whose theory has shifted from the individual to the interest group as the basic unit of societal organization and social investigation, and as republicans with a constricted notion of civic virtue.

The most influential pluralist writer within political science literature over much of this period has been Robert Dahl. It's not hard to see why. Dahl is a writer whose ideas are clearly articulated and closely reasoned, one whose thinking has undergone important evolution over the years, even if he does not always acknowledge some of the changes. Here we will look at Dahl in his pluralist phase, one that also has elite implications for his democratic theory. Dahl, however, is a transitional figure who (as I will show in chapter 15) moves toward a more comprehensive view of political power and subtle understanding of the problem of political inequality as his career progresses.

Dahl's main contribution is to develop what he calls "polyarchy" as a theory able to account for empirical observations about the practice of democracy in modern, complex societies, generally western, liberal, capitalist, parliamentary polities. In doing so, Philip Green argues, Dahl has countered the cynicism of some writers in the tradition of Joseph Schumpeter, who sometimes viewed the " 'electoral mass' " as " 'incapable of action other than a stampede.' " "To this cynical view," Green points out, "Dahl more than anyone else has added the hopeful concept that democracy proceeds via the active influence of competing elites, representing the various minorities of which any large polity really consists."[1]

In his 1961 classic pluralist text, *Who Governs?*, Dahl asks,

> In a political system where nearly every adult may vote but where knowledge, wealth, social position, access to officials and other resources are unequally distributed, who actually governs?[2]

Dahl's foundational argument, spelled out in his 1956 A *Preface to Democratic Theory*, is that in modern democracies, "minorities rule," because in "all human organizations there are significant variations in participation in political decisions."[3] In *Who Governs?*, he wonders if much of the public, and especially nonparticipants, comprehend or share democratic values. Abstention by such people can be functional for polyarchy.

Elections are critical. Although they don't fully indicate majority preferences, they provide for elite competition and serve as a mechanism of democratic control.[4] Consensus on basic democratic values is vital on two counts. Although minorities rule through elite competition, it is the majority that sets the terms of the consensus and this gives the system its essential democratic character.[5] Consensus among the politically active, moreover, is necessary to absorb the stress of democratic competition.[6]

Perhaps the most important norm of the consensus is political equality, defined as the equal opportunity to influence decision-makers through some form of political participation.[7] In his 1970 book *After the Revolution?*, Dahl points to political inequality as an important problem for democracy, while still concluding that American polyarchy "looks very much better when it is compared with other political systems that have actually existed."[8] Elsewhere he writes, "In every polyarchy, consequently, and more emphatically in the U.S. than in some . . . full-time politics is distinctly a monopoly of the white-collar strata." In *After the Revolution?*, written at the height of 1960s unrest, Dahl makes both of the following claims:

> until we reach much greater parity in the distribution of political resources, other steps toward democratization are like treating tuberculosis with aspirins.[9]

And:

> the greatest obstacle to democratization and reducing inequalities is not that . . . elite of wealthy men *themselves*, or even that military industrial complex . . . but rather the . . . American people.[10]

Note also the tension in his 1976 edition of *Democracy in the United States*. After listing "social arrangements, individual characteristics, and in representative governments, the very process of representation itself" among the causes of political inequalities, and claiming that they "help to produce differences in political *resources*, *skills*, and *incentives*," he later states: "In every political system, some citizens are much less interested and active in politics than others. Apathetic citizens disfranchise themselves; active citizens gain influence."[11] Inequalities produce the conditions for nonparticipation and apathy, and yet apathetic citizens freely choose to withdraw.

These incongruities reveal both his belief that American democracy is a functioning system of polyarchy and his attempt to draw out serious inequalities that manifest themselves, testing this belief. So Dahl both argues that we need much greater equality to ensure political equality and freedom, and still places the blame for political inequality ("apathetic citizens disfranchise themselves") on the "military-industrial–financial-labor-farming-educational-professional-consumer-over and under thirty-lower/middle/upper class complex": that is, the American people.[12] As Dahl's career progresses, political inequality becomes an increasingly important concern, as he first tries to reconcile it with polyarchy and then adopts a more critical stance by broadening his criteria for polyarchy itself. While he identifies structural sources for political inequality—even his earliest works, such as A *Preface to Democratic Theory*, correctly point to the Madisonian constitutional design as a successful, intentional effort to circumscribe majority rule—he still often roots toleration of inequality in individual political apathy.

His long-standing involvement with pluralist analysis, his intellectual commitment to and investment in working out a realistic theory of democracy (or polyarchy), his regard for behavioralism, and his individualistic conception of human nature, which is like Madison's notion that conflict "is sown in the nature of humankind," are reflected in his ideas on power, consent, and the possibility and value of political participation itself. These in turn shape Dahl's explanation of nonparticipation.

Why isn't political activity more rewarding for more people, Dahl asks; what is a realistic view of persons as political beings?

> man is not by instinct a reasonable, reasoning, civic-minded being. Many of his most imperious desires and the source of many of his most powerful gratifications can be traced to ancient and persistent biological and physiological drives, needs, and wants. Organized political life arrived late in man's evolution; today man learns how to behave as a political man with the aid and often with the hindrance of instinctive equipment. . . . To avoid pain, discomfort, and hunger, to satisfy drives for sexual gratification, love, security, and respect—these needs are insistent and primordial. The means of satisfying them quickly and concretely generally lie outside political life.[13]

Dahl's view of consent flows from these predispositions. While social training plays an important role in the formation of values, neither value development nor shared values stimulating a sense of collective responsibility play a significant role in his account of how consent should be established or maintained. In spite of the importance of social learning, therefore, the idea of civic responsibility has little power. While consent could be achieved by pressing hard for collective agreement on policies—here one is reminded of why Madison chose to preserve "liberty" by controlling the effects rather than the causes of faction—this is both unrealistic and potentially tyrannical.

The favored option becomes establishing consent only through agreement on process rooted in accepted democratic values. However much democratic practices may fall short, it is this kind of limited agreement that best fulfills ideal-type consensus.

Dahl favors the process of "procedural democracy," and in a 1977 essay, "On Removing Certain Impediments to Democracy in the United States," he lists five criteria for it:

1. *Political equality.* "The decision rule for determining outcomes must equally take into account the preferences of each member of the *demos* as to the outcome."
2. *Effective participation.* For point 1 to be effective, "every member must have equal opportunities for expressing preferences, and the grounds for them, throughout the process of collective decision-making."
3. *Enlightened understanding.* "In order to express preferences accurately, each member of the *demos* ought to have adequate and equal opportunities for discovering and validating, in the time available, what his or her preferences are on the matter to be decided."
4. *Inclusiveness.* The "*demos* ought to include all adults who are obliged to obey the rules of the association."
5. *Popular sovereignty.* The *demos,* through procedural democracy, can oversee (and change) the scope, domain, and procedures of decision-making that occur "outside" the domain of procedural democracy (i.e., technical, administrative, or judicial decisions).[14]

These standards by which to judge the quality of aspiring democratic polities indicate both growing concerns about inequality and an individualistic, almost asocial, conception of the development of human interests. In an otherwise very favorable review essay, written in 1977 just before Dahl's "Impediments" article, George Von der Muhll critiques Dahl's view of consent and human interests:

> When not altogether ignored, the binding force of a commitment to publicly defined values is either discounted without argument or reduced to a formula for realizing private preferences. Dahl's political actors pursue fixed goals derived from their personal utility curves. . . . authority itself is discussed in terms of personal needs and individual calculations of opportunity costs.[15]

People refrain from participating in politics, Dahl argues, when the opportunity costs of participating are greater than the gains. If it is in a person's perceived rational self-interest to participate, he or she will—unless obstacles increasing opportunity costs are placed in the way. Participation is often not perceived to be in the rational self-interest of the agent, with many factors mitigating participatory zeal: (1) people are not civic-minded by nature, and participation is not intrinsically rewarding; (2) citizens might not perceive important differences between the competing political parties; (3) they might have a low sense of political efficacy; (4) they might be content with the likely outcome of a political contest; (5) their knowledge is often limited; (6) sheer size discourages participation; (7) government is likely to be remote; (8) inequalities of political resources place formidable obstacles in the way of participation.

In *Modern Political Analysis*, even its second edition (1970), he emphasizes the first five items, while in his 1970 *After the Revolution?*, he stresses the latter three. While there is an important shift in emphasis as to what constitutes opportunity costs, especially political inequalities, there is little or no shift in the basic formula of how one calculates such costs, or what the value of political participation is. Dahl's conclusion remains, therefore, that nonparticipation is a problem in polyarchy only to the extent participation is needed to protect one's self-interest and fortify the basic consensus. Almost as an afterthought he adds, it is a "good norm."

Dahl's use of the concept *apathy* in the explanation of nonparticipation reflects these tensions. Sometimes, as with Berelson and his colleagues, apathy is equated with nonparticipation—"the apolitical stratum":

> in all polyarchies, it seems, a sizable number of citizens are apathetic about politics and relatively inactive: in short, apolitical.[16]

Recall also his comment that "apathetic citizens disfranchise themselves."[17]

In *After the Revolution?*, Dahl offers one of his more careful statements on the causes of nonparticipation and apathy:

> registration and voting laws and practices that make participation unnecessarily difficult, discriminatory laws and practices, severe lack of education, inadequate organization and mobilization, apathy produced by poverty or a group history of subjection and defeat—can be eliminated or at the very least greatly reduced [by reducing unequal political resources]. . . . in a highly egalitarian society . . . differences [in participation] would result more from the exercise of personal choice over an array of opportunities and less from *objective differences* in the opportunities available.[18]

Yet his other comments, with which this is in tension, leave substantial ambiguity as to what he really believes about the nature of political inequality. Taken as a whole, his earlier work simplifies the nature of political inequality, underplaying the ways in which institutional, structural, and ideological constraints may undermine freedom even if, as here, he seems sometimes aware of these. If we are not as free as Dahl, or as we imagine ourselves to be, our consent may be mistakenly given; what appears as consent may really be disguised confusion or alienation. And what appears to be nonparticipation born of apathy or indifference, derivatives of his foundational views about the relation between human nature, self-interest, and political participation, may instead reflect severe depoliticization.

Dahl's explanation of nonparticipation employing the concept of political apathy can be represented as follows:

> X (an individual, group, or race) is apathetic with respect to Y (politics, an election, an issue) if X, after calculating opportunity costs and benefits, becomes indifferent to or content with Y; or conversely if X suffers political inequality with respect to Y, causing opportunity costs to become greater than the likely benefits.

Even to this point in his work, Dahl's explanation of nonparticipation, and his use of apathy in it, are a marked improvement over Berelson's and Huntington's. Maintaining a conceptual distance between apathy and nonparticipation, and emphasizing political inequalities as causes, political apathy in Dahl's hands sometimes retains its classical function within discourse about democracy, leading him to call on democratic societies to remove impediments to participation.

Dahl also does not restrict the range of X to individuals—for example, in his analysis of the role racial discrimination plays in nonparticipation. By sometimes taking a broader view on the range of Y than Berelson and his co-authors, he helps us locate the reasons a person or a group may be apathetic about a specific issue that, arguably, should not be of great concern to people in their situation. Expanding the range of both X and Y helps us locate the reasons that stand behind observed apathy. However, note that between Berelson, Lazarsfeld, and McPhee and Dahl, there is a subtle shift in what needs to be explained. To their credit, Berelson et al. seek to account for (and, unfortunately, to reconcile) the anomaly of high levels of nonparticipation and apathy extant within a democracy. Reflecting his emphasis on human motivation as a calculus of costs and benefits, and asocial conception of needs, Dahl says, on the other hand: "Instead of seeking to explain why citizens are not interested, concerned and active, the task is to explain why a few citizens *are*."[19]

Presuming "that man is incapable of holding a social interest which conflicts with his self-interest," as Peter Bachrach argues, Dahl ignores the idea that participation may yield unanticipated benefits, going beyond the reward of immediately getting one's way.

> Dahl fails, in other words, to conceive of political participation two-dimensionally; as instrumentality to obtain end results *and* as a process that affords him the opportunity to gain a greater sense of purpose and pride in himself and a greater awareness of community.[20]

In *After the Revolution?*, Dahl begins to develop his now long-standing interest in greater citizen involvement at the workplace, developing criteria for authority—personal choice, competence, and economy—to enable him to construct an argument for greater workplace democracy and public control over corporations. Yet, as Von der Muhll points out, even these remain instrumentalist, in and of themselves only testing whether the process will advance or retard self-interest and not evaluating the "rightness" of a particular organization of politics. They are

> questions any instrumentally oriented consumer would rationally wish to ask of a public service agency. They do not differentiate decisional processes we support because they are effective in meeting our needs from those we regard as legitimately binding without prior assessment of their outcomes.[21]

And in his 1982 edition of *Dilemmas of Pluralist Democracy*, the cost-benefit calculus dominates. In systems comprising large aggregates of individuals, conflict is inevitable; therefore the impossible idea of civic virtue as pursuit of the common good should yield to the possible solution of "enlightened egoism." The ideal of "perfect complementary" interests becomes the realistic standard for civic virtue, where "the actions of each to achieve his or her ends would create benefits at no cost to the others."[22] Surely Dahl's own lifelong commitment to democracy is itself more an example of the type of civic virtue that Von der Muhll suggests, "legitimately binding without prior assessment of their outcomes," than even of enlightened egoism. It is this view of the common good, shared by many, that forms the real social glue that undergirds the commitment of most Americans to the democratic ideal—an ideal of the good society not reducible to a process for fairly assessing costs and benefits. Civic virtue remains more than the sum of individual calculations of "enlightened egoism."

Actually, a politics of the "common good" has room for political conflict in a way Dahl's view of virtue does not. As John Buell puts it, "properly construed," a politics of the common good recognizes that "political contestation is a part of such a democratic common good and is intrinsic to its continual refinement and elaboration in changing circumstances." What might initially appear as a cost, to use Dahl's somewhat stiff discourse on virtue, might actually contain a hidden benefit: a conflict could result in greater understanding, wiser policies, necessary adjustments.[23]

Dahl's instrumentalist horizon is reinforced by reliance on behavioral methodology. Using participation rates unreflectively to predict the potential of future participation or to gauge how basic political participation is to our nature, while pertinent, may beg a series of questions: What is the relationship between the rates and the quality of participation available? Can effective participation, once experienced, lead to increased appreciation for political participation as a component of community life?

His methodology is itself rooted, like those of Berelson et al. and Huntington, in a problematic conception of power. For Dahl: "A has power over B to the extent that he can get B to do something that B would not otherwise do." As Nelson Polsby describes this characteristic pluralist approach, we see if potential power is, in fact, exercised by studying "specific outcomes in order to determine who actually prevails in community decision-making."[24]

In analyzing whether power is exercised, therefore, the emphasis is on behavior, policies, and articulated preferences that have surfaced politically and have then been blocked. The scope of issues drawn, covert grievances and troubles, manipulation of consciousness, and barriers to new ideas and limits on action characteristic of particular social structures are theoretically invisible to this account of power. And when constraints are not self-evident, nonparticipation is too easily seen as a function of political apathy endemic to human nature.

The depth to which Dahl's methodology and his assumptions about power, political participation, and interests are built into his analysis is revealed in his discussion of political inequality in his "Impediments" article. Here, Dahl argues that corporate capitalism has established resilient "ideological barriers" against the idea of government control of business, and that corporate domination is an important source of political inequalities. His solution is to call for some redistribution of wealth and for the principle of "enlightened understanding"—"each member of the *demos* ought to have adequate and equal opportunities for discovering and validating, in the time available, what his or her preferences are on the matter to be decided." But "enlightened understanding" studies only the individual's ability to comprehend his or her self-interest within a given system, deflecting attention from how economic and social class, as factors, limit the kind of self-interest that is even conceivable.

Philip Green argues that Dahl's account of political inequality fails to see that the "maldistribution of political as well as economic power [is] . . . secondary to the existence of social classes that set boundaries to one's political existence":[25]

> The existence of any large-scale productive enterprise supplying social necessities, which is operated according to rules formulated independently of the people who work in it, live around it, or otherwise rely on it in any decisive way is incompatible with political equality.[26]

Softening Green's comment, I would suggest that corporate domination of the economy limits, channels, and constrains democracy, even as democracy tries to keep corporations responsive to the needs of the public.

About *After the Revolution?*, yet applicable to most subsequent writing in Dahl's pluralist period, Peter Bachrach comments perceptively,

> Pragmatically, Dahl has transcended the structural confinement of pluralist theory. Theoretically, however, it is clear that Dahl's contention has not departed in any major respect from the narrowly drawn pluralist concept of interest.[27]

As a result, he never effectively includes the idea of grievance into the range of Y—particularly covert grievances and vague troubles—perhaps because such would transcend both behavioral methodological and pluralist assumptions, respectively, regarding how a social scientist may study expressions of needs, and to what degree the political system blocks legitimate issues from surfacing. Both as cause and consequence, he also doesn't integrate the idea of social class into the range of X. While in his account inequalities may be severe, in reality the primary impediments to democracy may be structural and ideological constraints hidden to his enterprise. Taken together, the effect of these is to exaggerate, through political analysis, the amount of apathy related to the motivation of discrete individuals. Although far more perceptive than many of his followers', Dahl's analysis of nonparticipation, therefore, retains significant limitations.

Yet, beginning over two and a half decades ago, a healthy tension starts to develop in Dahl's work—as his awareness of political inequality grows, so does his understanding of how inequality blocks his ambition for America to become a robust pluralist democracy. To his credit, Dahl is willing to question basic institutional forms of American polyarchy as he becomes convinced that they inhibit effective political participation, and thereby political equality. He urges political scientists, for example, to examine the "constitutional system" itself, including developing a unicameral Congress, a multiparty system, and proportional representation.[28]

These tensions result in discomfort with the confines of classic pluralist and behavioral methodologies, since they restrain his analysis from helping him understand how best to fulfill his deeper commitment to real democracy. He later transcends some of these, as we'll see, revealing himself to be a transitional figure.[29] To this point in his career, however, Dahl insufficiently appreciates the relationship between political participation, discovering what is truly in one's interest, and freedom, and rates too low within democratic discourse the importance of the element of responsibility implicated in the concept of political apathy. Peter Bachrach suggests the reason for concern:

> The *real* interest of man is freedom: the freedom to discover himself and beyond that, the freedom to develop into a socially conscious human being. For this reason, democratic participation must be recognized as an integral moral value of contemporary democratic theory.[30]

⌷⌷ Chapter 7

The Rationality of Apathy

Dahl's tendency to reduce human interests to a calculus of costs and bene-fits is developed into an art form in the work of rational choice theory. If the goal of theory is to enhance our ability to predict political behavior, and this is the goal advocates of positivist social science postulate, then one needs a powerful model of human motivation to ground theory, with narrowly con-fined assumptions and clearly stipulated variables capable of spinning off pow-erful generalizations. This formidable challenge is taken up by rational choice.

The act of making a "rational choice," presumed to be the way persons interact in the political world, is one in which the individual most efficiently gains value, preference, or taste goals from a given set of political choices by analyzing relative benefits and costs. Driven by individually rooted motivation to enhance or protect self-interested wants, in rational choice theory the autonomous egoistic individual is the fundamental macro-unit of analysis, while individual values, preferences, tastes, and the like are the micro-units. The choice is purely instrumental to keeping costs to a minimum and benefits to a maximum—it has no value outside of this function. Even when groups are considered, it is clear that the logic of their collective action, their seeking of collective goods, and indeed their ability to form at all, is based on a collec-tion of individual calculations of self-interest.

In basic form with regard to political participation, a rational choice (R) is equal to the probability that participating makes a difference (P), multi-plied by the benefit the actor receives (B) should the activity be successful, minus the cost of participating (C): $R = PB - C$.[1]

When Anthony Downs introduced the idea of the rational voter in his 1957 landmark, *An Economic Theory of Democracy*, he immediately presented the theory with an important internal problem. Since the probability that the act of voting in any election by any individual has virtually no chance to affect the outcome of an election, why would anyone vote?

Similarly, when Mancur Olson in his 1965 pathbreaking *The Logic of Collective Action* tried to understand how groups form, he uncovered the "free-rider" problem. Why would anyone join a group if that person would enjoy the benefits of what that group does without incurring the costs of joining?

Indeed, in both cases substantial evidence refutes the clear logic of the models. How then can these models be reconciled with empirical observations?

Carole Jean Uhlaner argues that Downs introduces what she calls a deux ex machina, by stipulating that one consider the voter's desire to preserve democracy as a new type of benefit.[2] William Riker and Peter C. Ordeshook introduce a "D" term as a benefit, where "D" is citizen duty calculated by a "citizen duty" scale. Thus Downs and Riker and Ordeshook both allow for voting to be motivated by factors independent of the outcome of an election.[3] Uhlaner suggests that "both Downs and Riker and Ordeshook reconcile theory with observation by introducing consumption terms into the voting calculus," and concludes both still fall short "in their inability to explain why people would participate at non-zero rates."[4]

The Irrationality of Democracy

In *Liberalism Against Populism*, William Riker sets up "a confrontation between the theory of democracy and the theory of social choice." His goal is to use the technique of social choice theory—"a theory about the way the tastes, preferences, or values of individual persons are amalgamated and summarized into the choice of a collective group or society"—to test the adequacy of competing liberal and populist definitions of democracy.[5]

Under what he calls liberal or Madisonian democracy, "the function of voting is to control officials, *and no more*."[6] The burden carried by the collective decision of an election is light because no claim is made as to the "quality" of the decision. In populist or Rousseauistic democracy, the burden carried by voting is extremely heavy. Decisions made represent no less than the "general will," embodying the liberty of the people, capable of justifying broad strokes of political action, including repressive acts.

What if, however, what appears to be a strong majority decision based on clearly articulated, freely arrived at, coherent individual choices, under scrutiny from the theory of social choice, dissolves into a series of groups of minority preferences that cannot be logically aggregated into a coherent majority view? Then the collective voting decision forfeits the imprimatur of "majority rule." This "paradox of voting," discussed by theorists such as Duncan Black, Kenneth Arrow, Robin Farquharson, and originally discovered by Condorcet in the late eighteenth century, is captured by Riker as

> the coexistence of coherent individual valuations and a collectively
> incoherent choice by majority rule. In an election with three or more
> alternatives (candidates, motions, etc.) and three or more voters, it may

happen that when the alternatives are placed against each other in a series of paired comparisons, no alternative emerges victorious over each of the others: Voting fails to produce a clear-cut winner.[7]

Riker argues that our choices are either to accept the intransitivity of the result, in which case the choice as *social* choice loses an important element of rationality, or to impose transitivity by privileging the position of one of the contestants, creating a quasi-dictator. Because voting outcomes may or may not be "accurate amalgamations of voters' values," and may or may not be manipulated, and because we can "seldom know which" in either case, we can't expect either accuracy or fairness. Therefore, he concludes, "Outcomes of any particular method of voting lack meaning."[8]

Can the theory of democracy survive this confrontation with the theory of social choice? Only by moderating expectations as to what degree the democratic method can accomplish democratic goals. Populist democracy does not survive, Riker says, because voting simply fails to sustain the great moral burden placed upon it. Only liberal democracy—and, as we'll see, a highly circumscribed "liberalism" at that—passes the rigorous testing of Riker's theory.

Considering Riker's critique of populism as well as his formula with Ordeshook for calculating the rationality of voting, his paradigm of political apathy—of losing interest in politics—can be explicated as follows:

> X (an individual) is rationally apathetic with respect to Y (an election) if the probability that participating makes a difference, multiplied by the benefit of participating (PB), plus the reward of citizen duty (D), is less than the cost of participating (C).

Under these restrictions, R is likely to be less than zero, and political apathy, freeing time and energy for other more rewarding pursuits and not putting moral demands on electoral outcomes incapable of bearing them, is likely to be both rational and supportive of democratic institutions.

Liberalism Against Democracy?

Riker claims,

> The liberal interpretation of voting thus allows elections to be useful and significant even in the presence of cycles, manipulation, and other kinds of "errors" in voting. . . .
> The kind of democracy that survives is not, however, popular rule, but rather an intermittent, sometimes random, even perverse, popular veto. Social choice theory forces us to recognize that the people cannot rule as a corporate body in the way that populists suppose. Instead, officials rule, and they do not represent some indefinable popular will. Hence they can easily be tyrants, either in their own names or in the name of some putative

imaginary majority. Liberal democracy is simply the veto by which it is sometimes possible to restrain official tyranny.[9]

Is the fundamental proposition of the paradox of voting valid, however— the idea that a social choice consists of the combination of discrete choices of individuals, which bear no internal relation to each other or to the social choice itself? What, in fact, is an "election" and what act does "voting" constitute?

Prior to and a condition for the question of whether elections or voting methods can issue in a general will is the fact that most people agree to them as a preeminent form of conflict resolution. Therefore, the question social choice theory poses for democracy is itself based on a prior group choice, minimally that of what Jane Mansbridge calls "adversary democracy" as a fundamental institutional form and matrix for American political culture.[10] If this choice is likely to have been incoherent, doesn't social choice theory also deny legitimacy to the founding of the American republic, and with it Riker's liberalism as well?

Has Riker succeeded in demonstrating that democracy today cannot aggregate a public interest? If we accept my characterization of elections as human enterprises and acknowledge, as Mansbridge and others argue, that taken alone, adversary democracy is a limited view even of what now exists, we see that Riker at most has only demonstrated that one notion of democracy—competitive elections—and only one now suspect way of characterizing elections—as tote boards of the sums of the discrete wills of abstract egoistic individuals—are problematic as a guide to the popular will. As Jon Elster suggests, the idea of universal adult suffrage transcends not only instrumental considerations but those of commutative justice as well: "Society is indeed a joint venture, but the bond among its members is not simply one of mutual advantage, but also one of mutual respect and tolerance."[11]

Even if we allow Riker his findings about the questionable ability of elections to aggregate individual preferences, but deny him his anthropological assumptions about the constitution of societal institutions like elections, his case is weakened. If he is wrong about the coherency of elections themselves, it utterly collapses. Then Riker would really need to argue that the popular will, however arrived at, is likely to be flawed and should be given limited sway. Conservatives for centuries have taken on this argument, and many have made a far more straightforward and persuasive case than he has.

Riker does demonstrate that voting systems may not clearly aggregate preferences in an optimal manner, that ambiguities remain, that the whole is less than the sum of the parts. His work within these parameters is useful for students of schemes of electoral representation, and needs to be taken seriously by them.

Even with regard to electoral democracy, however, Riker's case is inadequate. Politics is simply not nearly as mechanical as Riker indicates. An elected representative may not truly represent the exact wishes of a majority on most critical issues, but, as Heinz Eulau points out, that representative is subject to pressures from groups and constituents, to which he or she responds based, in part, on calculations of political survival—and, I would add, not only his or her own interests, but often an assessment of the public interest. Moreover, the process of negotiation, which is often the heart of democratic politics, as Mansbridge suggests, often simultaneously includes both adversary and unitary democratic methods, which in different ways try to assess the public mood and the public good.[12] Negotiation, lobbying, protests, even compromise can all serve to repair the mathematical defects Riker identifies. Politically aware people are often willing to undergo the sacrifices entailed to achieve the best possible good in a political world that is far more imperfect than the electoral machinery itself.

Overall, the defects in Riker's theory stem from his approach to social choice in which society and even the idea of social choice exist for him only as an epiphenomenon of compiled individual choices. From where, then, comes Riker's own commitment to democracy? If his own account of the democratic method is accurate, his belief in democracy must be based on something more, as I suspect it is and believe it must be to be rational, and indeed to sustain Riker's convictions. But acknowledging there is "something more" begins to undermine the confrontation he has set up between democracy and social choice theory. If there is nothing more, then Riker's real claim should be that democracy is largely irrational, now revealed as mere ideology, and today constitutes a most massive exercise in false consciousness.

Riker himself tacitly acknowledges this problem elsewhere, when he discusses why anyone would vote when rational behavior would counsel abstention. In this sense his introduction, with Ordeshook, of the consumption term "D"—citizen duty—to be added into the equation $R = PB - C$, now to read $R = PB - C + D$, serves to explain why people, when they do in fact vote, are not behaving under the delusions of false consciousness. Of course he is also reconciling with the experimental facts rational choice theory's tendency to predict abstention. In order to salvage the theory, he takes the old-fashioned idea of obligation, in the form of citizen duty, and translates it, in effect, into a "benefit" (or at least a reduction of "cost"). Indeed, the very idea of citizen duty entails commitments that put great pressure on his anthropology, and citizen duty can only be understood as a component of what Riker derides as "popular will." Yet, this retreat weakens the central argument he levels against populism—that it creates an anthropomorphic concept (the will of the people) through which society acts. He claims liberalism escapes this charge by insisting "that individual people in the society choose, and what they individually choose is whether to support or oppose candidates."[13]

But in liberal polities, society "acts" through its choice of government, at a minimum; and for that government to earn legitimacy, it must be representing someone. In a liberal democratic polity, that someone must in some sense be the public. Now, if the claim is that the degree to which it represents the public is extremely uncertain, and that the actions it takes should be constricted through liberal institutions, those very limitations, in order to gain *democratic* legitimacy, still must be part of a design as to how the public thinks it is just to proceed. Even in their nonaction, governments following this plan ratify a particular construction of the "popular will," one that asserts that it is adequately represented in *existing* institutional forms and *existing* distributions of values and power.

Riker is straightforward about his belief that populist excess can undermine democracy; indeed, the twentieth century, he reports, is "a populist era worldwide" in which our "homegrown populists" persistently try and "may well succeed" in undermining our "fundamental constitutional limitations." The main thesis of his book, however, is not this standard conservative one against the dangers of populist excess.

By his own account, the theory of social choice does not prove that populism undermines liberty. What it proves is that the notion of the "popular will" can now be scientifically discounted, that populism as a *possible* theory of democracy is a fraud. But if the popular will cannot be ascertained, it then becomes incumbent upon us, as I have suggested, to ask the same question of liberalism and other theories that he asks of populism—can they demonstrate their legitimacy as theories of *democracy*? If Riker were right the answer must equally be "no." In that case, the only difference between populism and liberalism would be that false claims to legitimacy are more dangerous under populism than they are under liberalism. This, however, would do nothing to establish the democratic *bona fides* of liberalism, as understood by Riker, and it would still turn on the highly political assumption that constellations of power under present liberal regimes are more salutary than they would be under future populist ones.

The real reason populism is dangerous must lie in a more familiar place: in what mass movements, their leaders, or potential tyrants they empower may do to liberty and other cherished values in the name of "the people"— and not in whether the popular will can be scientifically demonstrated to exist. These dangers would exist all the same whether we can know the popular will or not.

Traditional conservative arguments about the illiberal havoc caused by populism remain central to Riker's case against it, after all. But the "confrontation" between social theory and populism is deployed adroitly to soften us up for the familiar kill.

It is not surprising, therefore, that in the end Riker makes an Olympic leap from his assertion that social choice theory demonstrates empirically that popular will is a dangerous illusion to the conclusion that

> The main defense against populist excesses is the maintenance of the constitutional limitations inherited from eighteenth-century Whiggery. It would probably help also to have a citizenry aware of the emptiness of the populist interpretation of voting.[14]

"Consequently," Riker claims, "the fundamental method to preserve liberty is to preserve ardently our traditional constitutional restraints," including a multicameral legislature; a separate executive; an independent judiciary; national and local governments, each with its own sphere of authority; limited tenure; regular elections; and decentralized parties. Believing he has demonstrated that majority will is an illusion—or, minimally, that there is no democratic way to discover it—he falls back on tried and tested institutions designed precisely to modulate the will he doesn't believe is discoverable.

The irony is palpable. Having constructed an argument based on denying the possibility of being able scientifically to study aspects of civilization that fall outside of the discrete wills of individuals, Riker falls back on institutions, of all things, to defend the type of democratic polity he uses his science to endorse. But democratic institutions may be the paradigm of popular will congealing in and giving legitimacy to social constructions of reality, which epistemologically may not be separate from living human beings, but which certainly live within them as a community instrument of civilized living. Commitment to these institutions inheres in assumptions that transcend the narrow bounds of both rational and social choice theory. Belief in the Constitution that the amalgamation of these institutions helps constitute is in part, but far transcends, the calculation that it gives one the opportunity to veto potential tyrants that may adversely affect one's interests. Indeed, it constitutes a way of life irreducible to individual calculations of self-interest, however much self-interest may play a role in commitment to it. Riker knows this, of course, and himself calls constitutional structures places "where participants' values are amalgamated."

Up until his leap of faith, his position is truly minimalist: People share values, but there is no known way to determine authoritatively what they are. If this is true, however, Riker's liberalism must be denied legitimacy for the same reason he denies it to populism: Liberal institutions, which after all are collective value formations, reinforced by both authority and power, cannot be shown to represent the will of the people.

One can go further and assert that Riker is really questioning the possibility of any kind of politics. If the idea of a popular will itself is an illusion—that is, not merely an illusion as an artifact of technical inability to unearth it through elections—what would be the basis for legitimacy for any democratic political point of view or any democratic society? These are some reasons his leap of faith is necessary.

It remains amazing, however, in one respect. Riker writes as if he is invigorating a Madisonian defense of liberalism with the theory of social choice. Although Madison also feared manipulation, he differs from Riker in one essential way.

The institutions Riker points to were designed by Madison and others, as Riker fully understands, not because the Federalists didn't believe one could find out what the majority really wants, but because they were terrified the majority would find a way to know what it wants and take it—and do so democratically. They were afraid of the "tyranny" of a majority that actually might discover itself, coherently aggregate its individual preferences into a popular will, and act in terms of it.

His return to institutions is not surprising politically, for institutions and the social practices they embody are an essential source of predictability in human affairs, and this predictability is enhanced by the very fact that there are popular expectations about what behaviors are in certain roles. Indeed, by proposing the formula $R = PB - C + D$, Riker is advancing his view of how the popular will sees normal behavior. His return to institutions is more surprising methodologically in that he roots his choice analysis in the discrete motivations of individuals.

Frank C. Zagare analyzes Riker's work in a way that helps explain the relationship between Riker's methodology and his dependence on institutions. Riker's view of politics and democracies "is that of a world characterized by an incoherency that is practically and theoretically unavoidable" and subject therefore to manipulation.[15]

Because of this indeterminacy, Riker draws certain conclusions about the enterprise of political science itself. Riker writes:

> the hope, from a scientific point of view, of finding political equilibria is that one might isolate political phenomena. . . . The achievement of that ideal depends, however, on the pieces in fact being self-contained . . . specifically on the political process being independent of the morass of participants' perceptions and personalities, which are features of the world entirely outside the political abstraction.

Unfortunately, Riker believes, there is an absence of equilibria, suggesting that matters exogenous to the political abstraction also need to be considered, such as "perception and personality and understanding and character." Political outcomes are

> not simply a mechanical, impersonal, unbiased amalgamation of individual values . . . [and] . . . the notion that political outcomes are the will of the people must be revised to say they are the will of the smarter, bolder, more powerful, more creative, or luckier people.

Consequently, disequilibrium for Riker issues both in "philosophical (or ideological) disappointment,"[16] and the further disappointment, as Zagare puts it, "that the power that comes from scientific knowledge is well nigh unobtainable for political abstractions."

In spite of this "scientific" disappointment, Zagare concludes, Riker "goes on to deny that a science of politics is impossible," but instead "seems to suggest that scientific knowledge is possible but only within narrowly defined limits set by institutional arrangements that induce temporary equilibria (and hence permit short-term explanations and predictions)." Zagare reasons that Riker thus "implies" an argument, old both to Riker and in political science, "that political science should return to its earlier tradition and reconcern itself with the study of institutions," a point Riker makes in such an "oblique way" that it "is certain to invite misinterpretation."[17]

I would extend Zagare's point in the following way. Riker's methodology and political proclivities reinforce each other. His desire to predict encourages him to push outside the domain of science phenomena such as perceptions, willpower, intelligence—indeed, it seems some aspects of power itself—in order to base inquiry on firmer footing. Nevertheless, he recognizes that these phenomena affect, in fact, help constitute, politics. His political fear of "popular will," now wedded to his methodological concern that one can't be an objective political scientist except if one holds constant these exogenous properties, leads him to strongly endorse firm institutional restraints on the sway these properties, exhibited through widespread political participation, will have in influencing the political world. His conservative brand of liberalism and his view of what a science of politics entails go hand in glove.

Riker's methodological and ideological commitments also affect his understanding of the concept *power* in ways that serve to undermine some of his genuine insights:

> It is possible that alternative x (say, some political platform) repeatedly beats alternative y (another platform) so that one is fairly certain that x has a good majority over y. But suppose x wins only because z was eliminated earlier or was suppressed by the Constitution or by the method of counting or by manipulation. What then is the status of x? If x is as precise as a motion, then one can still be fairly sure that x at least beats y. But if x is as vague as an ideology, it is far from certain that a clear decision is ever made.[18]

More advanced than his colleagues who focus only on "observed behavior," Riker here insightfully probes the real nature of political power. Quite strikingly, he uses his insight not to discover ways freedom is practically restricted, but to develop a rationale for a diminished role for political participation based on the limited nature of political freedom as such, lending legitimacy to his version of Madisonian liberalism:

> The popular will is defined only as long as the issue dimensions are
> restricted. Once issue dimensions multiply, the popular will is irresolute . . .
> and that is why populism is an empty interpretation of voting and why the
> populist ideal is literally unattainable.[19]

That only the restrictions on agendas and ideology that *he* proposes
should be accepted without reference to whether they are illicitly sustained
by power is inexplicable. Like Berelson, Lazarsfeld, and McPhee, and Huntington, Riker puts forth a theory in which carefully circumscribed participation is not only not a threat to democracy, but actually is essential to it.

What is distinctive about Riker is that like many critics of his methodology, and unlike many positivist social scientists, he believes there are tight
limits within which we can "scientifically" explain and/or predict human affairs, leading to modest claims for his science. Yet he believes he has *scientifically* demonstrated such incoherency and that it can't be *scientifically* untan-
gled. Moreover, although he seems to believe that political science must
disappoint, his calculations of intransitivity and incoherency are used to no
less than discard most traditions of democratic discourse, from Rousseau to
Mill to Pateman, in favor of his narrow reading of Madison. Although he
acknowledges the limits of his science, he uses it nevertheless to fix politics
very carefully.

Rational Choice or Giving Reasons

Carole Jean Uhlaner is concerned with limited models of rational choice on
the model of Riker's, and develops "A New Approach." One objective of hers
is to reconcile the best in rational choice theory with the best in behavioralism:

> The rational actor approach to participation suffers from its failure to
> predict or explain actual behavior. The political behavior literature ignores
> interests and instrumental motivations in favor of focusing on "resources."
> A solution to the deficiencies of both sets of theories comes from
> incorporating within a rational actor theory a recognition that individuals
> identify with groups . . . [essentially by introducing] an alternative
> conception of rationality which permits us to capture within a rational actor
> framework affiliational motivations.[20]

As with Riker and Downs, Uhlaner begins with the problem that "in the
absence of consumption benefits, abstention maximizes utility." However, if
one considers the interplay of rational interchange of costs and benefits
among leaders, candidates, and voters, and then how individuals often see
themselves in terms of their "group identity," a powerful model can be developed with which to explain participation because "enhancement of a sense
of group identity plays a key role in that mobilization": "In other words, group

leaders have available, in addition to standard material incentives, a repertoire of psychological incentives."

Uhlaner then extends the way rational choice theory looks at rationality itself, in a way that uncovers "clearer benefits for individuals who respond to group appeals," by looking into "the content of the voters' utility functions." Here she tries to read into rational choice theory both an impulse toward rewarding cooperative behavior and the way culture determines individual wants, remedying the theory's defective focus on "self-aggrandizement and indifference to the structure of relations with others, except insofar as this structure increases goods."[21]

In perhaps her most perceptive insight, she suggests that a major theoretical defect of the standard model of rational choice theory is that it doesn't address the question of where consumption benefits come from:

> people do participate and . . . not on solely arbitrary consumption grounds. Instead, the group structure and the manipulation of material and psychological benefits link the individual, albeit via consumption benefits, with instrumental benefits accrued from the aggregation of individuals' actions. Our second version provides the foundation for such a linkage.

By reconstituting what should be considered rational within rational choice theory, including developing a social basis of rationality while maintaining the idea of individual instrumental behavior, she believes she deepens its explanatory power:

> Norms which dictate behavior to benefit the collectivity or which enhance awareness of embeddedness in some group are central, not incidental, to social organization and to this model. . . . The model presented here raises the question of whether private self-interest is distinct from a public, political interest. Do people shift their moral perspective, their sense of action, their sense of obligation from one mode, when considering themselves autonomous disconnected beings, to another mode, when considering themselves members of some community?[22]

Uhlaner believes that her work redresses "the imbalance introduced by focusing solely upon persons' egoistic impulses" by starting "from the premise that human beings have a motivation toward maximizing the extent to which they are included by others." Refocusing in this way "leads to questions about the characteristics of culture which tend to suppress or to enhance [impulses to inclusion] . . . relative to egoism." The payoff is that "actions inexplicable from the viewpoint of maximizing egoists become subject to prediction and to theoretical explanation."[23]

Jon Elster puts the point better: "Much of the social choice and public choice literature, with its assumptions of universally opportunistic behaviour, simply seems out of touch with the real world, in which there is a great deal of honesty and sense of duty." "If people always engaged in opportunistic behaviour when they could get away with it," he concludes, "civilization as we know it would not exist." And Elster believes this means that the purpose of political life is not simply to "devise institutions that can harness opportunistic self-interest to socially useful purposes" but, equally important, "to create institutions that embody a valid conception of justice."[24]

Uhlaner's work is surely an important attempt to rescue the power of rational choice theory from its tendency to oversimplify, even distort, human motivation and behavior to achieve that power. Yet as Brian Barry suggests, "It is no trick to restate all behaviour in terms of 'rewards' and 'costs'; it may for some purposes be a useful conceptual device, but it does not in itself provide anything more than a set of empty boxes waiting to be filled."[25]

One is struck by the fact that the more Uhlaner elaborates the theory—fills those "empty boxes"—by adding and refining the meaning of costs and benefits, and especially by recasting how we should view rationality itself, the further she gets from rational choice theory and the closer she gets to ordinary language. Indeed, theorists of rational choice restrict the terms in their equation precisely in order to allow them, in their view, to stipulate closely and objectively the conditions under which the theory can be tested. This is what leads Riker forthrightly to acknowledge that the best *science* of politics he can come up with will still disappoint.

Yet Uhlaner is right—indeed, she does not go far enough—to try to reinject political analysis with concepts that *seem* troublingly imprecise. What is precise, after all, about translating citizenship duty into the foreign language of a consumption benefit?

In reference to Anthony Downs's *An Economic Theory of Democracy*, Brian Barry implies that the "empty boxes" of rational choice theory actually are not empty even at the beginning of the analysis. When Downs claims that a citizen " 'is willing to bear certain short-run costs he could avoid in order to do his share in providing long-run benefits,' " Barry argues, he "commits a common fallacy in social science thought which most of the book turns on his avoiding." The idea of "doing his share," Barry correctly argues, "is a concept foreign to the kind of 'economic' rationality with which Downs is working." It means the citizen needs to think that, since his benefits "depend on the efforts of others, he should contribute too."

> This may be good ethics, but it is not consistent with the assumptions of the model, which require the citizen to compute the advantage that accrues to him from his doing x rather than y; not the advantage that would accrue to him from *himself and others* doing x rather than y, unless, of course, his doing it is a necessary and sufficient condition of the others doing it.[26]

The "boxes," then, are designed for a view of human nature presumed to be circumscribed by calculations of egoistic self-interest. It is their design rather than their filling that is problematic, and that is why, as Barry argues, an arena of human life as important as ethics doesn't fit in them.

Consider the following example. Paying off a loan is a material benefit to my creditor while not to me as a debtor. But it is also a benefit to me, in Uhlaner's terms, in that it allows me a sense of fulfilling a social obligation. I might now modify my language and say, for example, one is a material benefit, while the other is a social affective benefit attached to an economic cost, which itself has the economic benefit of preserving my credit rating. Perhaps the word *obligation*, or even *contract*, best captures the real relationship. Both words imply these ideas but are not completely circumscribed by them or by each other.

Perhaps hidden both to Uhlaner and Riker is that the perception common today—that no one any longer really operates out of obligation—may have insinuated itself in their theories. If we create theory in language that reflects these perceptions, however unwittingly, we sanction and reinforce them, especially if we claim for political theory the imprimatur of science and not politics. Is the model predicting reality? Or does it appear plausible precisely because it conforms to aspects of the reality from which it has been drawn, imperceptibly accenting them and reinforcing their credibility while implicitly discounting the value of more religious, communitarian, traditional conservative, or egalitarian aspects of ways to understand that reality?

In what circumstances, to take another example, is voting simply because it's the right thing to do meaningfully referred to as a "benefit" called "citizen duty," or taking the trouble to walk to the polls a "cost"? Perhaps in a society in which voting is intuitively viewed as something one does, however irrelevant to the real political fabric.

Like all theory, rational choice has an incipient notion of false consciousness. When, in pure form, it posits voting to be irrational—costs outweigh the benefits—its theorists can choose to conclude instead that the many people who vote are actually behaving rationally, which means that the theory is wrong. Or they can insist that the theory is correct, and that people actually are behaving irrationally, by which they must mean, out of a false understanding of what rational behavior entails. To strengthen the theory, Riker adds the "D" term and Uhlaner tries to reform the concept of rationality itself within rational choice theory.

Yet the implication of Uhlaner's revision of Riker's theory is that, even with citizen duty added as a benefit, it still fails to adequately explain why so many vote. Left where Riker leaves it, we can imply from Uhlaner that rational choice theory leaves too much false consciousness scattered about. So she expands the vocabulary of benefits further to include satisfactions of "group affiliations" and the like, to improve the model of rationality. Each move, however, seems to generate new problems. What about people who vote out of habit? Out of tradition? Out of irrational impulses they themselves can't understand? Out of loyal obedience to an ideology or political party that might patently harm their interests? And so on.

Uhlaner's quest will continue, I believe, because in the end, the language of costs and benefits is insufficient to convey certain aspects of human behavior, and is simply inappropriate for certain characteristics of human motivation. At a more practical level, there is another reason that her quest will continue. The instrumental language of costs and benefits, as she herself implies, is inadequate also as a *grounding* to the norms, conventions, and beliefs that help constitute social, political, and even economic life. If values depend on a richer understanding of motives, reasons, and rationality itself to retain their coherence and legitimacy, in the end translating them into the terminology of costs and benefits will be frustrating as well as misleading. New "benefits" will continuously be discovered. To the extent they seem to provide most accurately a language with which to explain human behavior, they will come closer and closer to the language of ordinary discourse, with its rich array of concepts that can ferret out causes, reasons, rationality, costs and benefits, delusions, commitments, responsibility, relations of power, concerns about manipulation, beliefs about what democracy should realistically entail, and why people do or do not participate in politics, and the implications of those causes and reasons.

Elster captures an important presumption of rational choice theory when he suggests that it "is first and foremost normative," telling "us what we ought to do in order to achieve our aims" but not "what our aims ought to be." But he does not go far enough. For in telling us what it makes sense to do, it *does* tell us how we behave, and indicates to us a vision of what *normal* people *should* be expected to do. Indeed, Elster continues, "From the normative account we can derive an explanatory theory, by assuming that people are rational in the normatively appropriate sense."[27]

Like behavioralism, rational choice has a role to play in explanation, for it does capture some important aspects of modern life.[28] But its role will be enhanced if it becomes aware of its normative point of view.

Behavioralism Against Rational Choice?

The famous behavioralist Heinz Eulau, no friend of participatory democracy, dubs *Liberalism Against Populism* a "curiously bamboozling book" whose central and weakest part (he praises the two other major sections) is the one I review here. Eulau argues, "That rulers in a democracy are, can, will or should be *responsive* to 'people' (interests, classes, support groups, influentials, or what not) is a notion not beyond the bounds of liberal democracy."[29] He suggests that Riker has set up in his rendering of liberalism and populism "two straw men," and is right as a liberal in fearing that Riker's caricature is more likely to drive people away than to draw them to liberalism.

Yet Riker's methodological reasons for tightly limiting what can count as scientific data, allowing him his narrow political conclusions, is not different in kind from why behavioralists look to statistical regularities, rather than peering into the mind to discern motivations. Both seek to limit inquiry to what they perceive to be the facts of the case, but this view in both accounts is predicated on a notion of social science that believes facts and values can be distinguished without entailing theoretical and even political implications.

Eulau and Riker share unacknowledged assumptions relevant to each's methodology about the nature of social science and human nature itself. Each in his own way sees political society as a collection of "atoms,"[30] as it were, and the enterprise of social science as one of attempting to explain human action with scientific tools, which themselves are objective in the sense they are not implicated in any particular and rationally debatable worldview. Thus, while both would acknowledge theories they discover may have political implications, both would deny their methodology as such is implicated in their conclusions, which therefore can gain the status of scientific objectivity. Political science, in both accounts, is an enterprise through which we can learn how to maximize values we somehow hold, such as democracy, but it does not establish the nature of those values, and because proper methods do not derive from commitment to anthropological or political assumptions embodied in them, its methods are neutral with respect to them. It is precisely this view of political science I have been contesting throughout.

The Limits of Positivist Social Science

The epistemological assumptions of all the thinkers considered so far in this work rest on a common and problematic view of the nature of explanation and prediction in the social sciences. Where rational choice theory attempts to develop a meta-theory from which we can (deductively) predict human behavior, behavioralism seeks to accumulate data from which we can (inductively) predict human behavior, and empirical democratic theory attempts to forecast, based on its observation of existing behavior, how much participation it is wise to design into a political system. All these efforts have as their goal the development of refined techniques of systematic analysis through which can be developed lawlike generalizations of political activity, with the same epistemological claim to objectivity, if not the same precision in practice (indeed Riker believes far from it), as the natural sciences.

First of all, social science is incapable, in principle, of attaining the kinds of predictions positivists believe are available to natural science, and the belief that it is capable is based on a flawed understanding of human ontology, social science, and natural science itself. Second, viewing social science as an enterprise in which prediction becomes virtually a sufficient condition for explanatory precision unwittingly serves to turn it into an exercise of control.

To take the second claim first, "positive" social science seeks to explain (usually meaning *stipulate*) the conditions under which certain political behaviors rather than others will occur. Explanation is closely allied if not always thoroughly identified with the ability to predict. But building up bodies of predictive political knowledge is most useful for the purpose of organizing people within complex industrial societies in which political administration and control over people and the economy seem necessary for productive activity, and politics itself becomes a technical enterprise. Brian Fay argues that "it is *because* of its conceptual connections with the idea of control that a positivist social science has the relevance and institutional backing that it has in modern life."[31]

In fact, one way the endorsement of control in positivist social science comes is via its claim not to endorse particular ends (and to deny that its methods do). Its actual concepts derive, nevertheless, largely from the repertoire of dominant practices—indeed, its very focus on defining explanation largely as prediction *is* one such practice. In claiming for its predictions the status of epistemic reality, it implies a view of what kind of behavior is natural and, therefore, what kind is abnormal and subject to appropriate control. It may make accurate predictions. But to the degree its explanations are judged solely by the accuracy of the prediction, they uncritically may more reflect than explain the conditions that made the prediction likely. Note the following similarities between branches of positive theory within political science: it catalogues political behavior from political behaviors observable within the present systems of politics (behavioralism); it devises a theory of rational behavior from dominant ideological predispositions of existing society (rational choice's predilection for cost-benefit analysis); in order to make democratic theory realistic, it revises it to conform with societies it presumes to be as fully democratic as humanly possible (empirical democratic theory).

Now to take the first claim. When he explains that there is a "systematic unpredictability" in human affairs, Alisdair MacIntyre captures the impoverished notion of subjectivity within positivist social science in a way that bears directly on its foundational epistemic claims. He suggests four sources of unpredictability. First, he claims, radical conceptual innovation can't be predicted because to do so is to discover the innovation. One can't predict the discovery of the wheel, or explain it, until the discovery is made, which is not to say that its discovery is inexplicable. Second, I also can't predict what decision I will make among several choices, for unless there is inherent unpredictability, they are not meaningfully called choices. Now someone else may be able to predict what I will do, but because, like me, he can't predict what he will do, and what he does may influence what I do, "It follows that insofar as the observer cannot predict the impact of his future actions on my future decision-making, he cannot predict my future actions any more than he can his own; and this clearly holds for all agents and all observers. The unpredictability of my future by me does indeed generate an important degree of unpredictability as such."[32]

Third, even though aspects of life resemble the game theory of political scientists, interactions among people with interests have an "indefinite reflexivity" that undermines the "scientific" enterprise. In any contest, each participant tries to make his or her behavior unpredictable at the same time that each must try to predict the other's behavior, and each tries to hide information from the other. Moreover, we can't be sure if, in the real world, we're all playing the same game. I may be a union negotiator who is seeking a political appointment; you may be a government mediator who, in fact, is seeking union votes; she might be a corporation head who, in fact, is a corporation head.[33] Lastly, there is the unpredictability of "pure contingency." What was the effect of Cleopatra's perfect nose on Marc Antony, and therefore on Roman history?

"Given then that there are these unpredictable elements in social life," MacIntyre argues, "it is crucial to notice their intimate relationship to the predictable elements," of which there are four kinds: (1) coordinating or scheduling of social activity; (2) statistical regularities (we may or may not know the cause); (3) "causal regularities of nature" (e.g., snowstorms); and (4) "causal regularities in social life" (may have definite causes; for example, educational opportunity in Britain in the nineteenth and twentieth centuries has been "determined" largely by social class).

The claim, then, is not that human behavior is incapable of being predicted or, less, or being caused; but that in the human sciences, predictions and explanations cannot have the status of objective lawlike generalizations. Thus, understanding the nature of generalization in the social sciences means coming to terms with the inherent need, capacity, and inevitability of both predictability *and* unpredictability in human affairs: "It is at once clear that many of the central features of human life derive from the particular and peculiar ways in which predictability and unpredictability interlock." Without predictability we "would lack the basis for many characteristically human institutions. . . . But the pervasive unpredictability in human life also renders all our plans and projects permanently vulnerable and fragile."[34]

MacIntyre traces this lack of self-understanding in social science to the Enlightenment propensity to see unpredictability stemming from the "character of the material environment and our ignorance," to which the "Marxists added economic competitiveness and ideological blindness."

> All of them wrote as though fragility and vulnerability could be overcome
> in some progressive future. And it is now possible to identify the link
> between this belief and their philosophy of science. The latter with its view
> of explanation and prediction played a central role in sustaining the former.
> But with us the argument now has to move in the other direction.[35]

There is no future in the state of social scientific discourse in which this fact of life will or should change. He writes,

> It is necessary, if life is to be meaningful, for us to be able to engage in long-term projects, and this requires predictability; it is necessary, if life is to be meaningful, for us to be in possession of ourselves and not merely to be the creations of other people's projects, intentions and desires, and this requires unpredictability. We are thus involved in a world in which we are simultaneously trying to render the rest of society predictable and ourselves unpredictable, to devise generalisations which will capture the behaviour of others and to cast our own behaviour into forms which will elude the generalisations which others frame.[36]

In principle, human life is not as predictable as positivism, or Marxism, believes it to be. Nor is it subject to lawlike generalization. Yet the claim that it is, especially by a social science that is self consciously normatively neutral, still suggests a view as to how normal people behave—but positivism hides that fact to social science, to itself, and to others.

This dilemma extends to techniques, as I suggested earlier with regard to definitions of "rational" behavior, but rational choice techniques are hardly alone. Survey questionnaires encounter similar problems. The less deeply questioners probe into attitudes, the more the answers tend to reflect dominant appearances. The more these answers get publicized, the more they cast a range of normal attitudes or opinions within which people should arrange themselves. The less deeply they probe, therefore, the more they ratify current perceptions and, in fact, reflexively re-create them. Yet the more deeply they probe, the more difficult it becomes to quantify the results or, within current canons of social science, make credible claims of social scientific accuracy, and the more likely they are to be accused of imposing their own ideas upon the respondent. And the more widely their questions range, the more likely the questioners are to be accused of framing them from an ideological viewpoint, precisely because what they would then ask slips outside of dominating ideologies. And, most subtly, unless respondents can foresee other ways of ordering their reality, which is difficult enough to come up with, let alone volunteer to an interviewer, they will assume that the present context of expectations will not and perhaps cannot change, and their statements about happiness and contentment, or cynicism and alienation, will be framed from that point of view. Indeed, it may not be until respondents have a chance to discuss the interview later among themselves that there may be a shift in the terms of comparison.[37]

The problem of lack of social scientific rigor of this sort is very difficult although not impossible to work through, but it involves a rethinking not only of technique but of the social scientific enterprise. Beyond interviewing in more depth, the interviewer might need to be exposed to alternative theories that then would be tested in the interview,[38] which then would also per-form the educational function of exposing the subject to alternative theories. This raises fundamental questions about what one needs to do to make sur-veys truly social scientific.

All theory, not just positivist theory, casts a vision of what society is, or should be, and how people behave, or should behave or are likely to behave under certain circumstances, and the techniques chosen as appropriate to theories help create data for that vision. And while explanations may support predictions, or flow from behavior that has become predictable, or help make behavior become predictable as they become publicized, they also must take the form of giving reasons as to why the claim is true, which entails assump-tions by the person studying. Even explanation that is given only in the form of prediction can be made to reveal hidden commitments.

For explanation to be circumscribed thoroughly by prediction, and really become reliable *lawlike* generalizations, restriction of freedom as a prior condi-tion would be necessary. Since this can't be accomplished ontologically—intentionality can't be abolished; prediction can't really circumscribe expla-nation—it would have to be done politically. However marginal in the larger sweep of history, and however innocently, one small way may be in the claim that positivist social science is a value-neutral science of society compiling objective laws of political nature.[39]

Writing about rationalism but applicable generally, I think, to positivist social science, William Connolly concludes,

> in the name of reason, it construes the unfamiliar to be unreason; in the name of criticism, it closes off avenues to self-criticism; in the name of the universal it celebrates the provincial. To avoid recognition of the deficiencies in this perspective the rationalist must either treat a particular set of ends and priorities as if they were universally acknowledged by all peoples, or treat particular character traits and purposes prevalent in one society as if they reflected orientations that all people everywhere would endorse if only they knew themselves more thoroughly. . . . It tries to establish on *a priori* grounds that which must be established through historically specific inquiry. In doing so it fosters a reified view of one set of social processes, identifying them as the universal norm against which others are to be appraised.[40]

Chapter 8

Plain Democratic Theory

E. E. Schattschneider argues, straightforwardly, that those who do not participate in politics do so because the present scope of political organization and debate does not speak to their needs. His major work, *The Semi-Sovereign People*, written in 1960, is an excellent early attempt to explain the existence of widespread nonparticipation in American politics. Written in accessible commonsense terms, his work is a classic for good reason.

Against the dominant analysis of his time, Schattschneider argues that pluralists exaggerate the extent of consensus that exists because they ignore fundamental, though submerged, political cleavages. Indeed, the existing consensus is itself a particular distribution of power because *"the definition of the alternatives is the supreme instrument of power."*[1]

> All forms of political organization have a bias in favor of the exploitation of some kinds of conflict and the suppression of others because *organization is the mobilization of bias.* Some issues are organized into politics while others are organized out.[2]

The Mobilization of Bias

In the American political scene of his day, this bias resulted in forty million Americans rejecting electoral politics, with an overwhelming majority having no place in the system of pressure groups. These facts are of fundamental significance to American democracy and how we study it.

> It is a great deficiency of the group theory that it has found no place in the political system for the majority. . . . The vice of the groupist theory is that it conceals the most significant aspects of the system. The flaw in the pluralist heaven is that the heavenly chorus sings with a strong upperclass accent. Probably 90 per cent of the people cannot get into the pressure system.[3]

The participation of the nonparticipants could dramatically alter the scope of politics. For Schattschneider, the "struggle for democracy" was no longer over the right to vote, but over the organization of politics itself, and especially over the terms of the present consensus. To the extent writers view nonparticipation only in terms of ignorance and lack of interest, in his view, they are rationalizing the present organization of politics, deflecting attention from the need to change it.

> There is a better explanation. Abstention reflects the suppression of the options and alternatives that reflect the needs of the nonparticipants. It is not necessarily true that the people with the greatest needs participate in politics most actively. *Whoever decides what the game is about decides also who can get into the game.*

It turns out that "every study supports the conclusion that nonvoting is a characteristic of the poorest, least well-established, least educated stratum of the community."

> Unquestionably, an expansion of the scope of the present system would bring a new kind of voter into the community and would change the balance of forces.
>
> The question is: Has the quarrel that underlies American politics been so defined that it excludes a major segment of the nation from the political system?[4]

The relationship between nonvoting and the scope of politics, for Schattschneider, is "the most important datum about the political system, much more important than the distinction between Republicans and Democrats."[5] The democratic challenge is to develop a "public policy about politics" to use "political means" to overcome the extralegal, social, procedural, structural, and organizational biases of the political system. The democratic goal must be nothing less than to bring the disenfranchised into the electoral and interest group political arenas.[6]

With simple brilliance, Schattschneider suggests that the present bias of the political system is drawn on conflict lines in which none of the antagonistic positions really speaks to the needs of the disenfranchised. There are alternative lines of conflict with their own catalogue of political issues, although latent, which would motivate the politically marginal. Presently, however, they are *displaced* by the existing lines. He asks, "If the political system is dominated by the cleavage AB, what can the people who want another alignment (CD) do? One thing they may do is to stop voting."[7]

The historic function of government in a democracy is to help redress imbalances in power, particularly between unequal economic power and the political power deriving from the principle of political equality embodied in one person, one vote. How can this be done? By responsible political leaders and organizations undertaking the task of broadening the "socialization of conflict"—moving it away from issues that represent narrow private interests to encompass different and broader concerns. Powerless voters and nonvoters

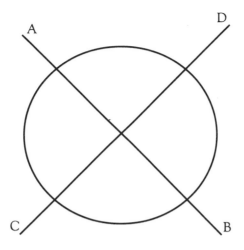

The Displacement of Conflict

alike would then develop a greater stake in the system and break the present domination of business interests. Democratic government could then serve its historic function of counterbalancing the power of private wealth, and democracy would be preserved alongside corporate capitalism.

Schattschneider's "mobilization of bias" is the classic exposition of a normal thesis of depoliticization. He explains nonparticipation through this thesis as follows:

> X (individual, group, race, "subjective" class) does not participate in politics when there are no significant Y's (political issues, overt grievances) that meet X's needs. Political apathy is not a central explanation of nonparticipation for Schattschneider, but here is how I think it enters his model: Apathy *may* explain X's nonparticipation when no Y's significant to X are being kept out of the political arena.

The Bias of the Bias of Conflict

In contrast to Berelson, Lazarsfeld, and McPhee, who misuse and overuse the concept of apathy, and Dahl, who often does, Schattschneider virtually dismisses it. To reject by rational, conscious abstention is not, at the outset at least, to be apathetic.

Instead, Schattschneider uses concepts that have precise critical meaning, such as "mobilization of bias," "rejection," "suppression," and "abstention" itself, in order to locate the systematic exclusion of identifiable groups from the political process. For Schattschneider, X rejects politics because Y (the range of issues) under the present two-party consensus does not meet X's needs. The problem is not just that political inequalities exist, as Dahl has described it so far, but that the normal working of the political system routinely spins them out and they congeal in a biased political agenda, a most difficult "inequality" to contend with.

Schattschneider's explanation, therefore, restricts the too-loose application of the concept of political apathy. If X is conceived as a disparate individual, John, who seems not to be involved in Y (conceived generally as politics), all things being equal, political apathy seems a reasonable explanation of John's nonparticipation. If X is now viewed, as Schattschneider suggests is more plausible, as a social group or class for which there are Y's, now seen as issues or concerns typical of that group or class but not represented as issues within "politics," then political apathy loses its prima facie plausibility as an explanation. Apathy becomes a reasonable explanation, in Schattschneider's account, only after we have determined that such group or class-based grievances do not exist.

Schattschneider's explanation of nonparticipation, however, has important limitations. He draws too narrowly the concepts of power and interests, reinforcing his tendency to confine the range of X and Y, and also actually to underuse the concept of political apathy.

For relations of power to operate in the Schattschneiderian conflict model, as in the pluralist account, there must exist A doing something to constrain the choices of B, or, as is absent in pluralism, an agenda that is in the subjectively felt interest of A and against the subjectively felt interest of B, which constrains B's political freedom regardless of whether A actually has to do anything. The second is what he means by the *bias of conflict*.

Interests for Schattschneider are essentially the same thing as the subjectively felt needs of persons, excluding what Lukes has called their "objective interests." There is no room for discontinuity between what someone believes to be in his or her interest and what actually is, nor is there an appreciation that felt troubles may exist, reflecting unmet "objective interests" (or even future false interests) that are not yet coherently developed by the person into a clear statement of subjective need. Lewis Lipsitz, for example, suggests that grievances may be latent—that is, as the individual or group may not yet be fully aware of their terms, their preferences are not yet articulable.[8] Grievances may also be overt but, drawn in the language of contemporary political discourse, be constructed only in personal terms, leading a person to therapy or other nonpolitical solution. Left as vague troubles, or clear but personally defined grievances, these discomforts may not presently stimulate political organization, although, through a broader reading of power and interests, they could in the future.

Unresolved in his account, therefore, is the following question: Might a political agenda reveal its bias, not by thwarting a group's definitions of issues, but by derailing either the development of coherent issues out of troubles, or, even more powerfully, by denying people the experience of other ways of thinking about political life, which might actually lead them to reassess their real interests and turn to views different from those they now hold?

Sexual harassment at work was certainly for some women, let's say in the 1950s, a clear political issue but with no available political forum; for others, a privately held grievance they weren't sure they had a legitimate right to remedy; for still others, a severe discomfort for which a critical language was not yet available; and for others, the way the world is, perhaps not even harassment at all. Yet from the point of view of someone who believes sexual harassment is a clear political issue deserving of crisp legal remedy, as most women in American do today, all of the ways sexual harassment was kept off the agenda in the 1950s potentially were exercises of power that manifested themselves, in part, in the way women (and of course men) defined their own political interests.

These theoretical difficulties regarding interests and power, and his political focus on the role of government in democracy to redress power imbalances between economic groups, also come into play in limiting Schattschneider's view of what constitutes politics. In Schattschneider's discussion, politics is confined primarily to party politics and government, even though he is fully aware of the enormous influence of business on the political agenda.

Consider hierarchical job structures, racial and sexual divisions of the workforce, and atomistic lives in a liberal polity as a context within which to test Schattschneider's view of power, interests, politics, and participation. Power is organized in ways that may exclude many important concerns from what Schattschneider calls politics. The populace may be politically fragmented, making it more difficult for members to locate common structural sources of problems that may appear to be personal (loneliness in a suburban housing development made possible by huge federal subsidies to highway construction), economic (a family loses its source of income because the company that employed the breadwinners moves to another location), or private (a person resents the limited responsibility assigned in a job, while incorrectly believing that having a narrow job like his or hers promotes economic efficiency).

None of these discontents is created by what appear to be political relations of power. None was debated in government. None is viewed by the disadvantaged themselves as political issues. These presumptions concerning the nature of the political arena, power, and interests, first, deflect attention from issues that others might claim to be political and, second, glance past more subtle power relations that may inhibit participation.

Without translating latent or explicit grievances, whether personal, private, economic, sexual, or racial, into explicitly political ones, the bias of conflict may remain biased even if grievances clearly understood to be political are now given their proper place within the agenda. Of course, what should be included as political is always contestable and, in fact, is often at the heart of politics. Yet a broader construal of politics, interests, and power helps us explain nonparticipation by looking at the bias of conflict in new ways.

To illustrate, let us consider how the concept of political apathy might come into play in Schattschneider's analysis in ways unintended by him. Let's suppose for the moment that nonparticipants and participants alike, in spite of class and educational differences (Schattschneider's clue that they have different needs), actually have similar overt grievances but participate at different rates. Lacking sensitive enough concepts of interests, power, and politics, and now missing the cue of different felt needs, Schattschneider's analysis here ironically puts pressure on itself to overexplain nonparticipation as apathy related to free choices.

In his actual usage, however, Schattschneider greatly underutilizes the concept of apathy in both its faces. He is unable to explain the more subtle ways social positioning may inculcate a posture of apathy that has little to do with choice, apathy as a condition of political life that is surely a subtype of depoliticization. It also remains important not to eliminate by fiat the possibility that people may be responsible for allowing their will to wane or for making other political choices that render them apathetic about concerns, we would maintain, that should be important to them.

For Schattschneider, the primary question for political theory and strategy is why so few people participate and even fewer have influence in politics. He is a democratic theorist of the first order because he sets his sights squarely on trying to understand why and how "popular rule" is being limited, and does so with great insight.

Duality of Interests

Peter Bachrach has also devoted his life to uncovering limits on popular rule. While indebted to Schattschneider's mobilization of bias thesis, Bachrach broadens the scope of essential concepts, especially interests, power, participation, politics, and democracy itself.

Bachrach's early analysis of power is similar to Schattschneider's. In a famous 1962 essay, "The Two Faces of Power," written with Morton Baratz, he suggests that power relations exist when there is conflict over issues or over what grievances should be allowed to become issues. An exercise of power may be found to exist whether or not the exercise is intentional and obvious. Its most subtle manifestation, not observable through rigid behaviorist methodology, occurs through "nondecision-making." Can the student of politics safely ignore the possibility, for instance, that an individual or group in a community participates more vigorously in supporting the *nondecision-making* process than in participation in actual decisions within the process? Stated differently, can the researcher overlook the chance that some person or association could limit decision-making to relatively non-controversial matters, by influencing community values and political procedures and rituals, notwithstanding that there are in the community serious but latent power conflicts? To do so is, in our judgment, to overlook the less apparent, but nonetheless extremely important, face of power.[9]

In his paper "Interest, Participation, and Democratic Theory" (1971), he refines his notions of power and interests, suggesting that a power relation exists when nondecision-making prevents the development of *explicit* grievances as well as of coherent political issues.[10] Increased participation itself, he suggests, may undermine certain values and raise questions about previously accepted relations of authority. There is a revealing ambiguity in his work, however, in that, also with Baratz in 1970 in *Power and Poverty*, he claims that nondecisions must be "observable" and that covert grievances, in order to be recognized by a student of politics, must have the coherency of articulated preferences.[11] Somewhat defensively, he responds to criticism of his original and superior position on nondecisions, claiming that "a decision which results in prevention of conflict *is* very much an event—and an observable one to boot."[12] Even here there is ambivalence.

> The observer may find that no one is *aggrieved* in the community. In that event, he would be ill-advised to search for evidence of nondecision-making. If there is no conflict, overt or *covert*, the presumption must be that there is consensus on the prevailing allocation of values, in which case nondecision-making is impossible.[13]

Yet there may be potential groups, although today powerless and uninterested, "who are likely in the future to become active and capable of exercising power."[14] Bachrach here indicates that objective conditions, not immediately comprehensible to the actors, may undergird power relations. He does speak of "ideological barriers,"[15] authority in a pathological state reproducing pathology, and brainwashing (as an example of how power can be turned into "authority"), indicating discomfort with having to demonstrate the existence of an observable grievance or overt conflict in order to determine that a relation of power exists.[16] He remains unsure.

> Suppose the observer can uncover no grievances, no actual or *potential* demands for change. Suppose, in other words, there *appears to be universal acquiescence* in the status quo. Is it not possible, in such circumstances, to determine *empirically* whether the consensus is genuine or instead has been enforced through nondecision-making? The answer must be negative.

> Analysis of this problem is beyond the reach of a political analyst and
> perhaps can be only fruitfully analyzed by a *philosopher*.[17]

Resolving his doubts here in favor of behavioral methodology, Bachrach implies that relations of authority may have been established by power, and even be illegitimate, yet once fully established, they are not subject to inquiry by social scientists.

In "Interest, Participation, and Democratic Theory," he moves decisively away from this emphasis on observable conflict as essential cue for the existence of nondecisions and grievances, further from behavioral methodology, and closer to his original formulation of nondecisions. Here he argues for a "dual conception of interests" that "recognizes that not all expressed wants reflect real wants."

> Failure to delineate the real from articulated interests of lower strata
> individuals implies that their *political apathy* reflects the relative absence of
> personal concerns. Such a conclusion repudiates what we know to be true:
> that people consumed by the hardship of everyday life . . . possess neither
> the energy nor capacity to transfer *moods of bitterness and futility* into
> articulated preferences.[18]

Now employing the "duality of interests" standard, Bachrach finds the system rewarding those most able to articulate and press for their preferences—that is, it responds in inverse proportion to actual need. This in and of itself does not render the system less democratic, for the key question, he explains, is whether the system provides adequate participatory structures to enable all groups to articulate their interests—this for him is the key criterion of democracy.

Arguing that the raison d'être of democracy is freedom, he now believes political participation is necessary not only to promote one's preferences, but also to develop one's interests, and for freedom itself. Democracy, therefore, must promote participation.

If the most disenfranchised also seem least interested in public affairs, what kind of participatory decision making is likely to spark their concern, and actually help them develop their real interests? Unlike public affairs, which appear remote and beyond influence, issues arising at the workplace are salient. If large corporations "authoritatively allocate values," they should be considered as political institutions and subject to decentralized public authority and democratic control, including expansion "in participation in decision-making among members within their constituency."[19] Increasing participation in this way would not necessarily bring about progressive social change—workers seem fairly conservative—but it would dramatically diminish the power of nondecision-makers and allow new issues to emerge.

Bachrach broadens Schattschneider's political analysis. First, he offers a developmental view of political participation. Second, by developing the idea of nondecisions and broadening the concept of grievance to include not yet articulable troubles, he offers what Lukes calls a "qualified critique" of the behavioral concept of power. Third, he extends the pluralist idea that politics entails the "authoritative allocation of values" to another important arena of power, the modern corporation. Fourth, in supporting the idea that direct participation helps develop one's interests, he breaches the fences contemporary political and economic divisions of labor place around both participation and what should be called "political." Fifth, he also calls into question Robert Dahl's conclusion that sheer size of large polyarchies limits participation by refocusing political attention on the local workplace rather than on "public affairs." Finally, the question of political equality here goes beyond Dahl's concern with resource inequalities and Schattschneider's mobilization of bias, to encompass how we can come to know our real interests through equality of power grounded in genuine participation:

> whether democracy can diffuse power sufficiently throughout society to inculcate among people of all walks of life a *justifiable* feeling that they have the power to participate in decisions which affect themselves and the common life of the community.[20]

Nonparticipation as a Nondecision

Bachrach, like Dahl, is a transitional theorist, struggling with problems that seem to defy the bounds of his developed paradigm. Both ultimately shed these confines for rearranged theoretical quarters.

With Bachrach, as we've seen, the most important problems turn on the epistemological status of both nondecisions and covert grievances, and the emphasis and meaning he gives to political participation. Where the republican liberal school of thought sees but downplays the importance of apathy as a political problem—indeed, hails it as a solution—and where Schattschneider's brand of democratic theory submerges it to his concern for a biased political agenda, Bachrach resurrects it as a central concern: "We know that a predominant number of individuals in the lower economic strata are politically apathetic and ignorant. We also know that there is a positive correlation between social status and political participation."[21]

Bachrach's concept of political apathy in the explanation of nonparticipation can be explicated as follows:

> X (an individual, group, race, subjective class) becomes apathetic with respect to Y (issues, politics) when the polity denies X the participatory structures within which to determine the meaning of Z (overt and covert grievances, or troubles X has) in relation to Y. Thus, X becomes apathetic (ignorant and indifferent) because without such structures, X is likely to

lack the energy and capacity to see how Y and/or Z might relate to his or her real interests.

Bachrach is the first theorist studied in this work to begin to capture the sense of political apathy as a condition of consciousness, especially by introducing the idea of real interests and combining with it the need for participatory structures to help enable one to know them. When a person is presented with an array of issues not in his or her interest, he or she may become apathetic to the political order that continues to serve them. Nonparticipants do not always simply reject the present "mobilization of bias." They may also become indifferent to it because no significant avenues exist or are likely to exist through which they can express their needs or clarify inchoate troubles. For Bachrach, X may become apathetic to Y when Z is not sufficiently developed to do more than signal lack of interest for X in Y, *as well as* when X believes, over time, that there will be no way to influence the shape of Y. Adding Z to the equation, Bachrach displays a more subtle understanding than Schattschneider of how a mobilization of bias can suppress freedom.

In emphasizing the necessity for participatory structures to overcome apathy, moreover, Bachrach develops an idea that pluralist, democratic elite, and rational choice theorists ignore too often but repressive regimes know all too well: a dearth of political organizations with which to promote, develop, and sustain interests provides stability by ensuring quiescence. Finally, Bachrach develops a significant motivational analysis of apathy as a condition, which he suggests can result from the systematic exclusion of overt grievances from the political realm, prevention of covert grievances and troubles from becoming overt and clarified, and lack of participatory institutions that deepen political understanding.

Like Schattschneider, however, Bachrach does not adequately discuss apathy related to choice. It makes perfect sense to say that if X becomes apathetic about issue A because X has freely chosen issue B over A, we still hold X responsible for his or her apathy to the degree A should continue to be important to X, B notwithstanding.

Another difficulty relates to his commitment to a reformed behavioralism, especially a tendency to fall back on appearances when in uncharted terrain.[22] He too quickly accepts apathy as a condition as fact. It is surely possible, however, that some might have a coherent set of beliefs they choose not to articulate and press, simply because they don't feel anything good will come of it. The appearance of apathy, as Schattschneider shows, can mask a commonsense judgment to refrain from participating.

Of greater importance are inadequacies in his general treatment of the relation of power and interests. Are we to presume that the troubles a person feels reflect his or her real interests? A person may feel anxious because he or she has not been promoted along with one of his or her peers. Does the real interest of the person lie with being promoted and relieving the anxiety; or, hidden to him or her, is there an interest in doing away with those hierarchies that, for example, do not actually promote efficiency? Troubles themselves may reflect the beliefs, motivations, and practices of a particular social and economic order.

Bachrach tacitly moves away from simple need theory, as his intuitive understanding of real interests goes beyond the analytical category of felt needs. Because felt needs remain, at this point in his work, his stated analytic framework for determining real interests, however, he is open to the following criticism by Lukes:

> It is here assumed that if men feel no grievances, then they have no interests that are harmed by the use of power. . . . Is it not the supreme and most insidious exercise of power to prevent people . . . from having grievances by shaping their perceptions, cognitions and preferences in such a way that they accept their role in the existing order of things?[23]

To rely on felt grievances as the indicator of real interests, or to equate their absence with no existent interest, serves to underplay some of the most important power relations in a society. When explicitly apathetic roles are important models, people simply may be socialized into what may fairly be called a condition of apathy. People may also become apathetic because the grievances they experience never lead them to develop political strategies— either to overcome such grievances, or to overcome them without developing important new ones. Given acceptance of the ideology of meritocracy as both morally correct and operative, a person may assume an inordinate share of individual responsibility for being out of work during a recession, mistaking for personal sources what in fact may be political or economic causes. Or consider again the working person anxious about promotion. Suppose he or she successfully follows the desire to succeed, only to find after advancement there now exist a new set of peers to compete with, and new anxieties because former friends will no longer associate with him or her in quite the way they once did.

Now the most controversial aspect of political apathy: people may become apathetic with respect to issues that, I or others believe, *should be* important to them. Three possibilities emerge: (1) I may be incorrectly using the term *apathy* because, in fact, the issue under consideration, as the agent is insisting, is not and never will be important or in his or her interest. Or (2) apathy related to free choices the agent has made may be an apt characterization, in which my use of the term may prod the person, who bears responsibility and therefore some degree of freedom to overcome the apathy, to become more conscious of the choices made and their consequences. Or (3) if apathy as a condition obtains, my characterization is not likely to have immediate impact because the agent, in my judgment, is not in a position to freely assess what should be important to him or her.

How do we locate responsibility for nonparticipation and apathy? By Bachrach's account, we need to observe the relevant nondecision-making process before we make these determinations. However, the context of thought and practices in which nondecisions occur is often crucial to making relations of power appear legitimately binding and authoritative, removing them from scrutiny and thereby constituting a more important power relation than the nondecision itself.

When the cue of conflict is not given, Bachrach's method is likely to miss important structural and ideological sources—and agents responsible for them—of the apathy and nonparticipation observed. And by missing important agents and agencies, it magnifies the responsibility of those identified. Yet, the more successfully an ideology is established as a powerful value system, the less likely it is that any conflict will be apparent. A fundamental question will be missed: When is the authority of a social order, apparently grounded in consent, in fact illegitimate because it subversively fosters unnecessary apathy and nonparticipation, curtailing the interests and freedom of its members without their consent or knowledge in ways they presently don't fully understand? Not to go beyond the category of nondecisions, therefore, has the perverse consequence of relegating the study of a society successfully rearing "happy slaves" to the world of metaphysics and philosophy, removed from immediate political practice and relevant social inquiry.[24]

Tensions within Bachrach's own argument on this point are apparent:

> It is the central contention of this paper that a dual concept of political interest, *which recognizes that not all expressed wants reflect real wants, is an essential standard for determining the degree to which a political system is democratic*. In terms of this standard, a system is democratic to the extent it recognizes and enforces the right of the individual to participate in making decisions that closely affect him and his community.[25]

How are we to know when the participatory structures enable or disable the translation from apparent to real interests?

> The presumption that people from the lower strata have real interests—interests which they are unable to express, *let alone comprehend*—does not imply that elites nor anyone else know what these interests actually are.[26]

If people from the lower strata are unable to express their real interests, and elites (and "anyone else") do not know them, when is a *successful* translation taking place? The answer Bachrach gives, set up as a test, is only partially satisfying:

> when there is a blockage in the conversion process from feelings to articulated preferences for a significant portion of the population, there is

reasonable doubt that convergence between real and apparent needs is taking place.[27]

How are we ever to know that the participatory structures we put in place facilitate the effective translation of feelings into real interests, without having some conception of what those interests are? The problem is deepened when we consider that the agent's most basic feelings may be so confused or repressed that it would be fair to say he or she is unaware of what they really are and what they mean. Or that there are undoubtedly ideas and modes of life that the agent is unfamiliar with, which, if experienced, would prove to be more satisfying or normatively superior. Thus, even the agent's perception of the conversion process, while vital evidence, is not a conclusive test of the effective translation of apparent to real interests.

What type of participation will advance the ability of the person to freely ascertain his or her interests and press for them? Just as we cannot fully ground real interests alone in the agent's present articulated preferences, there is no easy, value-neutral way we can establish what type of participatory institutions and practices will advance freedom. Bachrach suggests that certain participatory schemes may be cooptative[28] and that equality of political power is an important standard to be brought to bear in order to determine, in fact, whether full participation obtains. But at the same time, any evaluation of real interests and the types of participation that truly advance freedom is an argument in favor of certain participatory schemes and a certain conception of interests. One standard of full participation should actually be the active involvement of agents in precisely these types of discussions.

Bachrach thinks he can avoid the behavioralist twin charges of elitism and emotivism by grounding his appeal for greater participation only in terms that do not themselves question the values actors hold. Yet Bachrach himself presumes that those who have difficulty articulating their feeling and comprehending their own interests are located in the lower economic and social strata. Consider the subtle tension this reveals in his work. On the one hand, he provides no contrast model through which we could know what their interests should be (his commitment to reformed behavioralism), but on the other, he must have one in mind against which he is judging his presumption of present misperception of interests by the disadvantaged (his transition away from behavioralism).

Identifying the images and values one's analysis projects is one hallmark of responsible inquiry. Mistaking an honest effort to understand for elitism subverts analysis and democratic discussion of those relations of power most opaque precisely because they are most formidable. Without more care in applying the idea of elitism one may unintentionally subvert one's own goal of a rational and democratic discussion of alternative political programs or unconventional ideas.[29] Questions and judgments like these are the essence of democracy and of good inquiry, and even for the political scientist, there are no neutral courts to submit them to for scientific adjudication.

 **Chapter 9**

The Subordination of Politics

What are the causes of political apathy in modern life? This is a primary question that C. Wright Mills, a sociologist, and Herbert Marcuse, a philosopher, tried to answer just as American society was awakening from the political torpor of the 1950s. Both were extremely concerned that the political space for any reasonable notion of politics was virtually disappearing, and both desperately sought ways to revive it. Both had an important influence on political radicals in the 1960s. Mills's critique of contemporary democracy was the foundational text of a seminal political guide of the era: the Port Huron Statement of the Students for a Democratic Society.[1] Marcuse's *One-Dimensional Man* was required reading for political radicals and the counterculture alike.[2]

Apathy as a Condition of Consciousness

Mills and Marcuse both cast very strong images of how pervasive and deeply rooted apathy is, and were severely critical of mainstream political discourse and scholarship. For them, the dialectic between structure and ideology, action and thought, come together to fashion a type of apathy very different from that celebrated by Berelson and longed for by Huntington.

Together, the work of Mills and Marcuse indicates three potential aspects of political apathy as a condition. The first two I put under the rubric *alienation*, but I use this term in the specific sense of conditions of political life that are *objective* within the terms of the theory. Objective alienation takes its most severe form in what I will call *absolute political alienation*, which in turn finds its most complete expression in Marcuse's *One-Dimensional Man*, to be discussed in the next chapter. Absolute political alienation exists when people have been so thoroughly manipulated and programmed that they lose the capacity for free intentional action, including the ability to think and act in ways that at some point may be politically relevant. Both Mills and Marcuse also offer what I consider a more tenable thesis of *relative political alienation*: the indefinite suspension of the consciousness to form *political* intentions and act in their terms.

From Mills's work, however, I draw a theory of *political subordination:* the scope of the political realm is so narrowly drawn, and the terms of discourse that find life within it so confusing and inappropriate, that it may be fairly said that politics is thoroughly subordinated to a matrix of depoliticizing institutions, ideas, and practices. Once modified, this theory forms the heart of what I later elaborate in chapter 13 as a thesis of complex depoliticization.

Publics and Power Elite

When we modify Mills's overtly political analysis with his imaginative sociological investigation of the role of motivation in human behavior and the contours of modern character structure, his concept of political subordination becomes distinctive, helping locate the social glue vital to depoliticized roles: *the active commitment of the actors to them.* In this manner, he helps account for their resiliency.

Political subordination occurs when people are denied counterideologies, political institutions, and modes of life that may help them form political intentions and act accordingly. In a society in which the prevailing ideology focuses on individual merit and achievement, in which the major political parties' programs are too similar, and in which "politics" is considered to be contained in the specialized electoral arena, distinct from work, culture, leisure, and family, troubles and grievances that emerge are unlikely to be translated into political issues. Left personal, or displaced onto inappropriate objects, such political moods leave the source of malaise untouched and deflect the formulation of accurate political analysis and smart strategy. Yet a clear reading of the shape of the social structure may indicate openings to a revived politics.

For Mills, the bottleneck of malaise and the faltering of reason spring directly from the development of mass society in America. His fear is that the community of publics characteristic of nineteenth-century America has been replaced by a "power elite" at the top, stalemate in the middle, and a mass society below. Comprising the top echelons of the corporate and military establishments, with the executive branch of government—the "political directorate"—as a junior partner, this elite, he claims, has concentrated more power in its hands than "any small group of men in world history, the Soviet elite possibly excepted."[3]

Gone is the political order characterized by a diversity of local publics, with power dispersed among the states, held in coalition by a weak federal center. The economy, too, no longer comprising a "great scatter of productive units" balancing one another, is now dominated by several large corporations. Military definitions of reality loom large as well in all political and economic decisions, as the military overcomes its meager origins colored by civilian distrust to become a full partner of the power elite.

The decline of publics is directly tied to the ascendancy of these centralized political, economic, and military institutions as they undermine four requirements of people as members of genuine publics: People lose the opportunity to express their own opinions, instead receiving opinions through the media in "one-way communication." They don't have an opportunity to answer the statements of others immediately and in public; nor can they base meaningful public action on such public discussion. And they lose the ability to protect themselves from the intrusions of large organizations.

In a public, discussion is the major medium of communication, and the media serve to link various primary publics. As publics dissolve into mass society, people no longer have a primary community within which to discuss problems and clarify their feelings or ideas about society and their position in it. Even the middle-level voluntary association—"the citizen's major link with decision" and the heart of pluralist analysis—is becoming remote from individuals and primary publics, and is stuck in a "semiorganized stalemate." To the extent politics exists, it is here, yet these group conflicts are those of second-rate provincial interests, not the great clash of dominant interests whose resolution, in pluralist theory, yields the public interest. Even here, there is increasing integration into the expanded state apparatus as bureaucratic administration displaces electoral politics and real legislation. United by psychological similarities, "the structural blending of commanding positions and common interests," and at times "explicit coordination," the power elite is able to dominate the American social structure. Without publics within which to develop alternative ideas and strategies, people and their opinions are successfully managed. The result is a permanent war establishment tied to a privately incorporated economy insulted by a "political vacuum."

> Within the elite as a whole, this coincidence of military domain and corporate realm strengthens both of them and further *subordinates the merely political man*. Not the party politician but the corporation executive is now more likely to sit down with military men and answer the question, "What is to be done?"[4]

Key institutions fail in their responsibility to democracy. The media do not help clarify the meaning of the narrow milieu of individuals in mass society.[5] Instead of helping "enlarge and animate the discussions of primary publics," they transform "them into a set of media markets in mass-like society."[6] The educational institutions themselves have become mass media, becoming job preparation centers rather than teaching citizenship, with "an ideology of 'life adjustment' that encourages happy acceptance of mass ways of life rather than the struggle for individual and public transcendence."[7] The political parties and voluntary organizations similarly fail to provide an effective link between the individual and public decisions. This failure is egregious because "these middle-level associations are the citizen's major link with decision. . . . it is only through them that he exercises such power as he may have."[8]

People become ripe for manipulation, unable to fully grasp even dramatic political experiences.

> experience of such a *structural* shift has to be organized and interpreted if it is to count in the making of opinion.
>
> The kind of experience, in short, that might serve as a basis for resistance to mass media is not an experience of *raw events*, but the *experience of meanings*. The fleck of *interpretation must be there in the experience* if we are to use the word experience seriously.[9]

The Last Radical Democrat of Modernity

A central focus of Mills's work was always the use of critical intelligence in the service of human progress. He considered that modern life—and modern intellectual life in particular—was characterized by a "higher immorality" precisely because, although knowledge was plentiful, critical intelligence was in short supply, too often not prized or even missed. This was what he strove to rectify. "Only where publics and leaders are responsive and responsible," he wrote, "are human affairs in democratic order, and only when knowledge has public relevance is this order possible." As Irving Louis Horowitz claims, to achieve this critical intelligence, "Mills called upon the 'classic tradition'—rational and enlightened tradition, in which mind is autonomous and independent of power but, nonetheless, morally related to the mainsprings of social growth." Although Horowitz would later temper his judgment, writing in 1967 he called Mills "the greatest sociologist the United States has ever produced."

> The main drift of C. Wright Mills' work is linked to the practical importance of an ethically viable social science. This is so because such a sociology confronts the facts with integrity, *and* confirms the integrity by *doing something* about the facts.[10]

Indeed, for Mills there was an intimate connection between the study of society and the issues facing it.

> To formulate any problem requires that we state the values involved and the threat to these values. For it is the felt threat to cherished values—such as those of freedom and reason—that is the necessary moral substance of all significant problems of social inquiry, and as well of all public issues and private troubles.[11]

Throughout his career,[12] Mills used what he considered the intellectual craft of sociology to search for a way for people to break with the "main drift" of American society toward increasing corporate domination, state and corporate administration, economic boom and slump, and ultimately war. The problem of how to generate real political participation and overcome apathy was always an important practical obstacle to his passion to see America become more democratic once again, and for it to fulfill the Enlightenment ambition of a society in which power was guided by reason. Overturning mass society, however, would require more than knowledge. It would also involve a coming together of organization, structural conditions, strategic location in the social structure, leadership, vision, and willpower.

In his early work, particularly *The New Men of Power*, Mills gives a more subtle analysis of the societal conditions that lie behind political apathy, and how they may be overcome. Writing in the economic and political climate of 1948, he suggests that unions could become a formidable agency of change, with union leaders playing a vital role. Backed by numbers and organization, they were in a unique strategic position both to organize the unorganized and to unite the power of labor organization to the ideas of "labor intellectuals." If the "character and timing" of the next slump created "appropriate conditions," Mills concluded, the masses could be moved.

There were formidable obstacles, however, including selecting leaders within unions who were "the last representatives of the economic man," and the "apathy and lack of understanding" of union members. Moreover, the state was taking over the task of regulating the labor force, and union leaders were supporting this development, narrowing the labor-capital struggle, serving as discipliners of the workforce and as go-betweens for workers, owners and managers, and politicians. Yet he had a hope. A major slump was coming, creating a "political interlude" during which union leaders could become decisive actors. The fact that economic struggles seemed increasingly to intrude into the political arena was itself a symptom of pending crisis. Mills proposed a program of increasing worker democracy in the economic sphere, workers' control of production, socialization of the means of production, and a party of labor to press for a program that would address not only the needs of organized labor, such as wages, but also those of the American public, such as prices and war and economic slump. For this program to succeed, however, a democratic mass base had also to be created, requiring "training . . . in the more direct democracy of daily life, in the shop and in the unions," especially allowing expression of creative impulses at work: "That is the basis for a politics of democratic socialism."[13]

Labor leaders were uniquely situated to unite alternative ideas to the power of organized workers, reject old legitimations, propose countersymbols, organize the unorganized, unite the unions, and develop a broad political program. Complete the task of developing an informed national union constituency, Mills warns, or the unorganized may be used against you.

> It is the task of the labor leaders to allow and to initiate a union of the
> power and the intellect. They are the only ones who can do it; that is why
> they are now the strategic elites in American society. Never has so much
> depended upon men who are so ill-prepared and so little inclined to assume
> the responsibility.[14]

Mills, in 1948, saw the apathetic public as neither the consenting abstainers of Berelson and his colleagues, nor the "cheerful robots" he himself was to later worry about in *White Collar*. Instead, he sees a range of depoliticized citizens.

The "underdogs" were "an important aspect of class relations in America"; for them to "endure this life requires a low level of aspiration which softens the will and creates apathy."[15] They could become politically engaged, however, through a "new type of union community" in which they would likely become "solid union members."[16]

The white-collar workers' numerical growth and bureaucratic indispensability had to be made politically relevant through union organizing, promoting their freedom and security. At present, they had "neither political awareness nor rudimentary organization" and their "occupational ideology" was "politically passive."[17]

Finally, the workers themselves had a "historic mentality of acquiescence," based on American prosperity and not broken completely even by the Great Depression. Yet would they suffer another depression without serious political engagement? Didn't advertising slogans that promoted business loyalty already seem banal, as market contraction helped undermine the dream of success through hard work? Although education was expanding, didn't the opportunity it afforded now mean less because there were an insufficient number of appropriate jobs? Mills asks,

> The personalization of success has been possible, but how long will the
> personalization of failure into individual guilt continue?[18]

Mills's hope was that changed circumstances, political space, leadership, and organization would help break the back of acquiescence.

> Political apathy is not a function only of leadership; certain *conditions* in the
> life of the worker, and in the history of the United States, lie in back of it.[19]

The capacity of American workers for political action, he cautions, should not be underestimated. Prefiguring Schattschneider's mobilization of bias thesis, he writes,

> The political apathy of the American worker is an apathy about engaging
> in electoral politics when there are no issues about which he feels deeply or
> understands fully. He votes neither for Tweedledee nor Tweedledum. Yet on
> more stirring occasions, the U.S. worker may "vote with his feet." The

American worker has a high potential militancy when he is pushed, and if he knows what the issue is. Such a man, identified with unions as communities and given a chance to build them, will not respond apathetically when outside political forces attempt to molest what is his.[20]

It was foolish, he argues, for labor leaders to complain about apathetic workers and support either of the main parties, who "alienate people from politics in its deeper meanings and demoralize those on the edge of political consciousness."[21] In those "who suffer the results of irresponsible social decisions and who hold a disproportionately small share of values available," labor had potential allies. But its leaders still had to choose to fight.[22] Only they could weld ideas to organization and "focus the deprivation politically, inculcate the truth about common interests and common struggles, and offer some hope of winning a better tomorrow."[23]

Despair

By the 1950s, with the increasing stability of capitalism and the integration of unions as interest groups within the corporate economy, Mills dismissed the "labor metaphysic" as a romantic illusion, concluding, as Herbert Marcuse also would, that the working class was now a conservative political force standing against structural reform:[24]

> the trade unions, have the pure and simple ideology of alienated work: more and more money for less and less work.[25]

If labor's recent history worked against Mills's hopes, the politics and consciousness of the white-collar worker met his fears. In this world, Mills found a "new little man," shaped by large centralized bureaucratic institutions, stuck in dull routines of enervating work and leisure, apathetic, and without political power. As persons in a mass without communities, publics, or traditions, the white-collar worker embodied the most profound apathy of his time.[26]

Unlike the old middle class, Mills reports, the new consists largely of dependent employees in salesrooms or offices, small-business people under pressure, and salaried professionals. The idea of the old independent middle class, confused by a dated "rhetoric of competition," now obscured the reality of a new dependent "middling class" of salaried employees.

> The broad linkage of enterprise and property, the cradle-condition of classic democracy, no longer exist in America. This is no society of small entrepreneurs—now they are one stratum among others: above them is the big money; below them, the alienated employee; before them, the fate of politically dependent relics; behind them, their world.[27]

Expanded by an increasing need to coordinate and dispose of the economic surplus, itself generated by leaps in productivity, the white-collar workforce had the essential tasks of manipulating the people who make things, the things themselves, and symbols in the form of paper and money, and turning all these into profits for owners.[28] Like Marcuse would, Mills sees a pervasive new ideology tied to increased productivity.

> The immense productivity of mass-production technique and the increased application of technologic rationality are the first open secrets of modern occupational change: fewer men turn out more things in less time.[29]

The bulk of the white-collar class falls into what he calls "the great salesroom" or the "enormous file." For both, the nature of their work life, leisure, communities, and culture keep them politically marginal and apathetic. With the decline of independence and real craft, work life becomes alienating and "whatever satisfactions alienated men gain from work occur within the framework of alienation; whatever satisfaction they gain from life occurs outside the boundaries of work; work and life are sharply split." Lacking true craft as a live contrast model, the white-collar worker is unable to determine independently the sources of dissatisfaction. To ensure steady work, enlightened managers propose relief that itself is alienating, conceived as a "human relations" problem of the personnel department. Legitimated "in the pseudo-objective language of engineers," these adaptive solutions allow "the personnel manager to relax his authoritarian manner and widen his manipulative grip . . . to conquer work alienation within the bounds of work alienation." Anticipating Jürgen Habermas's thesis of "motivation crisis" in advanced capitalism, he says management has "not yet found a really sound ideology" to replace the work ethic.[30] Instead, there exists a "curious contradiction" about the meaning of success—both a compulsion to "amount to something" and a "poverty of desire, a souring of the image of success."

The very meaning of a successful life in America is transformed:

> The governmental pension is clearly of another type of society than the standard American dream. The old end was an independent prosperity, happily surrounded by one's grandchildren; the end now envisioned is a pensioned security independent of one's grandchildren.[31]

Dependent on authoritarian hierarchy not only for income but for self-image, as Karl Mannheim observed, people will frantically grasp claims of status. The result is a "status panic"[32] and self-alienation:

> striving for the next rank, they come to anticipate identification with it, so that now they are not *really* in their places . . . status that is exterior to one's present work does not lead to intrinsic work gratification. Only if present work leads to the anticipated goal by a progression of skills, and is thus given meaning, will status aspirations not alienate the worker.[33]

As the home declines in importance as the worker's psychological center, it falls to leisure to prepare people for increasingly alienating work, and people segregate work life from real life. Rather than relaxing or regenerating creativity, however, leisure only diverts from the "restless grind" of work into the "absorbing grind" of glamor and thrills, encouraging distinct work and holiday images of the self: "The bright two weeks [of vacation] feed the dream of the dull pull."

With the decline of status in work, residence and consumption also gain as currency for prestige. But here, too, people rely on appearance in a "market of strangers" with whom one shares interests rather than descent or tradition, has contacts rather than relations, lives in a mass of uniformity, distant from work, rather than a cohesive community. Status claims must be continuously renewed. "Physically close, but socially distant," Mills writes, "human relations become at once intense and impersonal—and in every detail, pecuniary."[34] As ties become more superficial, self-respect is maintained through the display of the "token of economic worth," as Thorstein Veblen argued, "a struggle to keep up appearance."[35] But it is an unsuccessful struggle for status, on a "personality market" consumed by a "fetishism of appearances" that denies self-respect, alienates emotions from "inner feelings," and creates "self-estrangement."[36]

Popular culture also helps transform one's self-image from a producer to a "relaxed consumer." The relaxation, however, is illusory. As the gap grows between potential accomplishments and the forces that actually determine life chances, ambition takes the form of the "conscientiousness of the good employee"; leisure, of "consumer dreams" where the individual can "make no mistakes"; and life itself appears accidental, as a game or lottery, while success seems dazzling, beyond reach and something to be enjoyed vicariously.

Mills characterizes the message to the white-collar worker in this way: Work hard but expect little enjoyment from work and don't expect to go too far. When you fail, you will still be blamed for your inadequacies, and you will blame yourself as well. Don't worry, because success, you will be told, is not what it's cracked up to be, so do as you are told at work and seek your success in spiritual fulfillment off the job. You will try to find your satisfactions in consumption and vicarious living, your self-respect in competition over appearances, and your craft in molding yourself into a happy person despite your life. But you will fail because your position remains insecure, your relations transitory and shallow, and your self-esteem under constant assault.

White-collar workers, at the heart of mass society, are ripe for manipulation.

Hidden Power

In the popular imagination, Mills is perhaps most famous for his theory of power developed in his 1956 classic, *The Power Elite*. Mills's volume touched off a storm of debate and controversy, especially over whether he accurately captured the structure of power in American society, and over what power is and how one goes about examining it. Robert Dahl, for example, criticizes Mills for not putting his thesis to the "test" of discovering whether an elite in fact exists *"by an examination of a series of concrete cases where key decisions are made."*[37] While Dahl is surely right to look for evidence, his focus here on "decisions" not hidden to the researcher overlooks the way power can be deployed through what Lukes calls its second and third dimensions; therefore, Dahl much too narrowly constricts what is to count as evidence.[38] Moreover, as Horowitz argues, pluralist community power studies like Dahl's classic *Who Governs?*, even if accurate, do not disprove Mills's thesis. "Dahl seems to have deliberately decided," Horowitz writes, "that if Mills is right in the larger context it will be borne out in any community study. However, this is precisely what Mills's premises do not require."[39]

Criticizing Mills's theory of elite power more adeptly than Dahl, Peter Clecak concludes,

> In his desire to perceive the making of history as an increasingly conscious activity, Mills probably assigned too much weight to the elites at the top. Having done this, he was committed to overexplaining the powerlessness of other groups. The myth of consolation appealed to powerless individuals [especially intellectuals], but it implicitly subverted the creation of a new politics.[40]

In *White Collar*, however, Mills emphasizes a hidden, more insidious form of power.[41] Manipulation, he argues there, has become the chief form of power in twentieth-century America, and its ascendancy is directly tied to the bureaucratic context of decision making. Driven by a "managerial demiurge," "at the top, society becomes an uneasy interlocking of private and public hierarchies, and at the bottom, more and more areas become objects of management and manipulation."[42] Mills claims that, for the bureaucracy, the world is an object to be manipulated, and implies that the very idea of rationality has become a tool of manipulation.[43] Trapped in ever larger organizations ostensibly built on principles of rationality, carrying "out series of apparently rational actions without any ideas of the ends they serve," white-collar workers feel that life itself is arbitrary.

> The psychological heart of this mood is a feeling of powerlessness—but with the old edge taken off, for it is a mood of acceptance and of a *relaxation of the political will*.[44]

The result is "organized irresponsibility," a form of power that is manipulative precisely because it promotes the illusion that no one seems to bear responsibility. You are used for ends you cannot see, in ways you are unaware of, by people you do not know. You follow motives that are external to you, not because you believe in them, although you may come to, but because following them is how you function within the organization. You fit yourself in without clearly seeing how you are being fit in. And all this nurtures character development whose lack of grounded sense of self makes you ripe for further manipulation.

It is "the grand problem of the psychology of social strata," he writes, to explain the lack of correspondence between "political mentalities" and "objectively defined strata." Middle class largely in name only, white-collar workers have little power. For a social stratum to accumulate power, it must have a favorable interplay between

> will and know-how, objective opportunity, and organization. The opportunity is limited by the group's structural position; the will is dependent upon the group's consciousness of its interests and ways of realizing them. And both structural position and consciousness interplay with organization, which strengthen consciousness and are made politically relevant by structural position.[45]

Lacking the idea of craftsmanship as a contrast model, devoid of firm tradition, subject to the propaganda of one-way communication while "relaxed of mind and tired of body," living in a community of strangers, the worker of the modern metropolis has few resources with which to comprehend the white-collar world he or she inhabits. Without a clearly self-evident common group interest, shackled by an ideology and self-understanding that further deny such interest, left vulnerable by an easily manipulated character structure, white-collar workers will remain politically passive.

Apathy

The white-collar worker is Mills's prototype of the apathetic citizen. The most fundamental political difference between white-collar workers in mass society and citizens of a democratic society is that

> men in masses are gripped by personal troubles, but they are not aware of their true meaning and source. Men in public confront issues, and they are aware of their terms.[46]

Unaware of their own lives as biographical examples of a collective historical experience, unable to forge interpretive links between their life and their times, they are ignorant and apathetic, unable objectively to understand their position in American society or press independently to improve it. Whether joining unions or not, they are likely to remain "the little individual scrambling to get to the top" instead of the dependent employee banding together with others for a collective ascent. As people stuck in mass society, they don't truly observe their real experience, and their desires "often are insinuated into them":

> They may be politically irritable, but they have no political passion. They are a chorus, too afraid to grumble, too hysterical in their applause. They are rearguarders. In the shorter run, they will follow the panicky ways of prestige; in the long run, they will follow the ways of power, for, in the end, prestige is determined by power.[47]

To overcome their discomfort and dependence, they would first have to understand precisely what mass society so skillfully keeps from them: the relation between social structure and milieus of the individual. Only then could vague discontent be translated into political issues:

> It is not merely paradoxical to say that the values of freedom and reason are back of the absence of troubles, back of the uneasy feeling of malaise and alienation. In a similar manner, the issue to which modern threats to freedom and reason most typically lead is, above all, the absence of explicit issues—to *apathy* rather than to issues explicitly defined as such.[48]

The advent of the apathetic person as a dominant political and social type, for Mills, was a direct threat to American democracy. He asks,

> Can he be happy in this condition, and what are the qualities and the meanings of such happiness? It will no longer do merely to assume, as a metaphysic of human nature, that down deep in man-as-man there is an urge for freedom and a will to reason. Now we must ask: What in man's nature, what in the human condition today, what in each of the varieties of social structure makes for the ascendancy of the cheerful robot? And what stands against it?[49]

New Left

Before he died in 1962, Mills did entertain moments of hopefulness that a young intelligentsia could spark a New Left and become a catalyst for democratic change. Seeing worldwide dissent by young intellectuals, students, and other protesters, he charged intellectuals to become guides for the New Left then emerging: "*help* them to focus their moral upsurge in less ambiguous political ways; work out with them the ideologies, the strategies, the theories that will help them to consolidate their efforts: new theories of structural changes of and by human societies in our epoch."[50] Develop a "politics of truth," he urged, to counter the "crackpot realism" of the "NATO intellectuals" that was moving us toward World War Three.

Mills understood that youth, as an agency of change, were limited by lack of power in the social structure. He even wondered whether his hope was justified. "What's missing?" his assistant Saul Landau recalls asking him. "The New Left, that's what's missing," replied Mills.[51]

In turning to young intellectuals, Mills may have been trying to break out of the despair of what Peter Clecak calls "radical paradoxes"—the discontinuity between what one believes ought to happen and what is likely to happen. At times, he created an undemocratic mood within which to achieve democratic ends, perhaps in his anxiety that this was one last chance to rescue the opportunity for conscious, progressive history-making, now being squandered by elites with real power, from the "grip of fate" and avoid the slide into nuclear war. Yet, his turn to youth and young intellectuals was more than a delusion with which to escape "radical paradoxes." Before he died, it gave him hope:

> Let the old men ask sourly, "Out of Apathy—into what?" The Age of
> Complacency is ending. Let the old women complain wisely about "the end
> of ideology." We are beginning to move again.[52]

After he died, youth did become a significant agency for change. They were not powerful or wise enough, however, to be *the* agency he would have hoped for. Would he have been able to help them focus their moral outrage and discontent in politically relevant ways, as he goaded other intellectuals to do?[53] He died too young.

Mills on Mills: Social Structure

In endlessly reaching for agents of change, Mills undervalues his own analysis of social structure and how vital structural position is to the real power of potential agency. He writes at times as if both elites and intellectuals have more independent power than they actually do, then fails to suggest what reforms we might be able to expect of enlightened elites at particular times of opportunity:

> Far from being dependent upon the structure of institutions, modern elites
> may smash one structure and set up another in which they enact quite
> different roles. In fact, such destruction and creation of institutional
> structures, with all their means of power, when events seem to turn out well,
> is just what is involved in "great leadership," or, when they seem to turn out
> badly, great tyranny.[54]

Of course, Mills's political goal was to shake the power elite out of its collective irresponsibility, but when he tried to do so in this way, his ability to analyze power suffered.

Mills on Mills: Methodology

Writing in the quiescent 1950s and early 1960s, Mills offered tools to penetrate the silence. If it is a sad commentary on modern life that people's self-understanding could stand against their own freedom and reason, it is still a theoretical possibility that has to be faced squarely. His idea of the modern polis and his very American pragmatism forbade any compromise between truth and dispatch of method.

> If we take the simple democratic view that *what men are interested in* is all that concerns us, then we are accepting the values that have been inculcated. . . .
>
> If we take the dogmatic view that *what is to men's interests*, whether they are interested in it or not, is all that need concern us morally then we run the risk of violating democratic values. . . .
>
> . . . by addressing ourselves to issues and to troubles, and formulating them as problems of social science, we stand the best chance, I believe the only chance, to make reason democratically relevant to human affairs in a free society, and so realize the classic values that underlie the promise of our studies.[55]

Mills's later writings on the power elite and mass society, however, fail to fully incorporate key insights of his own earlier work, particularly on language and vocabularies of motive. In Mills's chapter on work in *White Collar*, for example, there is "*not one* reference to the feelings expressed directly or indirectly by white collar workers."[56]

In his early work, Mills suggests that inquiry follow a more sensitive path. Behind social behavior and interpretation lie basic values and vocabularies of motive that can yield discrepant meanings, mixed motives, motivational and value conflicts, especially in complex societies—what he later calls troubles in mass society—that can lead to revision of meaning and, consequently, of understanding and action. Within given historical eras and positions in social structure, therefore, social interpretation should explore the situational patterns within which people form motives and intentions:

> For men live in immediate acts of experience and their attentions are directed outside themselves until acts are in some ways frustrated. It is then that awareness of self and motive occur. The "question" is a lingual index of such conditions.[57]

In explaining conduct, analysts should look to construct "typical vocabularies of motive" that refer "to the typical constellation of motives which are observed to be societally linked with classes of situated actions." For "motives are the terms with which interpretation of conduct *by social actors* proceeds" and they "are circumscribed by the vocabulary of the actor." Mills writes, "This imputation and avowal of motives by actors are social phenomena to be explained. The differing reasons men give for their actions are not themselves without reasons."[58]

The implications for research methodology are significant. Researchers who "tentatively delimit the situations in which certain motives *may* be verbalized" and construct "*situational* questions" stand a better chance of not illicitly imputing motives to the actor.[59] And he cautions social scientists: "To simplify these vocabularies of motive into a socially abstracted terminology is to destroy the legitimate use of motive in the explanation of social actions."[60]

Political Subordination

For Mills, the modern threat of apathy takes the form of a direct ideological and structural assault on the potential to form political intentions and act upon them, severely constricting the scope of political thought and action. It is *political subordination*.

Apathy, in this sense, is a condition under which people suffer, caused by a suppression of political freedom through the subordination of political life itself. It is a complex form of depoliticization, hinged on the way mass society inhibits or channels political knowledge and restricts the ability to make use of it, and complicated by a dialectic between the present mobilization of bias and a complementary psychology, radiating through individuals, that helps social structure dynamically reconstitute itself. Overcoming apathy of this sort requires reconfiguring the present structural and psychological terrain of society. The role assigned women, as Mills put it, of "darling little slaves," the structure of work, the quality of leisure, the security of residence, perpetual vulnerability of self-esteem, the ability of society to manipulate wants—for Mills, all are latent political problems of contemporary social structure, all foster insidious political apathy.[61]

Read sympathetically in its entirety, Mills's work can help clarify how people in mass society help socialize themselves into apathetic postures. We not only learn ideologies that harm our interests; *we* pursue modes of life, in thought and action, that do so. Forms of social structure and outlines of ideology and vocabularies of motive set the parameters of the commitments we are positioned to make. Our awareness of self and motive and our active re-creation of roles, through commitments *we* make, then become themselves crucial resources for giving legitimacy to beliefs and ideologies, and this helps explain the resiliency of apathetic roles.

Taken as a whole, Mills's writing on nonparticipation allows for explanation that in principle may include the republican liberal focus on individual responsibility, the plain democratic concern with the mobilization of bias,[62] and the radical democratic preoccupation with the relation between social structure and consciousness. He distinguishes himself in specifying both faces of political apathy.

Mills's paradigm of apathy related to choice can be represented as follows:

> X (an elite, person, group, gender, stratum, subjective class, or society) can
> be considered responsibly apathetic with respect to Y (something important,
> of which knowledge is available, and something X could conceivably
> influence *if* X could *choose* to) if X does not care or demonstrate care about
> Y. (Mills uses this most clearly in reference to members of the power elite or
> to intellectuals.)

The suppression of the ability to use freedom and reason to make explicit
troubles that threaten these values can lead to the worst sort of apathy as a
condition:

> X (a person, group,[63] stratum, subjective or objective or mass society) is in a
> condition of apathy with respect to Y (something important, especially
> reason and freedom themselves) if X is *unable* to care about Y. (Mills most
> often uses this to refer to the members of mass society, especially white-
> collar workers.)

Political Alienation

In his darker moments, Mills carries too far his analysis of apathy as a condition, unable to substantiate it either theoretically or with reference to lived
experience:

> We know of course that man can be turned into a robot, by chemical and
> psychiatric means, by steady coercion and by controlled environment; but
> also by random pressures and unplanned sequences of circumstances. But
> can he be made to want to become a cheerful and willing robot?[64]

Here Mills pushes past the more moderate concept of political subordination, starkly suggesting that the very ability to form *political* intentions—
indeed, the ability to form intentions at all—could be severely alienated from
the person. Left where Mills leaves it, however, the idea of objective political
alienation remains acutely underdeveloped.

As a tendency, or possibility, apathy of the more extreme sort Mills describes should be considered a theoretical possibility of enough consequence
to deserve fuller analysis. This is exactly what Herbert Marcuse tries to do in
his famous and influential *One-Dimensional Man*.

Chapter 10

Absolute Apathy

In his 1964 *One-Dimensional Man*, Herbert Marcuse put forth this bold thesis: American society is rapidly becoming "one-dimensional" due to the indefinite suspension of structural contradictions within American capitalism and the eradication of the critical dimensions of thought, action, language, and character structure of its people. Only the dimension of the given social order remains, insulating the theory and practice of advanced industrial society from transcending critique, and the liberation it seemed poised to achieve.

The problem in need of explanation is this. Science and technology create the possibility for greater freedom, lessening the need for instinctual repression that under conditions of scarcity is necessary for survival. This creates a "specter of liberation," in which the social relations that continue to dominate under capitalism become unnecessary. Acceptance of such extensive but now *unnecessary* repression cannot be explained, Marcuse argues, merely by the manipulation of wants, but instead now must correspond to some deeply felt need. Otherwise, the pointless character of contemporary domination would simply be too transparent. Seyla Benhabib captures Marcuse's point well when she suggests that in his earlier *Eros and Civilization*, he "formulates the impossibility of social crises under conditions of industrial-technological civilization" by claiming, she writes, that "the very objective conditions that would make the overcoming of industrial-technological civilization possible also prevent the subjective conditions necessary for this transformation from emerging."[1]

Marcuse turns to Freud to help him answer the question, Why, in spite of the presence of the material basis for it, has a liberating transformation not occurred? For society to progress—indeed, for civilization to exist—basic conservative instinctual drives seeking pleasure and gratification must be repressed. This clash, the "reality principle," is ahistorical, he claims against Freud, really specific only to periods of scarcity. With much repression no longer necessary, today the disciplining force is the "performance principle." The greater the productivity and promise for freedom from alienating labor, the more of what now becomes *surplus* repression intensifies. The more repression is unnecessary, the more aggression is created and displaced into greater productivity or onto an "enemy" such as Communism or the underclass. The performance principle dynamically fortifies itself, fostering interclass and international capitalist harmony, an "economically essential and self-beneficial arms economy," while spurring further technological rationalization and integration of state, society, and the technical base. As John Fry describes it, "Both political apathy and economic prosperity are further ensured in a single stroke."[2]

Deeply buried under political apathy is extreme danger—the Nazi Holocaust in "civilized" Germany was never far from Marcuse's thoughts. Nor was nuclear war. The more productivity increases without allowing real gratification or enjoyment, the more repression becomes unnecessary, the more aggression is created, and the more productivity is needed on which to displace aggressive impulses, especially given the inability of the now weak conscience to discipline them. A "vicious circle of progress" is created. Should productivity falter, the severe aggression that repression causes in advanced industrial society could break free. With the world capable of achieving affluence and freedom, it creates instead the conditions for a modern barbarism.

Technological domination of society is extremely powerful, however, and conditions acquiescence right down to the instincts. With the strengthening of the institutions of technical reason over the family and the father, the superego is greatly weakened, the ego reified, losing its ability to mediate among the various instincts, reduced to "automatic reaction" to stimuli from the outside world, unable to distinguish the individual from the society, freedom from repression. The id becomes directly tied to this world through "repressive desublimation," a direct cathexis onto objects, losing the fantasy (and potential for critical distance) embodied in sublimation.

Productivity, consumption, and the enemy all become instinctual needs of the one-dimensional person, as technical reason becomes the ego ideal, the model for conduct, of the immature ego. Behavior is determined by "mimetic" adjustment to the needs, even rhythms, of the technological infrastructure, rather than by introjected codes of morality. The "multidimensional dynamic," he writes, ". . . has given way to a one-dimensional static identification of the individual with the others and with the administered reality principle."[3]

Marcuse's specific contribution is to attempt to show how one-dimensional society creates the *immediate and unreflective* identification of the needs of the individual with those of the technological apparatus itself:

> domination—in the guise of affluence and liberty—extends to all spheres of
> private and public existence, integrates all authentic opposition, absorbs all
> alternatives. Technological rationality reveals its political character as it
> becomes the great vehicle of better domination, creating a truly totalitarian
> universe in which society and nature, mind and body are kept in a state of
> permanent mobilization for the defense of this universe.[4]

In contrast to the expectations of generations of Marxists, as Jürgen Habermas puts it,

> At the stage of their scientific-technical development, then, the forces of production appear to enter a new constellation with the relations of production. Now they no longer function as the basis of a critique of prevailing legitimations in the interest of political enlightenment, but become instead the basis of legitimation. *This* is what Marcuse conceives of as world-historically new.[5]

Marcuse writes in his essay "Industrialism and Capitalism in the Work of Max Weber,"

> The very concept of technical reason is perhaps ideological. Not only the application of technology but technology itself is domination (of nature and men)—methodical, scientific, calculated, calculating control. . . . Technology is always a historical-social *project:* in it is projected what a society and its ruling interests intend to do with men and things. Such a "purpose" of domination is "substantive" and to this extent belongs to the very form of technical reason.[6]

> The point which I am trying to make is that science, *by virtue of its own method* and concepts, has projected and promoted a universe in which the domination of nature has remained linked to the domination of man.[7]

At once, Marcuse casts doubt on both optimistic moments of the Marxian dialectic: the forces of production in science and technology are no longer a means to unmask the now antiquated social relations of capitalism—indeed, they become the mode of domination itself; the working class is thoroughly integrated by them, and is removed as the historical agent capable of apprehending and breaking from obsolete capitalist social relations.

The political task is formidable, in Marcuse's view—to oppose, confront, and break "the tyranny of public opinions and its makers in the closed society." He writes, "it makes sense to say that the general will is always wrong—wrong inasmuch as it objectively counteracts the possible transformation of society into more humane ways of life."[8] For a radical democrat this poses a powerful dilemma, one which Marcuse confronts in his essay "Repressive Tolerance."

Tolerance, as now practiced, is really acceptance of a closed universe of ideas and actions that either clearly supports the status quo, or tacitly does so, however "negative" these ideas and actions may be in outer appearance.[9] This is what he means by "repressive tolerance." In contrast, Marcuse claims we need a "liberating tolerance": intolerance of destructive and oppressive ideas and deeds, and toleration of those of pacification and liberation—and this means "intolerance against movements from the Right [and "the estab-

lishment"], and toleration of movements from the Left." Not tolerating oppressive ideas may anger, and alienate those you seek liberation for—
including workers. However, they too have become functional units of a
system of total domination. Is Marcuse's theory of toleration a violation of
democratic principles? As long as the "general will is always wrong," he argues, "discriminating" tolerance must be part of the "struggle for a real democracy." This is the slim hope left liberation.[10]

> In the last analysis, the question of what are true and false needs must be
> answered by the individuals themselves, but only in the last analysis; that is
> if and when they are free to give their own answer.[11]

In advanced industrial society, they are not free to give it.

> The result is the atrophy of the mental organs for grasping the
> contradictions and the alternatives and, in the one remaining dimension of
> technological rationality, the *Happy Consciousness* comes to prevail.[12]

Apathy

For Marcuse, the explanation of what would normally be thought of as political nonparticipation is not really the issue. The question is, How do we explain the fact that so few people are engaged in liberating thought or action?
His answer (with respect to liberation) is that people are thoroughly apathetic, and his paradigm of apathy as a condition is the following:

> X (a subjective or objective mass, class or society) is in a condition of total
> apathy with respect to Y (something enhancing human liberation) when X
> *loses the capacity* to care about Y. Apathy can take the form of *absolute* or
> *relative objective political alienation*.

We have now come 180° from our opening discussion of Bernard Berelson's explanation of nonparticipation. The apathy that Berelson saw and celebrated as necessary for American democracy is now viewed through Marcuse's radical lens as profound false consciousness affecting "political"
participants and nonparticipants alike. There is an irony here because both
err decisively in overstating the amount of apathy present and in misconstru-
ing the nature of much of that which exists. In fact, Marcuse's work turns out
to be both explicitly an attack on technocratic (and positivist) theory and
modes of social organization and implicitly an argument that technocratic
social theory can become human practice.

Marcuse's work is important, however, as Jürgen Habermas points out,
for he helps answer a question vital to explaining how modern capitalism
retains legitimacy in a post–free-market era. Shorn of the legitimations based
on the "free exchange of equivalents," how will necessary state intervention
in the economic and social order, and the depoliticization that may be re-

quired for the state to proceed unimpeded, be made plausible to the inhabitants of advanced industrial society?

Let's now bring Samuel Huntington back in. Habermas's thesis of "legitimation crisis," which should provide some hope to Marcuse, would worry Huntington. Too many demands on a democratic political system, beyond what it is capable of achieving, would undermine the system's authority, in his view, wounding democracy itself. His solution, it will be recalled, is observance of rules of behavior for an advanced technological society, or what Marcuse calls technological rationality, overtly reinforced by a tempering of democratic ideals and tacitly by more apathy.

What Huntington wishes to achieve, Marcuse fears. The technocratic project is *most* dangerous because people *can* conform to its requirements. To what degree is Huntington's hope and Marcuse's despair justified?

Absolute Political Alienation?

Marcuse's thesis of one-dimensional persons taken literally, on its own terms, can be read as a thesis of absolute objective political alienation. While there is little doubt that he hedges on, modifies, and even sometimes contradicts it, Marcuse scholar Morton Schoolman takes the strict one-dimensionality thesis so seriously that he calls his book on Marcuse *The Imaginary Witness*: If society is truly one-dimensional, who is left to observe this fact? Marcuse writes,

> [Alienation] has become *entirely objective*; the subject which is alienated is swallowed up by its alienated existence. There is only one dimension, and it is everywhere and in all forms. The achievements of progress defy ideological indictment as well as justification; before their tribunal, the "false consciousness" of their rationality becomes the true consciousness.[13]

Critical of Schoolman's interpretation, Marcuse scholar Douglas Kellner suggests that there "are two ways to read Marcuse's theory of the one-dimensional technical world and society," "the primary focus" of *One-Dimensional Man*. One way is to see his "theory as a global, totalizing theory of a new type of society that transcends the contradictions of capitalist society in a new order that eliminates individuality, dissent and opposition." Indeed, I think the above statement by Marcuse lends some support to such an interpretation. Kellner argues, however, that because Marcuse criticizes one-dimensional society with alternatives that should be "fought for and realized, it is wrong to read Marcuse as a theorist of the totally administered society who completely rejects contradiction, conflict, revolt and alternative thought and action" and a "mistake" to understand *One-Dimensional Man* "simply as the epic of total domination in a quasi-Hegelian attempt to subsume everything into one monolithic totality."[14]

My purpose here is not to try to capture fully all of Marcuse's nuances, but rather to examine the viability of theories of total apathy through the example of his work. There is sufficient evidence, in my view, to suggest that Marcuse offers what I here call a strict one-dimensionality thesis of absolute political alienation, *and* a more tenuous thesis of relative political alienation, *and* an argument for continued political struggle, as Kellner notes. I would further suggest that all actually can even be found in *One-Dimensional Man* alone. While Marcuse's pessimism as a whole is closer to the theorist of relative political alienation discussed below, there *is* the still bleaker side to *One-Dimensional Man*, in which he advances a hypothesis of such radical alienation that it effectively eliminates subjectivity and constitutes a break with Hegel's metaphysics of the subject-object relation.[15]

One cornerstone of Marcuse's more extreme hyperalienation postulates in *One-Dimensional Man* is his inaccurate prediction of structural tendencies, such as long-term economic stability, mounting affluence, and domestic and international integration (in his later writings, Marcuse adjusts to account for evidence of problems and dissent—it gives him hope—but it challenges his strict thesis of one-dimensionality[16]). The essential problem is that Marcuse gives an overfunctional, almost teleological reading of social structure, privileging his ideas about the power and inevitability of technological hegemony over rumblings, present and past, of structural difficulties.[17] Typically, he looks at institutions such as welfare and trade unions simply as adaptive institutions, neatly functional for advanced industrial society. But this is a quick glance at them after they have been afforded enough legitimacy to appear integrated, and it misses the ways some demands are not simply adaptive and not easily conceded. If the "working class" appears integrated, this may have more to do with its inability to forge a common interest than its thoroughgoing integration. This fact points to Marcuse's account of subjectivity as a central problem within his work.

Alisdair MacIntyre reminds Marcuse that "the majority of men in advanced industrial societies are often confused, unhappy, and conscious of their lack of power; they are often also hopeful, critical, and able to grasp immediate possibilities of happiness and freedom." Underrating people as they are, MacIntyre warns, breeds "false contempt" and "underpins policies that would in fact produce just that passivity and that irrationalism with which he [Marcuse] charges contemporary society."[18] Writing about Theodor Adorno and Max Horkheimer, but Marcuse "in particular," Benhabib suggests that "their work is the best demonstration of how feeble the philosophy of the subject has become."[19]

Marcuse's problematic account of subjectivity is apparent both in his fear of total administration and in the hope for liberation that resurfaces in his post–*One-Dimensional Man* works, *An Essay on Liberation* and *Counterrevolution and Revolt*, written at the height of 1960s protests.[20] In hope, it becomes what he calls the "new sensibility," which manifests itself through Eros, the life instinct,[21] in students, third world rebels, minorities, and others he claims are "allergic" to domination. In fear, it is the thoroughly programmed instincts of "one-dimensional people" in mimetic harmony with the needs of advanced industrial society, their libido victim to repressive desublimation and their aggression harnessed to greater productivity.

Schoolman is right, I think, when he suggests that the subjective underpinning of one-dimensionality comprehends "social life exclusively in terms of the historical conditions, material factors, in the final analysis, structural elements *constituting* and *determining* the subject." Marcuse downplays Freud's constitutional factors of development and the development of the ego, focusing instead on the malleability of the instincts for social control.[22] I would add that this allows Marcuse to develop his theory of surplus repression, which in turn preserves his Marxian *cum* Marcusean hope that the freedom from necessity made possible by advanced technology is the base upon which liberation can *still* be built, once unnecessary instinctual repression is overthrown.

Marcuse's dilemma regarding Freud is this: Without Freud, he has an underspecified and somewhat impoverished subject. Yet with Freud, he can't identify the individual with the society in the way he wants to, either in the oppressive one-dimensional phase, or in the future liberated and communitarian one. So he adapts Freud. But in discarding Freud's psychological pessimism, he also discards his model of psychosocial development without replacing it with a more tenable one. The irony undoubtedly struck him when he wrote *One-Dimensional Man*: Freud's model of human development must have appeared to him an exercise in optimism in comparison to his own.

Habermas explains, however, that one of Marcuse's "most admirable features"—"not to give in to defeatism"—was enabled by "a chiliastic trust in a revitalizing dynamic of instincts." Marcuse could believe that the individual "is more and more swallowed up by a totalitarian society," that the "shrinkage of the ego is without any limits," and still "hope for the rebirth of rebellious subjectivity from a nature which is older than, and arises from below the level of, individuation and rationality."[23]

This belief, however, itself misapprehends important sources of rebelliousness—for instance, understating the personal reflection and political engagement that often are vital to alternative ideas. Many of the young student radicals of the 1960s, for example, were reared in privileged homes with non-repressive child rearing, which Marcuse sometimes thought allowed unrepressed instinctual energy to cause a thirst for liberation.[24] Yet their ideas, rather than being motivated by some vague "organic" foundation, were often extensions of those of their parents; and their radicalization was the result of what they perceived to be broken promises of liberal reform. In *Young Radicals*, Kenneth Kenniston reports that "what is most impressive is not their secret motivation to have the System fail, but their naïve hope that it would succeed, and the extent of their depression and disillusion when their early reformist hopes were frustrated."[25] Kenniston's conclusion concerning the students who worked in the "Vietnam Summer" of 1967 is consistent with a reading of the seminal statement of student protest of that era—the 1962 Port Huron Statement of the newly established Students for a Democratic Society. The most striking thing about this document is that it attempts to formulate and then heal the breach between American ideals and practice.[26]

There is also substantial empirical evidence to counter Marcuse's account of thorough worker integration. Schoolman claims that "technological rationality is frustrated by the rationality of subjectivity," severely limiting the capacity of technological rationality to impose its will—even at the workplace, the closest point to the technological base.[27] Industrial psychology literature since the 1950s has focused on "job rotation," "job enlargement," "participative management," "work teams," "human relations training," "sensitivity training," "job enrichment," "encounter groups," and even Eastern philosophy. While Marcuse would argue these are emblematic of increasing rationalization of the human mind to conform with technological rationality, Schoolman contends that "the increasing rationalization of production results not in more extensive domination but in increasing *resistance* to domination." The proliferation of such techniques points to their failure rather than their success, indicating a "contradiction between human nature and the nature of work in a rationalized society."[28]

Thomas Fitzgerald, director of employee research and training for the Chevrolet division at General Motors, writing in the *Harvard Business Review*, bluntly warned management that programs such as "job enlargement" will wear thin, requiring continuous development of new techniques, including the specter of meaningful reform such as "worker participation":

> Once competence is shown . . . and after participation has become a
> conscious, officially sponsored activity, participators may very well want to
> go on to topics of job assignment, the allocation of rewards, or even the
> selection of leadership. In other words, management's present
> monopoly—on initiating participation, on the nomination of conferees, and
> on the limitation of legitimate areas for review—can itself easily become a
> source of contention.[29]

Fitzgerald concludes, "History does not offer many examples of oligarchies that have abdicated with grace or goodwill."[30]

If human subjectivity is more complex than Marcuse's darkest (and brightest) moments allow, can a strict one-dimensional language thoroughly circumscribed by technological rationality be constructed? Marcuse's claim is that in conflating dialectically opposite terms, or in redefining critical concepts to conform to operational system needs, a thoroughly functional language is being created in one-dimensional society in which people follow either technical rules of behavior or other concepts whose moral content has been completely drained. Can action be reduced in this way to predictable lawlike behavior? The answer, I believe, is no, for such a language, at least as Marcuse describes it, would be incoherent and therefore not language at all.

Marcuse's legitimate moral concern, however, is not behind us. Recall when not too long ago, President Reagan dubbed the MX missile "the peacekeeper." Anticipating this kind of usage, Marcuse gives as an example of one-dimensional language the locution "preparing for war is preparing for peace," collapsing the contradiction between the two terms and thereby making criticism of war impossible.

But to the extent people accept the locution "preparing for war is preparing for peace," they do so precisely because they retain an implicit distinction between war and peace; actually, they accept the well-known deterrence theory of "peace through strength." That is exactly what Reagan's argument was. It was only intelligible to people to the degree that a conceptual distance was retained by Reagan and his supporters between war and peace. Marcuse needed to show what he did not and could not, that the term *peace* is fully defined by the term *war*, as in the locution "war is peace."

Marcuse's claim now can be coherently limited to say that pushing the locution "preparing for war is preparing for peace" too far is dangerous, undermines coherence, could be manipulated by elites sowing mass confusion and allowing what is really war preparation to continue. If the confusion spread to elites, we would have a society in complete interpretive breakdown, an extremely dangerous situation in an era of nuclear weapons, but in an important sense the exact opposite of a one-dimensional society. People would become dangerous to themselves and others in precisely the same way certain mental patients are. Indeed, schizophrenics sometimes develop a language along the lines outlined by Marcuse to cope with unbearable reality. But a mass insane asylum is not a one-dimensional society.

If opposite terms cannot be collapsed with the result Marcuse fears, can important normative concepts, like democracy, be reduced to technical terms? Again the answer to the strong thesis is no, for two reasons. First, to the extent they are, they simply lose their importance, ideological drawing power, and the ability to motivate behavior, perhaps replaced by other, newly ascendant normative ideals. Second, technical language cannot exist on its own because it is dependent on the language of human interaction to discover the purpose of the rules of technical behavior, indeed to define those rules, and for human subjects to follow these for some purpose not reducible to the rules themselves. Subjects following *only* technical "rules" would in fact be objects determined by "laws."

Marcuse's fear of hyperalienation of this sort does seem rooted in his worry that positivist theory can become human practice. Imagine, however,

MacIntyre suggests, that we are able "to build and program computers which are able to simulate wide ranges of human behavior." These are mobile, can gain, reflect, and exchange information, are competitive and cooperative, and can choose between courses of action—that is, make decisions. But they are also "completely specified mechanical and electronic systems of a determinate kind." Their closed mechanical character would seem to make them far better candidates to become one-dimensional—they *are* robots—than flesh-and-blood humans. Yet they would still be subject to the inherent unpredictability that MacIntyre identifies as ineliminable in human life: they couldn't predict radical conceptual innovation; nor the "outcome of their own as yet unmade decisions"; nor could they opt out of the game-theoretic tangles they would find themselves in, any more than we can; and they would be subject to contingencies, such as power failures.[31] He writes,

> It follows that the description of their behavior at the level of activity—in terms of decisions, relationships, goals and the like—would be very different in its logical and conceptual structures from the description of behavior at the level of electrical impulses. It would be difficult to give the notion of reducing the one mode of description to the other any clear sense; and if this is true of these imaginary, but possible computers, it seems likely to be true of us too.

He then adds elliptically: "(It does seem likely that we *are* these computers.)"[32]

If the behavior of mechanical beings whose circuitry we could fully specify has an inherent unpredictability to it, a strict one-dimensionality thesis would seem implausible on these grounds alone. A totalitarian universe of this sort would be one precisely in which there could be the kind of lawlike generalizations about human behavior that MacIntyre shows to be impossible.

Relative Political Alienation

Partly out of richness of thought and acute moral sensibility, partly out of lack of clarity, Marcuse also presents a useful although tenuous thesis of relative objective political alienation. The essential elements are: (1) a powerful apolitical ideology of technological rationality that limits human self-consciousness and freedom but does not itself become the categories of the human mind; (2) as part of this ideology, a host of "operationalized" concepts that trivialize and personalize grievances, and confuse but do not reduce moral ideas to technical terms; (3) a language that undercuts the potential for oppositional concepts to criticize society—for example, the MX as a "peacekeeper"—but that does not really collapse contradictory ideas (a modified notion of the "one-dimensional language" central to his more extreme thesis); (4) an adaptive mass psychology that defuses psychological discontent, both libidinally (what he calls *repressive desublimation*) and aggressively (in the "enemy," Communism or perhaps an "underclass"), but not a strict mimesis theory; (5) the production of expanding rewards that serve to focus satisfaction privately; (6) pseudo-political outlets for political thought, action, and discontent—for example, elections that really serve only as ceremonial plebiscites, and this called "democracy."

Robert Paul Wolff captures one of Marcuse's genuine insights on mass psychology, explaining Marcuse's theory of repressive desublimation in a way that is compatible with a modified one-dimensionality thesis. Within all people there exists a "psychical pool" in the unconscious that is permanent opposition to established society and that critical thinking taps in order to imagine a different society. The real genius of repressive desublimation is that it "absorbs" the opposition into dominant class interests by *refusing* to clamp down on these hidden impulses:

> Such a reaction [clamping down] only heightens the force of the repressed desires and, Antaeus-like, redoubles their energy. Rather, the appropriate move is to permit the specific, overt act, but to rob it of its unconscious significance by immediately accepting it into the repertory of permissible acts.

The act, therefore, is unable to mobilize the hidden psychic energy because it "ceases to serve as a surrogate for the entire unconscious."[33]

The constellation constituting Marcuse's thesis of relative political alienation, however, is an unstable one for a number of reasons. I will concentrate here on examining to what degree technological rationality as ideology, and the practices it generates, can help create enduring legitimacy for advanced industrial society.

The Limits of Integration into Technological Society

Machiavelli, who did as much as anyone to use the political arts effectively for purposes he supported, believed there was an ineliminable unpredictability to life. He called it "Fortuna." MacIntyre argues there are empirical and practical grounds for believing "Fortuna" to be permanent. An organization set up to minimize societal unpredictability would first need its leaders "to render the activity of . . . [the] organization wholly or largely predictable." But empirical studies show that effective organizations require initiative, redefinition of tasks, advice rather than command, and the use of knowledge whose location in the organization may itself not be predictable; they have an open quality about them, at least in being able to use fully—or exploit, if you like—their own resources. Thus MacIntyre argues "organizational success and organizational predictability exclude one another" and, therefore, "the project of creating a wholly or largely predictable organization committed to creating a wholly or largely predictable society is doomed and doomed by the facts about social life."

> Totalitarianism of a certain kind, as imagined by Aldous Huxley or George Orwell [I add Herbert Marcuse], is therefore impossible. What the totalitarian project will always produce will be a kind of rigidity and inefficiency which may contribute in the long run to its defeat [MacIntyre is prescient here about the Soviet empire]. *We need to remember however the voices from Auschwitz and Gulag Archipelago which tell us just how long that long run is.*[34]

Technological rationality does have a great strength, however, and that is that it doesn't appear to be ideology at all. Herein also lies its most important practical weakness. It doesn't have the solid moral resources other ideologies have at their disposal. Habermas argues that the "new ideology is distinguished from its predecessor in that it severs [I read this "attempts to sever"] the criteria for justifying the organization of social life from any normative regulation of interaction, thus depoliticizing them."[35]

But technological rationality cannot really eliminate the existential questions of why we do what we do, or why we should do or not do something, although it can help tell how, when, where, and what to do. The answer to the question "why" can be unreflective and assumed, but it cannot be eliminated. And it can't be answered only within the terms of technological rationality. One of the appeals of President Reagan was his ability to call into question not only the ability but the *right* of government to manage social affairs, deploying older ideas of a free market *against* technocratic rhetoric. When Daniel Bell follows his "end of ideology" thesis with a later call for a "public household," he is trying to reinsert an ethical dimension into a society in which *obeying* the rules of work and consumption nevertheless creates hedonism as a "cultural contradiction" of capitalism.[36]

In fact, technological rationality does have an ethical ally in utilitarian ethics, so that when most people seem to be accepting its logic, they are not really only producing for the sake of the productive apparatus itself, as Marcuse has it, but altruistically producing the greatest good for the greatest number, and self-interestedly maximizing their own rewards, as he sometimes does put it. Technological rationality remains subject, at a minimum, to a quasi-internal critique within utilitarian ethics.

Yet this ethical basis for a construal of human interests is a weak one, prone to being severely questioned when productivity falters. Stuart Hampshire argues that the alliance of social engineering and utilitarianism offers a constricted view of human purposes:

> when the mere existence of an individual person by itself has no value, apart from the by-products and uses of the individual in producing and enjoying

desirable states of mind, there is no theoretical barrier against social surgery of all kinds.[37]

Yet there are numerous examples, arrayed across the political spectrum, of vigorous opposition to "social surgery" on matters considered vital to constituting desired, perhaps competing, ways of life, such as sexual practices, customs of war, treatment of the terminally ill or the aged, and respect for life itself.[38]

Technocrats may themselves be morally uncomfortable with their roles, even from the point of view of their own self-interest. The technocrat is asked to view not only members of the public as objects to be administered, but him or herself as an objectified administrator. But while I, as a technocrat, may talk about my contribution of an idea for the more efficient accomplishment of a project as "input," I may well resent its rejection and become indignant if it is repeatedly rejected. I may then conclude that the system is unfair to people like me and search for those characteristics that constitute such a class, question a hierarchy that now only appears to be organized by true functional skill, question the legitimacy of the roles of those whose status is higher than mine, and maybe even question the technocratic model itself. Even technocrats sometimes try to answer the question, "why?"

There is, even more fundamentally, an important relationship between action, responsibility, knowledge, and self-consciousness that suggests technological consciousness cannot dispense with the need for grounding beliefs in values external to technological rationality. Consider that the job of the technocrat is to correctly apply technical rules, posing as a predictor of his or her own behavior, with the prediction circumscribed by the set of rules most appropriate for a given end.

But once a person predicts that something will happen because he or she is willing to follow the rules necessary to make it happen, and observes that prediction, a contradiction arises: because we are simultaneously observer and observed, once we predict and are conscious of our prediction, our role of observer contradicts our role as actor. Our prediction is necessary for us to know what we can achieve, but knowledge of our prediction now constitutes a *decision* on our part to do something. This dialectic of people as predictors and deciders, identified by Hampshire as a basic aspect of human action and self-consciousness,[39] can be obscured but not eliminated by technocratic roles.

If I as a social service bureaucrat say to you, "I predict I will take you off welfare because of raised eligibility requirements," we both probably know what I really mean is I have decided to follow the rules and take you off. The more aware I become of my decision, the more intentional my action, the more I persist, the more deliberate. If I tell you, "I have no choice," we both know that what I really mean is that I have chosen not to absorb the consequences of helping you, or that my helping you is futile because down the line your request will be stopped by someone else's choices. Clearly these choices are constrained, and we might even say predictable. In principle, however, language is always available to bureaucrats and technocrats (and all of us) to formulate the question, "What is it I'm really doing?" in following what seem to be purely bureaucratic or technical rules.

Subsystems of societies ostensibly organized only under what Habermas calls "purposive-rational" rules of behavior, that is, rules of technique, cannot rely on people to adopt only the role of predictors of their own behavior: Because people must decide as well, in principle, it must be possible to become aware of that role, heightening awareness of responsibility and freedom and forcing into the open the need for beliefs, external to the logic of prediction, to justify conduct. Such justification can weakly fall back on "I just follow the rules," or "it's in my self-interest to do so," or "following the rules helps the system run smoothly," or, less weakly, "it's for the greatest pleasure for the greatest number," or, more strongly, "it's for the greatest good for the greatest number," and, most strongly, "it is to enhance human life." Each step taken is one step away from a pure technocratic model, first into utilitarian ethics, and ultimately into more traditional ones. Each, however, calls into question the suppression of ethics and politics necessary for the depoliticized ideology that Marcuse argues is required to maintain the legitimacy of advanced industrial society. And Marcuse cannot (nor does he) abandon the centrality of such an ideology if he is to have any theory of one-dimensional society left at all.

⬚ Chapter 11

Race, Gender, and Explanation

When Samuel Huntington advanced his argument for a moderation of democratic ideals,[1] morally he rested it on his belief that the fundamental issues of political rights have been satisfactorily addressed. Many of the works we have discussed in Part I challenge that view, but their challenges fall short most when it comes to questions of how racial and gender disadvantages serve to depoliticize. And this is true in spite of the fact that the authors within the plain and radical democratic schools of explaining nonparticipation do develop substantial examinations of the depoliticizing effects of social class disadvantages, biased political agendas, and bureaucratic and technocratic ideological dispositions.[2]

My interest here is to suggest some ways the parameters of explanation need to be transformed in order to more fully capture depoliticization rooted in race and gender. In the section on race, I focus on how, since the Civil Rights era, the relation of structural limits, political choices, and attitudes of race served to weaken coalitions, slow real advances in political equality, and end increases in participation. In the section on gender, I focus on how certain notions of public and private roles, even those advanced by participatory democrats who have broad definitions of "the political," may limit real political equality for women and also limit their full participation. The territory covered, however, could be reversed. One could study the relation between assumptions about racial roles today to older racist ideologies. Why, for example, is it not viewed by some whites as a product of structural disadvantages, or at least peculiar, the fact that blacks are disproportionately concentrated in low-paid service fields like hospital care, nursing homes, or fast-food restaurants? Similarly, one could study the relationship between recent economic difficulties and the feminization of poverty, and how strains in the economy and in politics have served to weaken political alliances that might have strengthened women's political ability to defend and advance themselves.

Race and Political Equality

Even today Steven Rosenstone and John Hansen report, "decades after the passage of the VRA [Voting Rights Act], discrimination, harassment, and intimidation continue to make it difficult for blacks and other minorities to register and to vote."[3] In a more subtle and even more compelling way, African-American political power is limited, as Lawrence Bobo and Franklin Gilliam suggest, by the coming together of a number of decisive factors: advances in black empowerment have coincided with the decline in power of urban political machines; population and commerce were leaving the cities, where blacks were becoming concentrated, for the suburbs; federal programs were declining; obstacles to registering to vote continue; gerrymandered district lines that dilute black votes exist; there is "hostility to black candidates among a significant number of whites." And there are "persisting social segregation and economic disadvantages" suffered by blacks that "constitute structural bases for black racial identity formation," and as well for racial polarization over race relations, welfare policy, and "life satisfaction." They argue that while blacks have "made enormous strides in socioeconomic status and political influence . . . black progress and political empowerment are still partial and incomplete even though they have advanced far enough to affect how often, and why, blacks become politically active."[4]

Racism has been and continues to be a fact of political, economic, and social life in American society. For a brief period after the Civil War, and of course, especially in the 1960s, the American political system responded to pressure for civil rights and made important efforts to transform some of the legal and structural bases of racial stratification. The Civil Rights era did remove important obstacles to political equality, including establishing a real right to vote, run for and hold political office, as well as open up economic opportunities that themselves advance political power. By 1968, African-American voting turnout in the South equaled that of whites, as the Civil Rights movement effectively mobilized blacks to vote in a changing political and legal climate.[5] The civil rights movement, then, mitigated political inequalities between the races. Yet there are systemic reasons as well as human failures responsible for the faltering of this promising development.

Since World War I until well into the 1950s, with the need for cheap labor in northern industrial cities and the decline of the need for southern agricultural labor, there was a massive migration of African-Americans from the South to northern cities, where they often met racial discrimination on the part of employers and unions. This migration, shortly after the last major European immigration of the early twentieth century, brought blacks and their temporary allies from the 1930s through the 1960s—working-class whites—into close proximity, increasing racial tensions and making "race" an increasingly divisive issue.

The black population of major cities grew rapidly; at the same time, the nature of the economy changed, demanding higher skills and more education and making it more difficult for blacks to gain entry even when there was no overt racial discrimination. As Charles Green and Basil Wilson report,

"Whereas job losses in major northern metropolises have been greatest in industries with lower educational requirements, job growth has been concentrated in industries that require higher levels of education." Moreover, structural unemployment has been rising at the same time there has been a shift away from durable good manufacturing jobs toward finance, insurance, and service, including fast-food, health, and business. Most service positions tend to be concentrated in the lower-paying job categories and, unlike whites, African-Americans and Latinos tend to be concentrated in the lowest-paying service categories. Blacks, for example, "are more narrowly clustered [than whites] around a few industries that offer lower salaries such as hospital and hotel services, eating places, department stores, and nursing and personal care facilities."[6]

Increasing international competition also has played a significant role as, even in some areas where blacks gained entry, like autowork in Detroit, foreign competition undercut their newly won gains along with the position of white autoworkers as well. Moreover, private investment often withdrew from northern cities and invested in nonunion states, the Sunbelt, and southern and western regions benefiting from high military spending. In part these trends reflected a realignment of political strength, and where and how the federal government would spend its money, particularly after Richard Nixon's election in 1968. Some investment went to cheaper labor areas abroad.

Just at that period, therefore, that African-Americans were winning significant legal rights to work, vote, be educated in a nondiscriminatory manner, it again became more difficult to break in as capital was on the move, job requirements became more difficult, demographic change due to massive migration nurtured racial prejudice and tensions, and discrimination continued. As the post–World War II American economic boom petered out around 1969 and as the Vietnam war dragged on, consuming billions of dollars, political support for remedial progress withered, helping to create what Thomas and Mary Edsall call a "chain reaction" in America on the issues of race, rights, values, and taxes, most adversely affecting the New Deal coalition, and with it the ability of African-Americans to have a workable alliance through which to press their grievances.

As de jure discrimination fell to equal opportunity laws, and against an entrenched history of racist attitudes and practices, it was not a long leap for many whites to believe that blacks—now responsible for their own fate—were not taking advantage of the opportunities now available, and instead were engaged in special pleading. Looking at an economic world in which they had been told their own success was only limited by their ability, in which their perception was they never had received such help, and in which their success now seemed increasingly limited as the economy slipped in and out of recession, many whites resented these perceived demands. Equal opportunity in an expanding economy was one thing. But what they saw as special preferences at their expense, both in terms of jobs and taxes, in a stagnant, high-inflation economy was quite another. As the Edsalls point out, the simmering issues of race, rights, and values exploded in a "chain reaction" when the tax crunch became more burdensome, undermining the alliances African-Americans needed for programs of equity. Unlike the New Deal, and whatever the measure of reality, to many whites government seemed now to be taking more from them in taxes than it was giving back, and the money it was taking seemed to be going to those unwilling to do their share. The weakening of the political coalition that had advanced civil rights created the political opening for conservative ascendancy in the 1980s, and a significant attack on social welfare as well as civil rights programs and, as Kevin Phillips argues, an upward redistribution of wealth, hurting lower-middle- and working-class people, white and black. These changes had consequences for political participation.

Rosenstone and Hansen conclude that far and away "the most important drag on African-American voter turnout" in the 1970s and 1980s "was the atrophy of instruments of mobilization." As mobilizing institutions such as campaigns, parties, and movements "subsidized fewer costs and created fewer benefits, black voter turnout declined by 11.4 percentage points." Two thirds of the decline since 1968, they conclude, can be attributed directly to "curtailed mobilization."[7]

One specific factor that limited African-American as well as other minority turnout, and that by working-class whites, was the increasing inability of the Democratic party to hold them together and mobilize them vigorously and effectively (or even really try to). In some respects, as the Edsalls point out, the party did self-destruct, taking its white working-class base for granted, not creating a program at the level of presidential elections that could overcome racial divisions, and watching with confusion as race became a very effective "wedge" issue for the right.

There were, however, deeper forces at work. Not only had the will of government and the public for social programs waned, but America's relative world economic position slackened. Partly for reasons of ideological commitment to the idea of the "free market" and partly out of failure of foresight, and as fiscal pressures mounted, government did little to prepare much of the American workforce for the transformation into a postindustrial economy. Naturally, those in the most vulnerable positions again became the least prepared. Changes in the national and world economy were particularly harmful to core economic constituents of the New Deal coalition, especially industrial workers.

There were, then, important limiting constraints on government and on political movements themselves that made more difficult the possibility of a coalition strong enough to offset the effects of these economic and political forces. Perceived economic limits may have lured the party into making mistakes, such as not adequately protecting or, more important, helping adjust the economic base of its blue-collar supporters—or perhaps worse, not appearing to be sufficiently concerned about their plight.

It is not surprising that the Democratic party, the party of government social welfare activism, would suffer under these circumstances.[8] Nor is it surprising that race would be re-exploited as a dominant fault line in American politics. For all the tactical and strategic errors of the Democratic party, activists and politicians committed to civil rights, many of them (although certainly not all) Democrats, were faced with and had undertaken a truly heroic task, in trying to undo legal and extra-legal racism against African-Americans—that dated from 1619. Yet, passage of antidiscrimination laws and a "war on poverty" seemed to give many whites too quickly the sense that equal opportunity had been achieved, and this too added to the party's problems. Filtered through residual attitudes of racism, for some this belief became the lens through which other changes would be seen. Visibility of programs like affirmative action and busing, concentration of minorities in urban areas at precisely that time these areas were becoming most economically precarious, increasingly burdensome taxation on the working and middle classes, reinvigorated old prejudices, and kindled new resentments. As racial divisions grew, coalition and mobilization became more difficult. The lower the educational and class position, the more politically vulnerable, the more mobilization was necessary.[9]

Without mobilization, political participation would turn down. The more participation turned down, the less incentive there would be for political leaders to address these constituencies' concerns. The more participation turned down, the greater the opening for a conservative coalition to form, which could further weaken the authority of the government to steer the private economy in the interests of disadvantaged citizens. Eventually, under President Reagan, the very legitimacy of the government to do so became seriously questioned for the first time since the New Deal.

Furthermore, change within African-American civil society itself would contribute to these trends, reflecting structural, ideological, and historical factors that situate the issue of race in the late twentieth century. Writing about fundamental changes in New York City, Green and Wilson argue that government, unable to control important investment decisions, was faced with a situation in which

> the exodus of labor-intensive capital from the city concomitant with the continuing influx of unskilled labor into the city created the conditions for a burgeoning underclass . . . one that has become institutionalized in the sense that it is perfectly capable of reproducing itself. This underclass affects the ethos of city civilization as it is the source of street crime, gang violence, drugs, and general cultural decadence.

> The underclass in New York City is essentially African-American and Latino. The overrepresentation of black and brown people in the underclass is a critical factor in the rationalization of contemporary racism still rampant in white civil society.[10]

The separation of investment decisions from what is considered appropriate for democratic political decision making has as one of its core elements the idea that the generation of economic inequalities is a private matter. This makes it very difficult for the political or legal system to address racial disadvantages that are institutionalized in social and economic patterns that cannot be tied directly to intentional racist behavior or laws sanctioning racial discrimination. Many African-Americans and other minorities have made significant economic and political gains since World War II, but many of the most vulnerable were left behind in the "underclass," as William Julius Wilson named it, reinforcing racial stereotypes and hatred, creating resentments, and building further obstacles to coalition and mobilization, and thereby to political participation. The more participation remains low, the less likely it is that the political agenda will address the needs of minorities, the less real value of each of their votes, the less politically equal the marginally enfranchised are. In this way, America's racial history remains alive in today's politics of political nonparticipation.

Forgetting the Women

Abigail Adams was unsuccessful in persuading her husband, John, not to "forget the ladies" in the drafting of the Declaration of Independence, just as Mary Wollstonecraft was unable to convince the English shortly thereafter in her 1792 *Vindication of the Rights of Women*. Until recently, these demands also fell on deaf ears within much of democratic theory, as first Wollstonecraft's ideas were ignored, then John Stuart Mill's 1869 volume, *The Subjection of Women*, in spite of the widespread prominence otherwise afforded this thinker. This lacuna is not surprising, not only because of historic attitudes about the proper place of women, but also because—and these are related—of the central place of the Lockean liberal tradition in the development of society and of theory, and how women's roles have been fit into this tradition. Fundamental to the Lockean view is the idea that there can and should be a sharp separation between the state and civil society, in which the state is established for the purpose of allowing private affairs in civil society to proceed under a set of fair rules that will be enforced if necessary by the state. Ascriptive depoliticized gender roles are then nurtured by a particular manifestation of the liberal dichotomy of public and private spheres.

Carole Pateman, both a distinguished participatory theorist and feminist theorist, finds that analysts even of participatory democracy, including herself, have failed to understand the public-private distinction as it affects gender. Because participatory theorists challenge this distinction only with regard to work, their arguments

> remain within the patriarchal-liberal separation of civil society and state; domestic life has an exceedingly ambiguous relation to this separation which is a division within public life itself. In contrast, feminists see domestic life, the "natural" sphere of women, as private, and thus as divided from a public realm encompassing both economic and political life, the "natural" arenas of men.
>
> By failing to take into account the feminist conception of "private" life, by ignoring the family, participatory democratic arguments for the democratization of economic life have neglected a crucial dimension of democratic social transformation (and I include my *Participation and Democratic Theory* here).[11]

One can view the family, then, as both political, in the sense that it involves relations of power allowed and often enforced by the state and in the sense it also depends on public definitions of men and women's "natural" roles, and private as a sphere of life that involves intimate personal relationships that should be protected from state intrusion. Moreover, the sexual division of labor within the family is emblematic and helps reinforce the sexual division of labor in more clearly public arenas such as work and politics itself. Full democracy and participation require a fair chance to have equality of power, status, and the opportunities for self-development, and participatory rights, not only within the realm of politics and work themselves but also within domestic life. One therefore cannot discuss true autonomy of democratic citizenship without discussing engendered roles rooted in family relationships.

Similarly, according to Susan Moller Okin, there are "two major ambiguities" in the use of the terms *public* and *private*. Public/private refers to the distinction both between the state and civil society and between "nondomestic and domestic life." Where the state is paradigmatically public and domestic life private, there is the intermediate area of socioeconomic relations that is part of private relations (civil society) when compared to the state, but public (nondomestic civil society) when compared to the family. It is the family, then, that really is paradigmatically private in liberal thought. Okin argues that, as applied to questions of gender, the concept of public/private should distinguish between those relations of (private) civil society that are often viewed as public, such as the economy, and those that almost never are, such as domestic relations. Instead of focusing on public/private, it makes sense to think in terms of public and domestic, for it is really the continuation of "this dichotomy that enables theorists to ignore the political nature of the family, the relevance of justice in personal life and, as a consequence, a major part of the inequalities of gender."[12]

Consequently, she argues, the right to privacy in liberal theory that maintains a sharp distinction between public and domestic life actually has meant the right for men "*not* to be interfered with as they controlled the other members of their private sphere," and "no notion that these subordinate members of households might have privacy rights of their own."[13]

The hypothesis that a lack of rights could be contained just to the household is both implausible and goes against historical evidence. Okin cautions "those theorists who still seem silently to assume that female child-rearing and domesticity are 'natural' and therefore fall outside the scope of political inquiry" to bear in mind the following issues. First, "the domestic division of labor," especially male superiority and domination both in public and domestic life, and female responsibility for domestic life, especially child rearing, is "socially constructed, and therefore [a matter] of political concern." Second, these standard notions of domestic roles are "major causal factors in the gender structure of society at large," and "their continuance cannot itself be explained without reference to elements of the non-domestic sphere, such as the current sex segregation and sex discrimination in the labour force, the scarcity of women in high-level politics, and the structural assumption that workers and holders of political office are not responsible for the care of small children."[4] Like Pateman, therefore, Okin regards "the existing liberal distinction between public and domestic [as] ideological."

Pateman's and Okin's feminist critiques of mainstream liberal democratic theory have important implications for explaining nonparticipation. Understanding the relation between what is considered political and what range of issues, of interest to which class of persons, is displaced by such a definition, makes an analyst more sensitive to the possibility that women who appear apathetic about traditional "politics" may actually care deeply about nontraditional issues, now revealed through feminist analysis, as legitimately political. To the degree sexist roles within and outside of the family place women in a subordinated political position that creates a cycle of apathy, these roles may reflect apathy's second face—as an entrapping condition. In order to fully explore political nonparticipation among women, we should examine the ways in which women's political activity and interests are restricted both within and outside the family and through gendered ideas of politics and of power itself, and the way all these reinforce and reproduce each other. Just as Dahl saw economic deprivation leading to a cycle of apathy, and Bachrach saw worker powerlessness doing the same, so too can the subordination of women.

Part III

Overcoming Apathy

I now turn to sketch a framework for the explanation of nonparticipation based on the analysis in Part II and draw suggestions from that framework for the larger task of overcoming apathy and nonparticipation. In chapter 12, I suggest a way to study nonparticipation emanating from, but going beyond, the outline of political power put forward by Lukes at the outset. In chapter 13, I explore the foundational idea of a second face of apathy. In chapter 14, I examine the merits for democratization of empirical analyses of nonparticipation and reform proposals, and in chapter 15, some ideas for political renewal, all evaluated from the point of view of the explanation of nonparticipation developed in chapters 12 and 13. In the conclusion, I first argue that explanations imply not only values but strategies, and, second, suggest specific political proposals that I believe have the best chance of avoiding the traps of nonparticipation discovered in the explanation of it.

 **Chapter 12**

Real People and False Consciousness

Men and Work

In their richly suggestive work, *The Hidden Injuries of Class*, Richard Sennett and Jonathan Cobb criticize writers of both the left and right for too easily accepting the idea that economic rewards are a sufficient motivation for the integration of workers into industrial society. In studying the beliefs, aspirations, and motivations of workers, they find a far more complex relation between the appearance of worker integration and the reality of emotional damage in class-stratified society. Even those who have made it into middle-class life seem far from content with their achievements.

As we'll see, their work is a powerful indictment of writers like Marcuse and at times Mills, who sometimes analyze consciousness without seriously considering the actual beliefs that real people hold and the active role they play in helping create those beliefs.

How would Marcuse explain, for example, the feeling of someone like Frank Rissarro, who has climbed the ladder from the factory into the white-collar world but does not feel his new work is worthwhile compared to jobs that produce useful things? Yet he has climbed this ladder, in part, to gain dignity and respect. Or Frank O'Malley, who understands that success and respect require advancement over one's peers, and that this erodes comaraderie, the respect of others, and ultimately self-respect. Sennett and Cobb unearth a rich complex of aspirations, attitudes, and beliefs that, taken together, constitute what they call "the 'internalizing' of class conflict, the process by which struggle between men leads to struggle within each man."[1]

American workers, they argue, define their self-worth in terms of ability to succeed, educational accomplishment, personal sacrifice, and freedom. Yet they are caught in binds at every turn. They are free to advance, but if they do, they sacrifice friendship and respect, and if they don't, they risk their dignity. They want their children's lot to be better than their own and they will sacrifice for this goal. But when their children become educated, workers may feel betrayed by the status distinction now insinuated into their family, or be ambivalent about the kind of work their children do; they are sometimes even resented by their children—for these reasons and because their children never asked for the sacrifice in the first place. In order to maintain dignity and respect, the workers judge themselves and others, yet they don't feel qualified to judge. They feel anxious and often guilt-ridden about their lives and blame themselves for these feelings—"if only I had worked harder," "gotten that education," "sacrificed more." Whether they succeed or not, they often feel as if they have failed and they blame themselves for their failure.

Consider their passivity in this light. Rissarro has achieved much of what he considers the "good things" in life, yet after his superficial declarations of satisfaction, the doubt shows. He views himself on the receiving end of the good things, a *passive* agent who is not the cause even of his own success: "I was just at the right place at the right time." Far from showing modesty, this comment reveals that he feels he doesn't belong in the world he now inhabits, an outsider intruding on the middle class, illegitimate in his new situation and undeserving of respect. He explains his achievements to himself as luck. To explain them as deserved success would be to respect himself, but he is not confident of his dignity. Yet he wants respect and so he continues to judge himself and others in a social situation that will serve to reconfirm his doubt.

Rissarro may be viewed from the outside simply as acquiescent, or analyzed from the academy as a one-dimensional man. Indeed, he views himself as passive. He may well be politically apathetic. What is distinctive, however, is that it is *his active struggle* for identity and respect that is crucial in turning the blame for his discontents, not on the role society, elites, class structure, or ideologies may play in limiting his happiness, but *on himself*. Sennett and Cobb conclude,

> The examples we have so far given of assertion of individual ability in families point to three general results of such assertion: the search for respect is thwarted; the individual feels personally responsible for the failure; the whole attempt accustoms him to think that to have individual respect you must have social inequality.[2]

Acceptance of inequality limits the promise of democratic politics. And the binds that promote political apathy also restrict the freedom of democratic citizens. Passive acquiescence in this undemocratic fate is all the more insidious because it is made possible, and becomes more formidable, through the active participation of the passive person. Social critics, however, often overlook the power and responsibility this person has to free himself or herself from limits that are imposed on the self through the mediation of social structure by the self.

Women and Power

Jean Baker Miller argues that women in our culture are encouraged to believe that they "do not need power" and "are most comfortable using our powers if we believe we are using them in the service of others."[3] Therefore, women actually do possess a kind of power, one that empowers others through nurturing and caretaking roles. The location of power of this sort is often in the psychological, emotional, or intellectual realm rather than the political or economic. It is a complicated exercise: Because power in these roles is limited, and because they are roles that serve to empower others, women must be sensitive to changes in the relationship as the powers of the others grow in proportion to the success of the women's work. Miller writes, "Acting under those general beliefs, and typically not making any of this explicit, women have been effective in many ways."[4] Women, therefore, are powerful in ways undervalued by dominant definitions of what power should mean, uncomfortable themselves in seeing these as forms of power, and "do fear admitting that they want or need power."[5] Like Sennett and Cobb's study of working men, Miller's study reveals how women's active interpretive roles reshape dominant views of power but do so in a way that binds them to depoliticized roles.

Consider the experience of Abby, who had spent much of her life in the nurturing role of mother and wife and is now a low-paid health worker who sought therapy for depression. She was excellent at her job "largely because she approached her patients with the basic attitude of helping them to increase their own comfort and abilities and to use their own powers." She found she became most depressed not when things went badly but rather when they went well, "when she realized that she could *do* something more— for example, better understand and effectively act on a situation." She became most depressed when "she wanted to act for herself"—for example, by doing a procedure she was better at performing than the doctors, because "she helped patients feel more relaxed, more in control, and more powerful."[6] Virtually at the moment that this success led her to feel she was entitled to more recognition and pay, "she became blocked by fear, then self-criticism and self-blame." Externally, as a woman, she was occupationally trapped at the lowest rung of her field. Internally, an "even more complex bondage" was created. She was afraid to be "seen as wanting to be powerful," which provoked "notions of disapproval" and, "at a deeper level, evoked fears of attack and ultimate abandonment by all women and men." Moreover, "acting on her own interest and motivation" would make her appear "selfish" to others— "it was even more critical that she could not bear this conception of herself." With "selfishness" came a theme of inadequacy and the feeling "she should be grateful that anyone would put up with her at all, and she should best forget about the whole thing."[7] Inadequacy gave way to a stage in which she felt that she had "powers and could use them, but doing so meant, inescapably, that she was being destructive." This was revealed to her in "thoughts, fantasies, and dreams indicating destructiveness."[8]

There is another type of bind to which Miller's description also points. On the one hand, it is Abby's understanding of the kind of power that is appropriate for her to exercise—to comfort and empower others—that leads to her success. Given employment options available to her, the quiet type of selfless powers she exercises in her job is a rational way for her to channel her abilities. Yet these seem intrinsically related to her self-doubt: that she is not entitled to be in control, that to begin feeling that she is makes her selfish or destructive and will lead to rejection. Her powers are thus a source of her disempowerment as her reach for dignity is both made possible and frustrated by how, in her real-life situation, she has been and is capable of being powerful. She neither accepts fully the subordinate role assigned to her as a low-paid woman in the health field, nor overthrows it to adopt the doctor's conception of power as her own. She modifies both, making her less subordinate than she might otherwise have been but paying a heavy price.

Similar themes are discovered in the lives of Ellen and Connie. Ellen could think and work well in the house but could not bring these qualities to work, structured as it was for receptive and yielding behavior and leaving her unable to "bring my inside self outside," to really contribute. To do more would be to become destructive and overturn the situation—something she shouldn't do. Miller writes of women like Ellen,

> In each person such a theme forges its specific expression from the individual's history, but the basic theme occurs regularly in many women: To act out of one's own interest and motivation is experienced as the psychic equivalent of being a destructively aggressive person. This is a self-image that few women can bear. . . . it is more comfortable to feel inadequate. Terrible as that can be, it is still better than to feel powerful, if power makes you feel destructive. . . . On the one hand, this sets up a life-destroying, controlling psychological condition. On the other hand, it makes sense if one sees that women have lived as subordinates and, as subordinates, have been led by the culture to believe that their own, self-determined action is wrong and evil.[9]

Connie became blocked at finishing her work not when she was doing poorly but when she was doing well, for doing well would mean "I'd be too powerful and then where would I be. . . . I wouldn't need anyone else." While this fear was unnecessary, Miller writes, it "touched on a sense that is present in many women—namely, that the use of our powers with some efficacy and, even worse, with freedom, zest, and joy, feels as if it will destroy a core sense of identity." Where culture has encouraged men to deny the truth that "all of us exist only as we need others for that existence," Miller argues, "cultural conditions have led women to incorporate this in an extreme form." Again Miller seems to be describing binds in which women are caught: "[W]e women . . . have powers and the motivation to use those powers, but if we use them, we will destroy the relationships we need for our existence."[10]

These women all display, but exercise in ways that ultimately keep them subordinated, resources of subjectivity through which they try to relocate their relation to the idea of power itself and to the kinds of powers men typically dominate, especially of control in the areas of work, economics, and politics. Like the men Sennett and Cobb describe, their self-perception critically limits them in extending their powers. Unlike the men for whom major issues are "Do we deserve to be where we are? Is where we are worthwhile?," the judge for women is even clearer: It is wrong to try to do more. Both the men and women come to accept that they don't deserve more, should be grateful to be where they are. As we look at both, a similar paradox appears. Their passivity is not well understood as acquiescence into roles assigned by a dominant ideology. In some ways, they would be happier if they did passively acquiesce. Instead, it is enlivened by a dialectic of interpretation of emotional harm, which is triggered by the very effort to broaden the kinds of powers they should have, and the dignity and respect that they believe accompany new roles. The paradox is that their stretch for greater autonomy at once provides hope for change and traps them in the binds that make changes so difficult. Their passivity is extremely active.

For both the men and the women, there is one fundamental common bind. Society seems to teach that each individual is worthy of dignity and respect, that at the level of private emotions "all persons are created equal." In the real world, however, class, gender, and racial stratification promotes a type of emotional stratification. You are less likely to believe in your ability and self-worth not only because of role expectations drawn for you, but because of your own experiences of shaming, self-doubt, and self-disrespect as you try to advance your position based on the public philosophy of equal opportunity, the emotional damage hidden within meritocracy for all who fail (and probably many who succeed), and the specific emotional damage likely for those consigned to certain positions. Yet the hope remains that the person implicated in her or his own powerlessness has more power and responsibility to become freer than is often presumed by social critics.

There is a quiet ambiguity in Miller's work that, when listened to carefully, reveals a lot about power. Miller seems to suggest that the experiences of women have provided them with powers unsullied by male-dominated conceptions of power as control. These nurturing powers are pristine, selfless, generous, unique. Yet the women she describes seem to want something more. Is it simply for these powers to be recognized? Or is it that they want what should be coming to them—that is, they want their share of power, as defined by men, power as control? Can women both be selfless and want more for themselves?

Miller's ambiguity is creative. Clearly, her sympathies lie with the idea that women have a unique perspective on power and should assert it as they come to recognize its worth. But one can't help think that the assertive aspect trades heavily on what she seems to consider to be power as usually conceived by men, and, fortunately, she does not extinguish this tension in favor of her somewhat idealized version of the way women view power.[11]

Power to the Subject

Consider Miller's narrative now in light of Joan Cocks's assay of the "instrumentalist" view of power often found in radical feminism:

> The attraction of an instrumentalist analysis of power . . . is that it is highly gratifying, in certain ways, to subordinate groups. It allows them to say: "They have done this to *us*; *we* are innocent, *they* are guilty; *they* are evil, *we* must be good!" And in any relation of domination and subordination, there will be a great deal of truth to these charges. . . . But it is a long leap from the claim that a dominant group exerts a tyrannical agency in society to the claim that it exerts sole agency. It is an even longer leap from the claim that one group wields mastery over another in a system of social power, to the claim that group is the master of that system: that it has concocted the idea for it, designed it, executed it, and that it craftily has inculcated the group it oppresses and exploits with appropriately submissive beliefs, tastes, and preoccupations.[12]

Instead, Cocks argues, the real social power that groups may have within a regime does not imply complete freedom of thought and action on their part or complete subjugation of the subordinated. For the discursive and social power over thought and action of both dominator and dominated—in this case, the masculine/feminine—is a relationship of power in which women may be victims but in which they are not childlike innocent victims utterly incapable of complex and ambiguous feelings and desires. To view, as the instrumentalist radical feminists do, men as the "original genius" of the subordination of women, prime movers standing outside and over the society and assigning women roles that pervert the inherent goodness of their nature—this is to cast women precisely in this role. Instead, the roles and powers of both men and women exist within a "particular classificatory and practical order" in which "to the extent that consciousness is mastered, it will be so in the most fundamental sense as a comrade of its dominant counterpart under the same discursive regime, breathing the same ideological atmosphere, which is not to say (in fact, it is to say quite the contrary) that the regime and the atmosphere dictate identical self-images, proclivities, and passions to both parties."[13] Altering the presumption that anyone's thought or action can exist innocently outside of ideas and practices raises the profile of what Cocks calls "a new methodological rule of thumb."

> The initial movement one looks to trace is not from outside the bounds of an order of truth *in* (the sort of movement by which virgin minds are

inculcated with hegemonic ideas), but from inside the bounds of that order, where every mind begins, out.[14]

I don't here suggest that Miller has what Cocks calls an instrumentalist view of power—indeed, she seems to follow Cocks's rule when she describes the women's experiences. It is when she uses the concept *power* to analyze these experiences that she seems to import something akin to it, and with it the image of women waiting to break free of the evil "original genius" of male-power—power as control.

Cocks finds hope in a different place. While some humans clearly are political victims—and perhaps all are existential victims—in her view, onto-logically, we all are subjects. Subordinate and dominant alike, therefore, are capable of reflection on relations of power. The roles and relations of power of men and women—for power is relational—are implicated in one another even as men dominate women.

All cultural formations, whether of oppression or liberation, whether for oppressor or oppressed, discipline thought and action. Power and its disci-plines as abstractions are, therefore, neither innocent nor evil and are omni-present. So too, however, is the possibility of "any individual's making its way out, to some different and perhaps antithetical tendency of thought and action." Rooted in the capacity "for critical reflection and creative transfor-mation," both men and women are capable of breaking "from the dictations of Masculine/feminine." And yet it remains true that

> women rather than men . . . are the less likely (which is not to say they are unlikely) to be captivated by the notions of Masculine Self and feminine Other; who are the more likely (which is not to say they are extremely likely) to view the dominant Self with a jaundiced and cynical eye that does not see in the same way that the conventional eye does, and that on occasion breaks entirely with conventional vision.

Such are possibilities, not likelihoods, and there are countervailing tend-encies, such as becoming "over-exposed to the shocks and agonies that can lead to fatalism and despair but alternatively can trigger a sea-change in re-ceived interpretations."[15]

The Displacement of Interpretation

To assess what the grounds are for hope to break free of depoliticizing roles, let's begin by wedding E. E. Schattschneider's displacement of conflict thesis and C. Wright Mills's ideas on the roles of vocabularies of motive, language, ideology, social structure, and social psychology. Consider a prototypically apathetic person in mass society—for example, a consumerist. People who devote a disproportionate share of their time to consumption do so not simply because of advertising indoctrination or never-ending status panics, but because (aside from trying to gratify pleasures) in society as it is, the role of consumer is the most feasible arena in which to pursue freedom and dignity. In a mass-consumer culture, such pursuit is displaced effectively from the ethical and political and economic arena into one of consumption, due to a series of active resolutions of an inherent tension between thought and action. I think I am free and worthy of dignity; my society encourages me to think so. I act in situations in which my freedom and dignity are actually limited in ways that are opaque to me. I find areas of life where I can act in ways that protect my self-image as a free and dignified person. I interpret this quest in ways that protect this self-image, as well as inform it, in part borrowed from dominant political, economic, and social constructions of reality, but which I tailor to preserve a meaningful life for myself in the situation I am in as I perceive it. In the realm of consumption, I can exercise a degree of freedom unavailable to me in the same degree in politics and work, even though were I to have greater freedom in those realms I might ultimately also have greater real freedom in consumption than I now enjoy.

Political passivity can be produced and reinforced in much starker fashion. For an African-American mother on the very margin of survival, it may have been necessary to thoroughly revise—even during the Civil Rights era— dominant ideas about freedom to protect what little dignity she or her child could realistically hope for in life.

> Once a while back, maybe two years it was, my girl came home and said the teacher made them say that everyone born here in the country of America is born equal and we're all the same. . . . I was preparing their supper and I kept on thinking to myself how I could let my children believe that when that's not the way they're going to live. So, I called my girl over, and the other children too; and I told them that there is the white man and the black man, and the rich man and the poor man, and the sheriff and the rest of us, and there's the ones who have got a say and the ones who don't. That's what I told them, and you know what, I had them repeat it to me out loud, and they did; and I told them they should listen to what they just said, and they'd better keep repeating it to themselves, saying it, until the end of their lives like we all do.[16]

Frank Parkin suggests that the American political order may contain not only a dominant value system, based on aspirations for improvement within a framework of equal opportunity, but a subordinate system as well, which helps some understand their position when the facts of inequality are incomprehensible within the dominant system. The subordinate system is clearly accommodative—"its representation of the class structure and inequality emphasizes various modes of adaptation, rather than either full endorsement of, or opposition to, the *status quo*."[17] Here, "dominant values are not so much rejected or opposed as modified by the subordinate class as a result of their social circumstances and restricted opportunities."[18]

Nancy Fraser suggests that "members of subordinated groups commonly internalize need interpretations that work to their own disadvantage." She believes that dominant interpretations may be "superimposed upon latent or embryonic oppositional interpretations," and that this is "most likely where there persist, however fragmentedly, subculturally transmitted traditions of resistance"—for example, in some areas of the labor movement or among some African-Americans. Under what she calls "special circumstances, hard to specify theoretically, processes of depoliticization are disrupted," allowing political interpretations of what were formerly thought "economic" or "domestic" problems.[19]

I'm not sure that either Parkin's or Fraser's description captures quite enough of the way in which individuals are implicated in sustaining and perhaps even creating roles. People do not modify roles just to help them understand their situation or even to gain advantage, but also to help them *identify themselves* in the world and, unless there is pathology present, preserve and extend their dignity, freedom, and self-worth even as such definitions may be partially in terms of dominant or accommodative or even oppositional ideology. People become *committed* to such roles as ways of resolving conflicts about their identity and of finding meaning in their lives, and *this* is an important independent reason as to why depoliticized roles can be so resilient and so difficult to break free from.

How might interpretive displacements produce political passivity by dividing potential allies, thereby making it difficult for either to maintain enough political support to mobilize over the long run? Take the following hypothetical example of white and black working people, divided in a way that can only partly be explained by racial animosity. Imagine a white blue-collar male worker, who sticks with an unsatisfying job to help him and his family succeed, confronting an unemployed African-American man, whose implicit claim, it seems to the white worker, is that unemployment is caused by structural inequality based on race rather than personal failure, and therefore holding a job has little to do with merit. The white worker may feel this perception demeans the sacrifice he has built his life upon; in fact, it might lead him to question and even demean it himself. As William Connolly argues, "the worker's very possession of a job may appear to be more a matter of luck than of self-discipline and desert."

> The worker is caught in a bind. To repudiate the ideology of sacrifice is to lose the claim to respect available under present circumstances, but to affirm it is to set the worker against the very constituencies with whom he must be allied if significant changes in this undignified life-situation are to be generated. The ideology of sacrifice generates political orientations that

> help to perpetuate the worker's plight while the plight itself generates
> powerful pressures to perpetuate the ideology. Yet this bind itself cannot be
> acknowledged without undermining the identity available to the worker.
> The worker is thus under a double pressure, first, to accept the ideology and,
> secondly, to resist the suggestion that its role in securing his identity
> outstrips its truth value.[20]

As evidence piles up demonstrating that the worker's preoccupation with self-sacrifice may be an unfulfilling way to lead his life, possibly harmful in unintended ways even to those he loves, he may *suppress* these doubts rather than generate wisdom from them. A father who spends his life sacrificing for his son often does so with pure motives, but hidden to him may be the fact that this sacrifice is *his* way of carving out his identity in the world he was born into, and *his* way to protect his dignity and conception of freedom and power within that world. He does do it for his son. The fact he also does it for himself, however, may be obscure to him; and his son's resentment at the sacrifice never asked for (but the subtext for their relationship) may be beyond comprehension. When the son, believing his civics education, champions the struggle against racism and racial inequality, not comprehending how his father's attitudes are really sustained, perhaps blaming his father for being a racist, the father is challenged from the one place he was to be most secure: his home as a haven. What was formerly inexplicable turns to rage, confusion, and despair. This, I believe, was an important dynamic standing behind the so-called "generation gap" made famous in the 1960s.

Caught in binds, unaware of the limits of his ideological predispositions or of structural constraints on his action, the white working father is nevertheless confronted with the task of interpretation. The linchpin of his interpretation is his effort to construct, perhaps simply to locate, his identity in a world that seems to offer a robust market of identities, at least so it seems for others. Not conscious enough of his need for identity, insecure in his adopted identity, he misses how his need to find his place causes him to push away others unlike him; indeed, he constructs others as being more different from him than they may actually be—in fact, more different than dominant ideologies tell him they are.

In order to make sense of all this, he goes through a process of formation (sometimes transformation) and self-affirmation (sometimes abnegation)—a dialectic of ideological reconstruction and interpretive displacement that is always a process of self-constitution: Through his repertoire of ideas, intellectual and analytic skills, nostalgic remembrances, prejudices, and predilections, he rebuilds those formal ideological constructions of reality available to him to fit his life, needs, and passions. At the same time, perhaps gradually, perhaps idea by idea, interpretation by interpretation, political mood by mood, he displaces these formal ideologies and their constituent parts with his own reconstruction.

The fact that he does the reconstructing *adds power* to the new constellation of thoughts, anxieties, frustrations, fears. Defensively and reflexively reconstituted, his outlook doesn't encompass the real position of the son or the unemployed black man, for to do so would be to undermine his own. Because he lacks attractive yet realistic alternatives to ground his identity, his motivation to maintain this outlook is extremely powerful.

What is true of the white is equally true of the black. In a world in which to be good enough often means you must really be much better, in which self-esteem has a history of domination standing against it, in which pure racial hatred does exist, it is difficult to give up any source that can protect his identity. So he may cling to his oppression even in situations where it is not warranted, perhaps miss some opportunities that do exist. But he is caught in an even more terrifying bind. To fully compete with the cards stacked against him is to invite further ridicule. To hold on to the cards he's been dealt is to play an inherently demeaning hand.

On either side, his dignity is under assault, and there is a temptation to throw in the hand in a game he doesn't see he can win. His son, perhaps with more opportunities than he, perhaps having been in Head Start, perhaps benefiting from affirmative action programs, may find his father's accumulating resignation incomprehensible. He may take more for granted, expect more, be less resigned. Perhaps worst of all, his father may appear to him now as part of the problem. Like the employed white, the unemployed black is denied his haven.

Binds That Tie Us

The problems of the men in the above example are personal troubles, but at least some of the sources are political. The white son is angry at his father's racism, not seeing the father's "hidden injuries of class." The black son is angry at his father's passivity, not fully grasping the depth of the injuries of racism to his generation. The white resents the unemployed black, perhaps needing to explain the black man's unemployment as something the other deserves, in order to ward off the fear it might happen to him. The white resents the black son's assertion of power, fitting nicely as it does with his own attitudes about blacks engaging in special pleading. The inability of the black and white workers to form a common agenda is one reason for the atrophy of political vehicles that could mobilize their joint participation. The political indifference each son detects in the father is partly shaped by the political default of organization and leadership. And so on.

But there may be a dynamic hidden to all of them that, if made less opaque, might help heal the breach in these relationships in not only personally beneficial but also politically smart ways. This involves penetrating one's own attitudes about race and class and age. But it also involves exploring the way in which the acceptable range of political practices and ideological predispositions helps us, as active agents, formulate interpretations—indeed, reconstruct, displace, and thereby transform interpretations in ways that still do not serve us well.

There is in America a paradox of identity politics. American political economy and culture, the ideologies both of meritocracy and of equal opportunity, the economics of the market, the history of discrimination, the legitimate need to respond to discrimination by reasserting self-esteem and demanding a way to earn a living, all make it likely that the political goal of equality will be replaced by the priority of ensuring that the members of one's group are well positioned to compete effectively. The ideal of equality and the motivations behind it are themselves reconfigured, partially displacing the original ideal. In this process, *the drive for equality becomes transformed into the quest for difference, which selectively both inhibits and extends fuller equality.*

Programs designed to advance specific disadvantaged groups both solidify group identity *and* congeal outgroup resentment, reinforcing racial and gender attitudes and making broader political alliances difficult. The bind is this. To the degree outlook is limited in this way, we drive away palpable allies and ensure that such programs will never reach the most disadvantaged, including those most economically disadvantaged through race and gender discrimination. To the degree we don't limit our outlook, we embark on a risky strategy that may appear unlikely to bring *any* concrete results at all.

A cycle of depoliticization may be generated. Programs like affirmative action, for example, have sufficient rationality and support to become plausible solutions to problems, but have insufficient support to be a centerpiece of an agenda capable of extending not only participation but true equity. To the degree affirmative action remains limited to ascriptive characteristics, it fosters resentment and fuels the kind of identity politics that divide groups that might otherwise have broad economic and some social interests in common. In doing so, it produces short-term political motivation and, if not placed within the context of an agenda with broader appeal, may actually generate long-term depoliticization. The more divided these groups remain, the less support a program that could unite them will have, the more leaders who intentionally use narrow identity politics to promote themselves will seem rational and wise, the more programs will be portrayed in divisive ways by all sides, and remain at the center of political thrust and resentment. If separated from broader alliance, programs designed to service a disadvantaged group's needs will never have sufficient support to be extensive enough to reach to the group's most disadvantaged. With regard to affirmative action, the achievements can be important but will remain modest, restricted to those in a better position to benefit, while those in most need will have important needs unmet—and this will be true regardless of race or gender.

There will also continue to be a political price to pay. In limiting the reach of programs, one also limits the political support necessary to develop vehicles of mobilization and, once again, the most disadvantaged will participate the least without strong mobilizing efforts. For these reasons, the paradox of identity politics and the interpretive displacements that abet it simultaneously and selectively empower and disempower, generate greater equality for some and make equality for the most unequal perhaps even more remote.

If we want to address the lack of equity for those most harmed by race and gender injustice—for example, the poverty of the "underclass" or the feminization of poverty—we will simply not be able to do so successfully unless the range of people who participate in politics is widened. The range will not be widened unless programs with appeal beyond race and gender is put forward. Such universal programs will also reward society by creating unambiguous commitment to the principles of political and legal equality, and by nourishing depleted civic virtue. Binds that tie us to limiting the scope of political programs, thereby dividing constituencies, need to be understood as proximate causes of long-term depoliticization, especially for our most disadvantaged citizens.

Faces of Power

The three-dimensional formulation by Steven Lukes that we began this work with has been extremely useful in sorting out basic differences in methodological approaches to and political implications of the actual analysis of power, interests, and participation in western societies. In considerations of interpretive displacement, however, this paradigm encounters limits. Recall Lukes argues that, unlike the first and second dimensions of power, respectively represented in behavioralist and reformist conceptions, exercise of the third dimension of power

> can occur in the absence of actual, observable conflict, which may have been successfully averted—though there remains here an implicit reference to potential conflict. This potential, however, may never in fact be actualised. What one may have here is a *latent conflict*, which consists in a contradiction between the interest of those exercising power and the *real interests* of those they exclude. These latter may not express or even be conscious of their interests, but . . . the identification of those interests ultimately always rests on empirically supportable and refutable hypotheses.[21]

Jeffrey Isaac criticizes Lukes's overall conception of power from a "realist" perspective. "An adequate formulation of the concept of power," Isaac writes, "must recognize that the power one agent exercises over another agent in interaction is parasitic upon the powers to act that the agents possess."[22] Lukes's failure to understand this, Isaac charges, is rooted in his view of power as something that is exercised as caused behavioral regularities, rather than as a property that inheres in social structures. Like the behavioralists, Lukes fails to establish adequately a "structural dimension of power." "The primary object of theoretical analysis," Isaac writes, "would not be behavioral regularities, but the enduring social relationships that structure them"; or, as Anthony Giddens suggests about sociology, "the explanation of the properties of structures."[23] It is "these relations, rather than the behaviors that they shape, which are the material causes of interaction."[24]

Students and teachers, for example, are not two types who "happen to engage in interaction. . . . It is the nature of these social identities to be in relation to one another. As such it is their nature to possess certain powers, powers that simply cannot be conceived as contingent regularities."[25]

Contrary to Lukes's expectations, in power relations, there need not even be the potential of conflict between the interests of the power wielder and those of the subordinate. The whole purpose of the teacher's power over the student—reflecting interests of the teacher as well—is to develop the student's powers, an accomplishment clearly in the objective interest of the student. The relation is always, in part, a relation of power.[26] At times, the teacher may do the job most effectively by using a variety of power resources to control, discipline, manipulate, prod, command, impress the student in ways to aid learning. Sometimes, there may be an overt clash between what the teacher wants the student to do and what the student wants to do. Then, if the teacher is doing a good job, there may actually exist a perfect harmony between the real interests of the two, in spite of, in fact as part of, the deployment of power over the student by the teacher, necessitated by their differing (subjective) assessments of (real) interests. Lukes's third dimension of power notwithstanding, the teacher-student relation is but one example of a relation of power not predicated on a conflict between the powers deployed in the interest of the dominator and the real interests of the dominated.

"Realist" critics of Lukes are right, I believe, when they suggest that he underplays the relational aspect of power and seems to focus on power as caused behavioral regularities; concentrates too much on the locution "power over,"[27] and gives little consideration to "power to"; and mistakenly requires there to be a conflict of objective interests for a power relation to obtain.[28]

When Isaac discusses the relational aspects of power as the "material causes of interaction," however, he points to a difficulty within his own account as well as that of Lukes: the problem of agency. His purpose, of course, is to suggest an alternative to Lukes's emphasis on power as contingently caused behavioral regularities, to show that to really understand regularities, we need to understand how power inheres in social structure, relations, and roles. Power, then, is not really as Lukes would have it, A causing B to do something against B's interest, but A and B in a specific type of relationship in which each has certain powers in relation to the other and in which, in this example, A dominates and B is subordinate. The "cause" of B's subordinate behavior is not A's domination; the "material cause" is the structured relation between them.

But if Isaac is arguing that Lukes doesn't succeed in explaining the power relation between A and B—what the concept *power* is and how it is deployed—he also must be questioning whether Lukes can explain why A would choose to exercise power under certain circumstances in certain ways. Does understanding relational power as the "material causes of interaction" solve the problem of agency within Lukes's account or does it reveal one within Isaac's? Perhaps sensing this problem, he writes:

> But the exercise of these powers . . . is contingent, determined by the way particular individuals and groups *choose* to deal with their circumstances. . . . Thus, not only the exercise of power, but also the very existence of relations of power themselves can become objects of contention and struggle. . . . The reproduction of the relationship always involves their agency . . . with both dominant and subordinate groups mobilizing their specific powers and resources. A theory of power must analyze structural relations and the way they are worked out concretely by socially situated human beings.[29]

While this comment is a healthy effort not to endorse an overdetermined view of human action, Isaac's account remains better at understanding structural relations than it does "the way they are worked out concretely by socially situated human beings." It remains unclear what Isaac means—what he can mean within his analysis—by power exercise being contingent on *choice*. In Isaac, as in Lukes, the idea of choice remains, at best, underspecified.

Isaac seems not to have a theory of autonomy so much as a sociological explication of how contradictions within role relationships may work themselves out through human beings as bearers of role assignments that seem (over)determined for them by their structural position. Power in Isaac's account seems structurally overdetermined, in the sense that social "structures" are relationships of power that give various capacities to various classes of agents, are internally related to each other (powers to), and represented in the interests, practices, laws, and ideologies appropriate to sets of roles. If people's behavior with regard to others—their power over them—is parasitic on the powers they possess, where then does the power, capacity, ability to choose, indeed to choose wisely, come from? From the powers people possess by virtue of their position in the social structure.

Isaac also criticizes Lukes for stipulating "ideal democratic circumstances" as a way of discerning the "contingent" aspects of decisions, the arena of autonomous choice, *and* of helping to show how power may unfreely determine choice.[30] But without some conception of what a free person would do, how can we answer a key question of Isaac's own: Whether the kinds of powers that inhere in roles, and the kinds of power others have over us, are enabling or disabling?[31]

Interpretive displacement points back to the individual. It focuses on the nature of the powers subjects do have, locating an arena of choice that, while constrained by others, and by relations of power, is also directed by the individual, who retains and bears responsibility.[32] It shifts the focus from excessive consideration of structural relationships and ideology, to the social ontological quest for identity as an important independent source of *motivation* for thought and action, reason for *commitment* to thoughts had and actions taken, and as a way to more fully understand human practices.[33]

Interpretive displacement uncovers an important paradox within social inquiry: People *qua* subjects have greater power than often is presumed, but this power makes subjugation, when it occurs, all the more formidable. And yet, it holds out hope for greater freedom.

The activity it describes is socially situated but irreducible to social positioning, and seems especially characteristic of the times in which we live, in which both the capacity and the desire for self-consciousness is heightened, indeed, is more required as the self is cut loose from more traditional moorings of life's purposes. It is a kind of power people have (power to create or do), limited but not thoroughly defined by their position (power over others, and power to), and limited but not thoroughly defined by others seeking their own (power to) identity. These others are also sitting in a bath of powers (that both enable and constrain), one stream of which is the power over them some have achieved through their own quest for identity.[34] The very ways in which late modern life, ideas, and social structures motivate, channel, perhaps require such investment in the search for identity may help produce some of the apathy today that seems a normal part of political identity.

 **Chapter 13**

The Second Face of Apathy

Apathy has two faces, one related to unconstrained choices one makes or freely decides not to make, and one related to conditions to which one is subjugated and, at its worst, to a political-psychological condition one may even be said to have. If we can agree that someone actually doesn't care very much about some political issue that we think should be important to that person, and doesn't participate within a range of activities that he or she could participate in, and that we could mutually agree are political, then how are we to know which face of apathy we are looking into? In both cases, apathy refers to a loss or suppression of emotional affect with regard to, a listlessness, a loss of interest in, some issue, set of issues, or perhaps politics itself. Even in the first face of apathy, a person does not choose to become apathetic. Apathy is a relationship of emotion to an object, and however much it may result from other factors that condition decisions, or perhaps even other clear choices, it is not itself a choice. If we decide the motivational state is one of apathy, certain consequences follow.

When we say John didn't vote because he is apathetic, we rule out other explanations for John's nonparticipation, holding him responsible in a particular way. We imply that he has made some estimable choices as to what to concentrate on, or that he is a person of poor character who has allowed his will to wane with regard to important issues, or other reasons for which it is meaningful to say that John bears some responsibility for his motivational state and the behavior it produces, and could do otherwise, at least at some point, if he really wanted to. Indeed, one reason to tell John he is apathetic is to prod him out of his apathy. If it is the case that John is not responsible, ordinary usage needs further clarification or it tends illicitly to blame him. When the John who is apathetic turns out to be one who is a member of a family that has been stuck in a cycle of poverty and educational disadvantage for generations, his apathy is of another order.

The concept of political apathy, therefore, reveals itself to be an exceptionally rich one to use in explanation. In its nature, however, it has features that also lend themselves to ideological distortion, and it therefore presents special conceptual difficulties and requires extra care. Perhaps we can take that care by considering these questions.

First, to what degree do we hold John responsible for the constellation of factors and choices that are implicated in his political apathy? Second, to what degree do we believe John is able to break free of apathy; how pernicious is its hold on him? In global terms, the matrix below captures the key polarities, although usually we are considering a range of emotional states, and responsibility.

A1 and A2 are the most significant polarities. A1 indicates a person who is responsible for his or her apathetic state and capable of breaking free of it. A2 suggests the opposite. It is when A2 may be said to result from political causes that we have political subordination or objective political alienation. It could be the case, however, that A2 is caused by psychological pathology, or family dysfunction, or a host of other factors we would not want to insist were the responsibility of either the political system or the individual, but which resulted nevertheless in pervasive political apathy. I call this political subordination or alienation—nonpolitical, A2NP. It also may be that someone is apathetic due to political subordination but has the personal, familial, or even political supports and resources with which to break free. We have this in A2F. To the degree the apathy persists, we have more warrant to hold the person responsible even though we may believe the indolence was not

The Two Faces of Political Apathy

	1st Face Responsible	2nd Face Not responsible
Able to break free	Free political apathy—personal A1	Free political subordination A2F
Unable to break free	Unfree political apathy—personal A1U	Unfree political subordination or objective political alienation A2 Unfree political subordination or alienation—nonpolitical A2NP

initially his or her fault. Or, as in A1U, a person may be responsible for devolving into a state of apathy, now congealed into such a formidable obstacle that we think the person no longer has the resources to break free; indeed, if it persists, we may wonder whether the person doesn't really belong somewhere in A2.

These distinctions invite remediation of unnecessary apathy. Consider, however, that *activists* sometimes hold otherwise important issues in abeyance, creating emotional distance from them. Aware of such dangers and losses, they may accept these, sensing that trying to care about everything ends in caring about nothing—at once personal collapse and political default. This intuition reflects a deeper, ontological reality. Apathy is internally related to *taking interest* as such: Y's inevitably are excluded by the choices, moods, ideas, and institutions that constitute X's' inclusion. Some apathy, therefore, is best understood simply as *necessary*.

There is no simple way to settle the issues of what motivational state (and causal chain) exists, whether it is really apathy at all, whether it is necessary apathy or not, or whether it is personal apathy or political subordination. It is in this sense that apathy is a "contested concept," one in which broader political disagreements invest themselves. Someone I see as shuffling aside important issues, you may see as being constrained from caring about essential things. Berelson sees apathetic individuals; Mills sees "cheerful robots."

My interest is to focus on those practices and ideas which lead to a narrowing of how the subject conceives politics, and perhaps to an abandonment of politics as a practice itself. I make less strong claims as to whether the subject's conception of what is appropriate is a good one, except in the specific sense of whether it leads to lack of motivation and perhaps eventual inability to engage in political activity as he or she conceives it. Here, my primary interest is whether the subject is meaningfully *politically* engaged, rather than whether the subject is engaged in just the way I believe best. What is considered appropriately political, nevertheless, must remain part of the contestability of the concept *political apathy*, and when and how it should be applied.

The explanation of nonparticipation, of course, is not restricted to these ideas. There is an array of perfectly good concepts beyond these that can be used to develop coherent explanations, including abstention, rejection, contentment, loyalty, consent, depoliticization, and others. All responsible explanations of nonparticipation will account for this array, but may weigh concepts differently, and even find different meanings within the same concepts.

Complex Depoliticization

To explain the breadth and depth of nonparticipation, however, I have suggested we extend in two ways the normal depoliticization thesis of Schattschneider to one of complex depoliticization. First, this new thesis adds the way Lukes's third dimension of power can serve to depoliticize to the second dimension already incorporated in the normal thesis. Second, it suggests that depoliticization may take a more subtle form, perhaps falling within and between Lukes's second and third dimensions. Inquiry here needs to focus on the subject's active role through interpretive reconstruction and displacement in fostering his or her own depoliticization, and assessing the implications of this for strategies to overcome depoliticization. In particular I suggest we consider a *second face of political apathy* as a central form that complex depoliticization takes.

Nonparticipation is viewed here as a serious problem within democracy but not a hopeless one. The problem has roots in American political and economic development and liberal political theory, but the soil it grows in today is a formidable mix of political and economic power sustained by present institutional practices and ideological predispositions. But it is not a closed system of power. The inhabitants are seen ontologically as actively implicated and, in an important sense, as creators of these practices and these predispositions. Empirically, they are seen as having a high potential for self-consciousness and gaining a more thorough understanding of the situation they are in. In terms of the theoretical relation of people to society in late modern life, and the actual relation of Americans to their society, then this thesis, while troubling, still holds a measure of hope. Many people are politically quiescent but they are not merely passive.

Under the second face of apathy I include several distinct ideas. First, derived in its most uncompromising form from Marcuse's work is what I have called *objective political alienation* (to distinguish it from subjective feelings of alienation) and which I have broken down into relative and absolute varieties and subjected to very strict scrutiny and criticism (in chapter 10). *Absolute political alienation* is the abolition of the ability to form political intentions and act in their terms; indeed, the notion of intentionality becomes suspect as one becomes an object within a closed, total, and thoroughly unfree system. *Relative political alienation*, a more tenable idea, is the indefinite suspension of the ability to achieve and sustain political intentions due to the tightly spun web of depoliticizing ideology, language, social psychology, and technological and economic hegemony, which together form a mutually constituting and reinforcing system that for all practical purposes is closed.

Second, from the work of Mills I cobbled together what I consider his more plausible theory of the subordination of politics. *Political subordination* occurs when the political realm is so narrowly constricted that political deliberation and reflection is of little practical use in deciding how one lives in a political community. If political subordination becomes widespread, the idea of political community itself loses coherence. One set of ways in which politics is subordinated occurs when political thought, talk, and activity are narrowly constrained by ideology, imperatives of political economy, gender roles, racial and ethnic expectations, and other sets of beliefs as they develop within the interpretations of the subordinated persons—in ways that disable their efforts to make political sense of their lives. The inability to translate troubles into coherent political issues is a paradigm case.

When I use the term *political subordination*, I fix its meaning to a relation of power and the exercise of power. These fall roughly between Lukes's second and third dimensions of power, at times directly within the third dimension, and serve to narrow politics as a space in which democratic deliberation, imagination, and decision making can occur. However, it is a more subtle manifestation of power than is clear at first glance in Lukes's framework, and to the degree it places itself within his third dimension, it does so somewhat uncomfortably. In order to stretch Lukes's category to capture the kind of subordination of politics I have in mind, I have tried (in chapter 12) to elucidate the ideas of interpretive reconstruction and displacement, the agent's active role in creating the characteristic ways he or she becomes subordinated within a given time and place. The chain I am suggesting is the following: Within the general idea of complex depoliticization, we find the second face of apathy, which itself includes both objective political alienation (relative and absolute) and political subordination. I now want to suggest one particular form of political subordination, and profiles of types of interpretive displacements that help constitute it, that may have some explanatory value.

Political Mortification

A reading of the work of Jürgen Habermas might indicate that the high levels of political apathy that we seem to witness today may reflect part of a broader crisis of modern civilization. Habermas argues that at the present stage of the development of advanced capitalism, economic dislocations may be dealt with by closer and closer "technocratic" and "bureaucratic" intervention by the state. But the society pays twice. First, motivation in the performance of public and private roles, which already had their traditional bases of responsibility and commitment—in community, religion, and family—undermined by the dissolving effect of economic competition, further declines as the state cannot reinvigorate older motivations or come up with satisfactory new ones. Second, the legitimacy of the state declines and further undermines motivation as the state, constrained by the social relations of the political economy it is implicated in, cannot satisfy many of the constituencies to whom it is partly accountable. Yet its legitimacy with these constituencies is also dependent on their *not* fully understanding the real nature of the political economy that undermines the state's ability to serve them. Thus a bind is created. Legitimacy is undermined either by ignorance or by wisdom. As the economy stumbles, however, the state continuously is drawn in, and the norms of the political economy are thereby opened up to scrutiny that becomes more difficult to avoid because the intervention of the state itself makes appear political what were previously thought to be the unpolitical relations of the economic free market.[1]

Technological and bureaucratic roles and language can help obscure this political unveiling and serve to depoliticize, however, and even the repoliticizing tendencies are of a disaffecting kind. The state takes on and shows to be political important functions formerly thought to be economic, does not do a very good job, and therefore both brings economics into politics *and* discourages citizens who do not fully understand the great limits placed especially upon a democratic state in economic affairs from believing politics can solve what are now viewed as political problems. Even the repoliticizing tendencies Habermas points to, therefore, can easily create explicit problems for political motivation. Moreover, the general motivation crisis Habermas identifies also means that one of the roles people are less bound to is that of democratic citizen, further protecting the system from democratic intrusions. And as people briefly repoliticized see the inability of the state to meet its promises, a disillusionment in the possibility of politics itself sets in, opening the way for attacks against any democratic intrusions through government in economic affairs. Taken together, these represent structural pressures for and motivational receptivities to apathy as a response to modern political life.

The sketch Habermas draws has as its contrast model his ideal of democratic politics as that arena in which, unconstrained by illicit relations of power, the "forceless force of the better argument" would prevail. Under present conditions of political and economic life, such becomes increasingly difficult. There seems too much structural power arrayed against democracy.[2]

Would it make matters worse to suggest that the application of power in modern society is also like political death by a thousand cuts—relentless, persistent, minute? Here, the perspective of Michel Foucault has value. Terence Ball explains Foucault's view of power as "disciplinary power," which primarily is the ability to use knowledge generated by medicine, psychiatry, penology, criminology, and social science to create "a society of normalization," and "normal" subjects within that society. Foucault himself writes,

> On the whole, therefore, one can speak of the formation of a disciplinary society . . . an indefinitely generalizable mechanism of "panopticism." Not because the disciplinary modality of power has replaced all the others; but because it has infiltrated the others . . . linking them together, extending them, and, above all, making it possible to bring the effects of power to the most minute and distant elements. It assures an infinitesimal distribution of the power relations.[3]

Foucault's main culprit is the idea of the rational autonomous subject of the Enlightenment.[4] One aim is to study the specific discursive regimes that constitute specific social practices to show how Enlightenment reason and freedom, in reality, create rigid ideas of normality. And then to show how these are guarded by social institutions that serve an analogous monitoring function to that of centrally located guardhouses (panopticons) in specially designed prisons. As Ball puts it:

> This is not, however, a centralized or state-centered regime but consists instead of a highly decentralized array of "local" discursive practices operating in unsuspected and subtle ways in everyday life to produce "normal" subjects and, in so doing, to reproduce itself. This sort of "bio-power" or "micro-power" penetrates and circulates through the very "capillaries" of the social body.[5]

Yet, Foucault asks the question: "in what is given to us as universal, necessary, obligatory, what place is occupied by whatever is singular, contingent, and the product of arbitrary constraints? . . . [The answer] will separate out, from the contingency that has made us what we are, the possibility of no longer being, doing, or thinking what we are, do, or think . . . seeking to give new impetus, as far and wide as possible, to the undefined work of freedom."[6] As Thomas McCarthy explains it, then, the purpose of Foucault's genealogy is " 'practical critique' " motivated by an interest in overcoming or changing "allegedly universal and necessary constraints."[7] Foucault, in "his relentless scrutinizing of the impositions, constraints, and hierarchies that figure in rational practices challenges critical theorists to go further than they have in detranscendentalizing their guiding conceptions of reason, truth, and freedom."[8]

Is there a way to use Habermas to help elucidate how apathy may be generated through structural constraints and problems of motivation and legitimacy, while looking to Foucault for guidance with regard to the development of identity and, in particular, the "normal person"? William Connolly, I believe, engages in such an enterprise.

Connolly argues that the disaffection from the welfare state cannot be explained alone by the crises identified by Habermas, but also must be understood as resulting from a politics of "identity/difference." The first approximation of Connolly's argument might be that under conditions of economic dislocation or austerity, such as in the reindustrialization of the early 1980s and what we might today call postindustrialization and the global market, new disciplines will be needed to allow these economic projects to proceed. But these new disciplines are necessary because fundamental aspects of legitimating ideology—economic growth, and rising standards of living and the promise for a better life and more freedom—now are in tension with one another. Growth today requires sacrifice, which requires self-discipline or external disciplines. And these disciplines will be applied selectively to those less central in today's society. Thus, Connolly argues that to break this cycle we need to loosen our commitment to the religion of endless growth, particularly when growth focuses on production of exclusive rather than inclusive goods, and continuously turns old luxuries into new needs, creating an "imperative of consumption." We need to create more "slack" in the political economy by tempering the growth imperative, and thereby lessen the need for discipline, for normalization. For tightening the economic belt to allow growth ironically produces political support for more growth, which will require sacrifice and disciplines.

> The civilization of productivity—understood as those practices designed to promote economic growth and private affluence because they are thought to be good in themselves and essential preconditions to personal freedom and political democracy—finds itself pressed to subordinate all other ends to the interest of growth.[9]

In the most obvious political sense, these disciplines will narrowly constrict the range of political options that are viewed as reasonable and responsible under the pressure to limit state expenditures for the sake of growth. Further, they put pressure on the society to limit the role of democratic participation itself.

Yet why, Connolly asks, is it that the *welfare* state attracts so much resentment? If people are disaffected with what he calls the "civilization of productivity," but still want to see themselves as free, and if the welfare state is the one institution that is politically accountable and ostensibly capable of steering the economy to meet the promise of the "civilization of productivity," then

> we can construe ourselves to be free as a people only if we can believe that state officials could, if they were more honest or competent, steer the economy more effectively. Indeed, to see ourselves as potentially free, free as a people, we are encouraged to redefine issues and grievances so that they fall within the ambit of legitimate state authority. We then blame the state for unnecessary ineptness within the prevailing order, for that orientation holds out the possibility that new state officials might do the job more effectively and competently.

People, Connolly argues, express "covert disaffection" through declining worker motivation, drug use, divorce, endless litigation, hedonism, fundamentalist religion, child abuse, violent crime, "while our explicit expressions of disaffection are concentrated on the one institution which is formally accountable to the electorate."[10] And as we have seen, this resentment becomes particularly acute among non-wealthy white working men who see the liberal programs of the welfare state demeaning the sacrifice through which they establish their identities. However, today the state itself appears inherently unable to solve problems—not just as a defect of leadership or character—and this may lead to a profound apathy about politics because *it discourages even the displacement of freedom* onto the state.

Now a second approximation. Much democratic theory presumes the idea of reasonable and responsible human agency, which itself presumes the idea of a "normal" citizen. This is its Enlightenment heritage. But normalcy is established, in part, through power, applied as disciplines and codes in schools, prisons, asylums, corporations, factories, in books criticizing political apathy, and so on. That is, democracy itself creates an idea of what an identity should be like, which then seeks to punish "otherness" in some way. Identity then creates difference, but democratic theory does not generally recognize the way modern democracy itself requires and subtly deploys these powers of pushing others away, of defining difference, of creating intolerance.

Moreover, the modern individual is particularly susceptible to being enlisted in a normalizing regime. Even as the development of identity relies upon and spawns forms of difference, powerful urges in the modern self, including the fear of death in what Connolly calls a "post-theist world,"[11] press that self relentlessly to define every difference as otherness in need of therapy or punishment. The modern person's world is seen as a construct of human conventions, heightening the existential questions of meaning in life. The person tries to relieve this pressure first by taking responsibility for the suffering and then by displacing it onto others. First, *we* become the meaning in life. The world is one of human reason. Then we are responsible—are to blame—for our condition. Finally, others are responsible for creating doubt in ourselves about our own identities by being different from us. Yet, in focusing so much on the individual's responsibility, and closely stipulating the criteria, for the modern rational responsible self, we inevitably create a large pool of "others" available as targets for our displaced discontent. Connolly writes,

> The modern normal, responsible individual can redirect resentment against the human condition into the self, first, by treating the rational, self-interested, free, and principled individual as morally responsible for willful deviations from normal identity and, second, by treating that in itself and other selves which falls below the threshold of responsibility as a natural defect in need of conquest or conversion, punishment or love. The modern individual, in short, contains resentment against the human condition in its own identity, and this comes out most clearly in the intensity of the resentment it expresses against any others who deviate significantly from that identity. For such deviations, if they proliferate, make the self-identical self appear to be a sucker for accepting the disciplines and restraints required to maintain itself in this way. Only if these deviations are false or evil can it see itself as true. Resentment against injuries to oneself flowing from the standard of self-responsibility becomes translated into rancor against those whom one construes as escaping the dictates of that standard.[12]

Now let's return to politics. Connolly argues that certain programs such as busing, welfare, affirmative action, criminal parole and rehabilitation, and others "often encounter virulent opposition, indicating that they touch the identities of the opponents even more than their interests."[13] We are now in a position to give the full answer Connolly has in mind as to why the politics of resentment cuts so deeply.

People who are asked to bear the burdens of ameliorative programs resent both the conditions under which they now live and their existential condition as modern people. Take the example of white working-class males. They are already "subjected to a variety of disciplines and burdens that limit their prospects, but liberal programs devised since the 1960s tend to treat them as responsible for their own achievements and failures." The subtext is this: Professional and corporate males have "earned their position." Women and minorities are victims of discrimination and deserve more than their position; "only one group *deserves* to be stuck in the crummy jobs available to fit: white working-class males."[14]

Their identity is under a triple assault. Once, as modern people responsible for their life's meaning. Twice, as working men who failed to do better with the opportunities others (especially liberals) seemed to think they had. Three times, as suckers when others—for example, welfare recipients—seem to escape the disciplines and self-responsibility they couldn't or wouldn't escape.

I want now to suggest contours for an important subtype of the second face of apathy in the late twentieth century in America, which I will call *political mortification*, and place within the more general category of the subordination of politics. *Mortification* is a strong term and I want to fix how I mean to use it.[15] I use a strong term here because I believe that modern society does produce severe anxiety, doubt, shame, feelings of inadequacy, humiliation, insecurity, and other injuries that often result from the emphasis on an isolationist posture with regard to individual responsibility for the self. These injuries are also directly related to the operative philosophy of meritocracy— ideally the equal opportunity to compete in a harshly competitive race. Sometimes the race is clearly not (in the case of women, racial and ethnic minorities, the disabled, gays and lesbians) fair, and this is apparent at least to the fair-minded. Sometimes this is less apparent (in the case of disadvantaged white men). But these injuries result *even when the race is thoroughly fair*. Indeed, "failing" when you have no obvious disadvantages means that *you* are the disadvantage, and if the contest is the primary measure of worth in your society, *you are an abject failure in life*.

I use the term *mortification* here for two reasons. While today it tends to mean humiliation, more so than I intend here, the word also implies a kind of self-injury and, in its more archaic sense, means death of the flesh, its root implying death itself. Thus, political mortification is that subtype of apathy as a condition that is produced through: (1) the quest for identity in posttraditional society; (2) the normalizing pressures one is under and one takes on due to both the imperatives of economic growth and democracy itself as a system with ideals about the normal responsible citizen; (3) how these come together under the intensely competitive ideology of meritocracy; (4) how these come together under conditions of greater global and domestic competition; (5) the doubts these generate about one's ability to engage effectively in politics, the idea of freedom that is then displaced on the state to preserve it as an ideal, and the despair that ensues when the state seems incapable of free action; (6) how the self—in response to these needs, disciplines, pressures, and doubts—disables its own sense of its capacity and right to deliberate and come to political resolution of troubles the self feels.

A bind is generated. As pressures proliferate, the need for disciplines increase, the number of "deviants" becomes more obvious. For those who accept the pressures and bear the disciplines, they can either witness the others avoid what they have failed to avoid, and feel like fools. Or they can intensely resent those who deviate, rigidify their view of them as others not to be valued—indeed, as ones to be disciplined. In the first case, they interpret their troubles as private problems, blame themselves for not solving them privately, and understand their situation in ways that ward off political explanation, and undermine feelings of political efficacy or worth. In the second, they become intolerant of politics, especially democratic politics, and likely push away potential allies, feel their troubles deepen, and watch their political efficacy further erode.

Our search for identity is within the boundaries of a certain historical time and kind of society, and within our place within both. We displace dominant ideologies with ways of thinking that we actively construct within these boundaries and to which, therefore, we become all the more committed. Today these interpretations sometimes injure our capacity to engage effectively in politics. Our disaffection from politics is emblematic of our disbelief that we can change things, but not only because of how the world is, although that is often what we say, but because of doubts we have about ourselves. Then, we push others away from us who are probably more like us than we can afford to acknowledge, close off potential alliances, reinforce the self-fulfilling prophecy of our political self-doubt, and further weaken our capacity and deplete our desire to engage in democratic politics. Already overburdened with our sense of existential responsibility, economic responsibilities, and responsibilities, it seems, for designing and holding onto our identities, we naturally become less willing to take on political responsibilities. Our political sensibilities wither quickly under the assault of these pressures.

We become apathetic. We cling to this posture. It even becomes part of our political identity in a world in which disaffection itself begins to seem normal.[16] But sometimes this apathy is rooted in pain.

Chapter 14

The Empirical Basis of Democratic Reform

Much rigorous empirical work has been done by political scientists on the reasons for nonparticipation in politics and, in particular, on the causes of nonvoting. Often the project consists both of investigations of fact and proposals for reform. We now turn to the work of some fine political scientists to answer the questions: Do the facts of nonparticipation, and particularly of nonvoting, suggest the need for reform? Is there an empirical base upon which to build democratic reform?

Why Americans Don't Vote

In his informative 1992 work, *The Disappearing American Voter*, Ruy Teixeira "empirically" tackles four questions: Why is turnout here so low? Why has it been dropping since 1960? "Do these low and falling rates significantly bias American politics?" What can we do "to increase anemic levels of voter participation?"[1] He concludes that feelings of political disconnection are a primary reason for the precipitous decline in voting since 1960.

Teixeira argues that the low rates of electoral participation in the United States result from the fact that American electoral politics is a high-cost, low-benefit affair.[2] Benefits normally accrue from the structure of electoral competition which in the United States is "turnout inhibiting." Single-member plurality winner-take-all districts at the local, state, and federal legislative level, as well as the electoral college, all ensure that voters in districts or states where their candidate loses see the benefits derived from voting greatly diminished. Structures of electoral competition thus produce "electoral disproportionality," which he defines as "the amount of disparity between the votes cast for a minor party and the number of seats that party receives in the legislature."[3] Turnout is lower in countries with high electoral disproportionality. Turnout is also lower if the structure of political institutions fosters perceived compromise of voters' choices, such as through negotiation typical of bicameral legislatures and coalition governments in multiparty systems.

Finally, the degree of party mobilization—"the extent to which parties have direct links to voters through social groups, community institutions, or organizational networks"—has an important effect on the expressive benefits derived from voting, "through its impact on voters' sense of the meaningfulness of partisan choice." In the United States, party mobilization is low; consequently so are the benefits.

With the exception of multipartyism, cross-national comparisons indicate that "the U.S. system is structured in such a way as to *increase the costs* and *decrease the benefits* of voting."[4] Since 1960, Teixeira finds a drop in voting across all demographic groups, although "somewhat more rapid among those groups least likely to vote in the first place. . . . turnout rate gaps by income, education, occupation, and age have all widened over time."[5]

Teixeira argues that nonvoting "makes relatively little difference to policy outcomes . . . at least in an immediate sense," since policy differences between "voters and nonvoters are simply not large enough to seriously skew the signals sent to policymakers through elections."[6] This claim later turns out to be essential, for it is the foundation upon which he constructs an argument that rejects what he calls "radical" reforms and proposes what I believe are far too modest ones.

After weighing the factors contributing to almost 50 percent of eligible citizens not voting in the 1988 presidential election, he estimates that (1) 5 percent results from "frictional nonvoting," not related to costs or benefits but to the "inevitable scattering of personal problems or idiosyncrasies among the population"—"sickness, accidents, insanity, sudden travel, unusual work schedules, and so forth"; (2) a maximum of 15 percent comes from high costs, especially personal registration; (3) low benefits cause approximately 30 percent, of which the influence of party mobilization contributes 10 percent and the structure of electoral competition also about 10 percent and other low benefits another 10 percent.

He concludes that the "substantial and serious" decline in turnout since 1960, in spite of an easing of costs like voter registration, has been caused largely by decreased "*perceived* benefits of voting" that can "be traced in large part to trends in the individual-level characteristics of citizens": while an increase in education has pushed turnout up, decreases in social connectedness (an electorate that is younger, less married, less church-going) and political connectedness (especially "declining psychological involvement in politics and a declining belief in government responsiveness") have pushed it down, with "the ongoing process of political disconnection appear[ing] to have played by far the largest role."[7]

Reform

Lowering the costs of the present system of personal registration, he says, would have a positive effect on turnout ranging from 4 percent to 15 percent; he estimates likely benefits at around 8 percent.[8] But lowering the costs would increase turnout to a maximum of 65 percent, still leaving the United States "15 points lower than the average among other industrialized democracies." Focus should be placed, therefore, on increasing the benefits by addressing the problem of low voter motivation.

He rejects "the big fix approach" aimed at the "legal structure of voting [except for some voter registration reform], the structure of electoral competition, and the level of party mobilization." He opposes making voting compulsory or providing monetary incentives; or using proportional representation or eliminating the electoral college (both lowering electoral disproportionality); or augmenting the degree of party mobilization "through the development of dense and penetrative party organizations along European lines and much stronger party linkages to social groups and organizations."[9] Despite some empirical evidence that such "big fix approaches" would indeed increase turnout, he rejects them as too sweeping, difficult to implement, and radical, not justified simply by the goal of increasing turnout: "With such radical changes," he suggests, "one runs a real risk of having the cure be worse than the disease."[10] He concludes that "nonvoting . . . is simply not harmful enough by itself to the body politic to justify taking such a substantial risk."[11]

He offers instead the following proposals, one type he calls "top-down" (and somewhat grandly) "structural" reforms, and the other, "bottom-up" "voluntary reforms," both of which he believes can increase "political connectedness" and with it voter motivation by "reforg[ing] the links between Americans and politics": augmenting psychological involvement, sense of responsiveness by government, information about parties and candidates, and citizen duty. "The question now becomes," he argues, "how the political environment can be altered to promote these changes."[12]

The structural reforms Teixeira supports are familiar to us, and take aim at the media and campaign finance practices to lower financial cost and improve content of campaigns. Acknowledging that most democracies do not allow paid political advertisements on television during campaigns, he dismisses this solution as "excessively drastic," "antithetical to the 'more like us' approach" (inconsistent with American political culture), possibly even depressing turnout by eliminating stimuli and information. Instead, he supports legislation structuring political advertising, such as providing free or reduced-rate television time, and the elimination of production materials and promotion of "talking heads" formats for ads. These reforms "over time" "might increase the influence of ordinary citizens (real or perceived) in the electoral process," while they would improve the political system itself, by encouraging "more informative" discourse, discouraging manipulative discourse, tempering the role of money, and allowing greater competition.[13]

To these ends he suggests: (1) "if campaign spending is to be limited," limits should be "flexible and set high enough to ensure adequately competitive campaigns"; (2) "partial public financing should be considered"; (3)

"contribution limits should be cautiously set, so as not to further advantage incumbents and deter grass roots activities" while raising those for individuals and party committees "to counter the influence of personal wealth and special interests"; (4) tax credits should be given to individual small contributors.[14]

Voluntary reforms will make these structural reforms more effective. The media need to focus substantive coverage on positions of both candidates and parties, and show the links between issues, politics, and citizens' lives.[15] Party reforms should work to strengthen the citizen-party connection, including, for example, Larry Sabato's ideas of placing party "ombudsmen" in key constituencies and establishing party mobile offices, rather than ideas trying to strengthen the party itself.[16] Finally, he points to a "Kids Voting" program originated in Arizona, "a substantive, issues-oriented promotion of voting participation [that] should help increase students' psychological involvement in politics as well as their sense of civic duty."[17] Taking into account "the basic system of representation and political culture in the United States," he believes an upper limit of about 70 percent (in presidential elections) may be attainable "under a best-case scenario," leaving "U.S. voter participation below average—though *respectably* below average as opposed to *abysmally* below average where the United States now is."

The Hidden Agenda

Political archeology, a kind of hermeneutic dig into Teixeira's work, reveals sedimented clues as to how the American political system should be reformed to make it more democratic. It also provides a stronger argument for doing so than he acknowledges.

He writes in the very beginning of *The Disappearing American Voter* that the reasons to seek higher turnout are "found in less dramatic but still vital concerns about the type of democracy we wish to have," concerns "rooted in the link between those governing and those governed." This link becomes weakened in two ways by low and declining turnout. First, "the extent to which government truly rests on the consent of the governed is eroded."

> As a result, elected officials may *believe* they do not have sufficient legitimacy to pursue desired policies, and citizens may *believe* that government is not legitimate enough to merit support.

Note here the tension between his claim that government "truly" resting on the "consent of the governed" may become eroded, with the subsequent suggestion that the real threat to legitimacy, and his prior concern, is that the *belief* that government is not based on the consent of the governed could be damaging. Second is "the problem of agenda setting." Political agendas in a democracy "should ideally reflect the needs and interests of the people as a whole." Otherwise some segments of the population may be disadvantaged by these alternatives, even if their specific preferences about them differ little from those of the rest of the population. Low and declining voter turnout may contribute to this problem of an unrepresentative policy agenda because nonvoters and voters do differ from one another in *attributes that reflect individual needs and interests* such as income, even if their *specific policy preferences* generally do not.

In the short run, policy decisions may reflect immediate preferences, "but in the long run the policy agenda may only poorly represent the segments of the population that vote the least."[18]

Teixeira's second point, perhaps the most insightful in his work, and the tension within his first, call into question his argument against stronger reforms. If the political agenda is biased with regard to the objective interests of nonparticipants, as he suggests, contemporary political practices don't seem to be enabling nonparticipants to see the disjuncture between their real interests and the policy alternatives offered. Democratic legitimacy is undermined in a way that goes beyond perceptions and beliefs: long- and short-term needs may not be being met and, more insidious, political practices, including the policy agenda itself, seem to be disabling nonparticipants from accurately discovering these needs and registering them in articulated political preferences. Yet the view that more fundamental change is unnecessary must rest upon the conclusion that not voting does not adversely affect the interests of nonvoters because their interests are similar enough to those who do vote.

There are two methodological problems. Teixeira seems to have a commitment to behavioral methodology that tends to obscure discussion of the long-term interests of nonparticipants as well as felt discontents not yet clearly articulated, or at least to which the survey design is not sensitive enough to alert the interviewer. There is also the presumption that participation per se is not that important to help one come to know one's interests.

At the same time, the economistic rational choice categories he also relies on unreflectively reinforce what seem to be political predispositions. Note this curious claim. He argues that, while eliminating costs like cumbersome registration requirements can be defended on the grounds that "everyone has a right to exercise the franchise without incurring unreasonable and artificially high costs, it is more difficult to argue that everyone has a right to be motivated." This suggestion becomes less self-evident if the rigid distinction between costs and benefits cannot be maintained in the way he tries to; if whether and how one draws such lines, hides a more textured reality or, worse, itself has important political implications.

Costs and benefits are different things and they should be distinguished. If cumbersome voter registration requirements are a cost—that is, their absence does not motivate behavior but their presence constricts it—then it makes perfect sense to say one has a right to have them eliminated, virtually regardless of their impact on politics. If a competitive party system with low electoral disproportionality is a benefit, then it makes perfect sense to suggest one does not have a *right* to have such things. Preventing unfair burdens is one thing. Dishing out entitlements is quite another.

Yet, from another perspective, one should have the right and real opportunity to create and have access to institutions and practices that do in fact motivate participation. This is another way of saying that constructing practices and institutional supports that help one to fulfill aspirations and discover real interests and organize in terms of these interests is the very soul of democracy. Hidden in Teixeira's language of costs and benefits is a theory of rights, which lends legitimacy to the types of reforms he calls for and depletes it from those he opposes. The nature of the *political* debate becomes obscured by these ostensibly social scientific categories.

In the end, Teixeira's analysis is important and his reforms would do some good. But he falls short of being able to explain depoliticization, rejecting those reforms most likely to be able to contend with it. Perhaps sensing these difficulties, Teixeira suggests that "the largest impact . . . on turnout" would come not from his reforms but from a government that develops "real solutions" to problems, "and parties and politicians whose positions on issues are easily identifiable and meaningful to the average voter," both of which he believes unlikely "given the political dynamic that has developed over the last several decades."[19]

Democratic Reform

Contrast now Teixeira's conclusions with those of Frances Fox Piven and Richard Cloward in *Why Americans Don't Vote*. In their view, voter registration procedures, once established, directly blocked people from voting and "eroded voter participation among working people." Political parties stopped trying to win their support through issues, candidates, rhetoric, and strategic appeals, creating a political culture that "reinforced their tendency to abstain," and completed the circle "when the political parties that had been shaped within this constricted electorate then defended the barriers to electoral participation that worked to limit the electorate."[20]

The political world today, therefore, has a decided impact on the *attitudes* of nonvoters:

> Parties . . . do not put forward either the symbols that resonate with the
> culture of the worse off, or the policy options that reflect their life
> circumstances. . . . Political attitudes would inevitably change over time if
> the allegiance of voters from the bottom became the object of partisan

competition, for then politicians would be prodded to identify and articulate the grievances and aspirations of lower-income voters in order to win their support, thus helping to give form and voice to a distinctive class politics.[21]

If Piven and Cloward are right here, Teixeira's protest against the "big fix approach" as too "radical" becomes even less convincing. What can he mean when he says we must weigh the "costs" of reform against the "benefits" of improving the quality of the polity? Costs to whom and to what? What is the cost to democracy to continue, at a minimum, to deny nonparticipants—and participants, I would add—ways to help assess and determine their interests and shape the long-term agenda? While no one wants "political disruption of unknown magnitude," as he fears might come in the wake of proportional representation, for example, a biased political universe does warrant democratic transformation. His own cross-national comparison demonstrates the feasibility of some of the big-fix approaches, showing they already work well in many other democracies today. Proportional-representation expert Douglas Amy supports this conclusion:

> During the last hundred years the worldwide trend in electoral systems has been away from plurality and majority systems and toward proportional representation. With hardly an exception, democratic countries have been replacing these unrepresentative systems with various forms of proportional representation—not vice versa.

Teixeira also presumes that what he claims to be American "political culture" is not a candidate for change in spite of his evidence of disconnection from it. There is certainly nothing wrong with wanting to be "more like us," as he says; indeed, I will later argue that social reforms will not be successful if they are not grounded in American ethics, ideals, and practices and that these are generous enough to ground such changes. Culture, however, is a complex phenomenon, and when applied to politics, it can mislead. Political culture refers to a history of power as well as present consensus, in the form of dominant ideas, institutions, and practices, congealing over time, gaining legitimacy, later looked upon as having the authority to settle previously unsettled questions. But culture as sedimented authority also privileges—in fact, often helps form and nurture—certain construals of human interests over others, certain ways of thinking about the political world, this political agenda as opposed to that. Political culture often refers to those political practices that have gained such broad acceptance, they appear apolitical.

Proportional representation (PR) is not today a significant part of American political culture. As Amy points out, however, "for most of our history the use of single-member districts has been the exception in elections for state legislatures," where multimember at-large districts (although not PR) were most often used. Moreover, the choice of single-member districts over proportional representation has political consequences. For example, if PR existed here, possibly a Green party and a Libertarian party and certainly a Perot party would win seats in the Congress in the next election. From the point of view of these party members, to remain "more like us"—what Teixeira calls political culture—is actually unvarnished political power preventing a more rigorous test than presently of whether their message actually is antithetical to the values of Americans. And as Amy suggests, proportional representation would make legislative bodies more fairly representative by race, ethnicity, and gender, as well as help increase voting turnout, thereby *also* decreasing its class bias. For all these reasons it would advance democratic legitimacy. In fact, he concludes, proportional representation is more consistent than single-member plurality elections with American democratic principles such as "political pluralism, fair elections, and equal representation."[22]

Consider now Teixeira's treatment of political parties. Fully conversant with the voluminous literature detailing how highly mobilized parties both cross-nationally and historically within the United States have tended to produce high voter turnout, he still concludes that such a goal is not a wise one in the American context "because the salience of parties has been generally declining in American society" and "citizens' *affect* toward parties and candidates may have some quite serious limits." Instead of strengthening the parties themselves, therefore, we should enhance citizens' ability to gain information about parties and candidates: "Information, at least, is something U.S. society can supply to its citizens in abundance."[23]

Walter Dean Burnham has constructed an argument against what Sidney Blumenthal has called "the permanent campaign" that is now relevant. Burnham describes the permanent campaign as the substitution of "personalism and a variety of imagistic appeals" for the political party's declining ability to affect voters' "cognitive reactions" through historical memory of party identification, "and long-term collective commitments that permit relatively easy individual calculations of utility at election time." Party coalitions, under such conditions, form separately within the legislative and executive branches of government, leading "to intractable problems of accountability and governability," while electoral choices become fragmented and campaigns personalized, with external political efficacy and party identification in decline. As politics becomes "every person for himself," feelings of disconnection increase as the idea of "collective will" and the electorate both diminish, but selectively:

> Long ago, Maurice Duverger argued, "Parties are always more developed on the Left than on the Right, because they are always more necessary on the Left than on the Right." This perfectly valid remark reflects realities of differentials in power and political consciousness in any class society

between the better-educated, better-off owning classes on the one side and the less-educated, propertyless, and poorer classes on the other.

Moreover, while "the Democrats fall apart" and try to "shift their appeals 'upscale' in the information society's evolving structure of classes and strata," turnout decline since 1960 is among those who voted least even before 1960, "people who, if they had any reason to vote at all, would vote mostly Democratic."[24] From a behavioral perspective, it is unclear how more information, without other substantial reforms directed at providing a context for it, will do other than increase the political disadvantage of being less educated. Moreover, from a social choice perspective,

> If people are left to their own devices in a society with marked inequalities on all relevant dimensions of political consciousness, education, and information, some people will remain far better positioned to make accurate utility calculations than others. As the vast literature on the development of parties attests, it was the whole purpose of party-as-team and party-in-the-electorate to reduce this particular inequality as much as possible through organization, political education and mass mobilization.

In partially dissolving these "linkages," the "permanent-campaign era" ensures that such inequalities will grow "until the situation approximates a political 'state of nature'—a state that it was the entire purpose of party builders to end."[25] Elite electoral power and general political power grow in direct proportion to the territorial reach of the state of nature.

Piven and Cloward's strategy of increasing voting turnout through voter registration reform is explicitly tailored to overcome historic distortions, like these, within American democracy. While the United States ranks twenty-third out of twenty-four nations on voting turnout in national elections when the voting age population is considered, it ranks a much healthier eleventh, at 87 percent turnout, when percentage of *registered* voters is considered.[26] Registering more voters, they believe, would mitigate status differentials between voters and nonvoters. For example, in 1984, 79.1 percent of the most educated voted, while only 42.9 percent of the least educated did; yet 94.4 percent of registrants in the highest educated category voted, while 80.3 percent of the lowest educated did. Where 36 percent separated all potential voters in the highest from the lowest educated categories, only 14 percent separated the highest from the lowest educated registrants. Easing voter registration requirements would increase the number of registrants and voters and relieve class bias and its political consequences in the political agenda, policy choices, and politics.[27] They seem to believe that expanding the range of participation will broaden the debate, improve the chance of winning, turn voting turnout up, as more less financially secure people vote, and more candidates and parties appeal to their concerns. Voter registration reform could congeal into political power capable of defending the reform and the policy changes it brings about. Piven and Cloward's call for public-agency–based voter registration, or indeed automatic voter registration, would certainly be good steps; the recent more limited "motor voter" registration, which they strongly supported, may, in a limited way, help test their thesis.

Burnham traces, as do they, the present problems of disaggregation of the political parties and their weakened ability to serve as democratic political instruments to the 1890–1900 decade. He stresses, however, not rules changes such as personal voter registration, but the inability of the earlier political parties to adapt to the exigencies of full industrialism and large-scale organizations. Stuck with a democratic consciousness and mass organizational structures based on ideas of "middle-class individualist democracy," the parties were unable to provide a collective response to the "functional collectivism" of the society and economy under industrialization, or even to recognize the conflict. The result, he concludes, was "the displacement of democracy, not of industrial capitalism."[28]

Burnham contends that "the systemic forces at work" were probably more important to the general depoliticization of this period than all the rules changes "put together." The changes allowed "a large and possibly dangerous mass electorate" to be managed and controlled "within the political system appropriate to 'capitalist democracy.'" "But," he concludes, "they were not the ultimate causes or origins of the conditions which made possible such a remarkable solution to the problem of adjusting mass politics to the exigencies of industrialism."[29]

Piven and Cloward, of course, agree with much of this emphasis, but "nevertheless think that over time, voter registration arrangements came to carry much of the burden of sustaining a system of limited electoral participation."[30] They argue that as the economy today enters a postindustrial and international phase, as with the rapid changes of the late nineteenth century, the issue will again become "how government will intervene and who will benefit." Two key factors affecting potential political responses will be whether racism will continue to influence the voting choices of white workers, and the degree to which a "new working class" of low-paid service workers, largely women and minorities, can be mobilized to participate electorally. For Piven and Cloward, the goal now is to try to facilitate the participation of new constituencies, force the parties to adapt, create pressure to find new leaders and better programs for them, ultimately reorient "the Democratic party toward the new service proletariat."[31] If reform can activate those becoming less and less active, especially minorities and northern lower-strata whites, a "major electoral convulsion" would be possible, one that could "result in a party system capable of articulating the issues that divide American society."[32]

Burnham also suggests that, unlike among Republicans, there is a "very strong" relation "at the margins" between Democratic voters and "the party of nonvoters." As a result,

> marked social-structure bias in turnout and nonvoting is thus paralleled in politics by a no less striking asymmetry in the mobilizing capacities of the two rival parties. The two are indissolubly linked, appear to arise from the same systemic causes, and are becoming ever more manifest.[33]

Why are the Democrats so susceptible to these changes in turnout and this vicious circle? Burnham's description of the party, I believe, provides part of the answer.

The national Democratic party, he writes, has been a "periphery party" cobbling together various interests through federal programs in Washington. The Republican party, on the other hand, is more representative of the "center of society and political economy." While also reflecting these values, the Democrats represent constituencies that have fought to bring in the federal government to moderate the harshness of industrial development. Thus, while the United States has a "genuine Right" it does not have a "genuine Left," as the Democrats are a party really of the middle that also serves as a less than coherent left—and, indeed, as a less than coherent party. Since the late 1960s, the "glue" of the federal government, which the Democrats used to hold the center and left together, has been dissolving. A "politics of provincialism," therefore, Burnham suggests, has naturally enough re-emerged among Democrats, with "the peripheries that the party largely represents" becoming "dissociated and go[ing] their several ways" in the 1980s.

Suppose, however, registration reforms did expand the party's mass base. What would now replace the lost federal "glue," particularly in the changing global economic climate? Increased voter turnout through mobilization of new constituencies as defined by Piven and Cloward suggest a platform of policy changes still framed from the point of view of the welfare state. More demands upon government to strengthen redistributive social programs, without policy proposals to increase productivity, might deplete capital from the market; create pressure for unemployment, deficit spending, and perhaps inflation; then drain legitimacy from the welfare state proposals, weaken the political position of their adherents, disillusion their supporters, drive turnout down, perhaps even open the political opportunity to reverse the registration reforms themselves.

It is doubtful that cleavages based upon a "service proletariat," and the political ideals and policies it suggests, could or should be the new center of ideational coherency for an alternative, although the workers Piven and Cloward are referring to would certainly be an important constituency for change. Whatever the merit and need for redistribution, to be politically sustainable it needs a larger base of support than its beneficiaries, and needs therefore to be part of a policy program that addresses itself not just to redistributing but also to producing—in fact, to broader quality of life concerns that cross racial, ethnic, religious, gender, and even class lines.

Out of the Political State of Nature

For Burnham, the modern political state of nature *is* the permanent campaign. He agrees with Blumenthal that its ascendancy since the late 1960s is of such importance that it might rightly be described as a critical realignment in American politics, "leading to the current 'sixth electoral era,' " in which there is "the partial displacement of the parties as organizers of politics by the technologies, operatives, and candidates" of "the permanent campaign."[34] In contrast to Teixeira, he argues that "the ultimate key to the problem of mass abstention clearly lies in the broader problem of American electoral politics and its modern party system." Even if new challenges demand collective responses to problems, and even if politicians thereby gain the incentives to lead collective action, solving this problem "would require the elimination or at least the radical transformation" of the "permanent campaign structure" that has developed, "a task of the most awesome magnitude." It is one needed, however, to stop the general "decomposition of the American political regime."[35]

Benjamin Ginsberg and Martin Shefter argue that America is now entering "a *postelectoral era*" as politics goes "by other means" than elections.[36] Even if "political forces" lose elections or don't compete at all, they are "able to exercise considerable power" using "such weapons of institutional combat as congressional investigations, media revelations, judicial proceedings, and alliances with foreign governments." Indeed, the turn to these new weapons may be part of the cause for the decline in parties and in electoral competition. As elections fail to "confer the capacity to govern," and as various interests gain footholds in diverse governmental and extragovernmental political niches, government loses the ability to develop coherent public policy and, they contend, America's position in the world weakens. Ginsberg and Shefter conclude that what is singular about the new means of political combat is their inherently undemocratic quality, inaccessible as they are to most citizens.

To break free of Burnham's "state of nature," then, would also require a recommitment to elections as instruments of democracy, which itself has severe obstacles in its path, including the self-interest of both political parties. Where revelations and investigations have the short-term benefit of driving opponents from office, "expansion of the electorate" jeopardizes Republican domination of the presidency; "whatever the potential benefits" for the Democrats, "an influx of millions of new voters would create serious uncertainties for current officeholders"; some "interests allied with the Democrats" (Ginsberg and Shefter suggest), such as environmentalists, public interest lawyers and antinuclear activists, might lose their influence under heightened mobilization.

> Finally, though it is seldom openly admitted, the truth is that many members of both the liberal and conservative camps are wary of fuller popular participation in American politics. Conservatives fear blacks, and liberals often have disdain for working- and lower-middle-class whites.
>
> As long as these conditions persist, the path of electoral mobilization will not be taken . . . and America will continue to pay the price of its undemocratic politics.[37]

How then can we break out of the political state of nature in all its facets? The virtue of Teixeira's proposals for reforms is that they are achievable; the vice is, they are so because they would be limited in what they could accomplish. Piven and Cloward's reforms have more teeth and should be supported; but even if they could be implemented, it is unclear they could sustain the political burden of hope placed upon them. While persuasive, Burnham's case feels too much like a lament—indeed, is one if America did reach in the 1980s a kind of "end point," as he suggests it might have, in democratic development.[38]

A first step is to view "the permanent campaign" and "politics by other means" as performing a function similar to the rules changes that Piven and Cloward and others have identified as characterizing the system of 1896. Just as those rules changes created favorable political conditions for certain interests in a changing political economy in that time, these political changes too create conditions within which the present restructuring of the American economy may proceed unimpeded by too much democratic interference.

But just reforming the electoral system to break away from what we might call "the system of 1968" in itself will not ultimately succeed, unless it creates and is supported by a new political center of gravity that can offer another, more reasonable direction for American politics, economics, and society. Back in 1970, Burnham addressed this issue saying we may need to construct "instrumentalities of domestic sovereignty to limit individual freedom in the name of collective necessity." But to occur democratically, he argued, such "would require an entirely new structure of parties and of mass behavior, one in which political parties would be instrumentalities of democratic collective purpose." This seemed inconceivable to him "without a pre-existing revolution in social values" that would most likely be "overwhelmed" by "those urban and suburban whites whose values and perceived material interests would be placed in the gravest jeopardy." Given the irrelevance to policy choices of still dominant Lockean ideology and institutions, and under the pressure of severe domestic and international transformation, he feared the middle class would be ripe for an appeal from the extreme right. He asked, "who proposes to make a democratic revolution against a class which constitutes a majority of the population?"[39]

Yet the choice is not, as he implies, properly understood as one between individual freedom and the general welfare. The real liberty of *individuals* also depends on improving the overall quality of life in society; and enhancing life's quality requires doing so in a manner that protects individuals from extensive and overzealous "collective necessity." Are there, then, ideas within American values, ideology, and practices that can politically sustain a pro-gram of democratic renewal—ideas that have a good chance to be embraced because they advance quality of life through a process of enhancing individual political freedoms?

Chapter 15

The Ideas Behind Reform

Much good work has been done in democratic theory with practical implications for democracy. Less work by political scientists has been done explicitly in strategy for democracy, but some sophisticated work here has been done by political journalists. I now examine, in turn, the recent democratic theory of Robert Dahl and Peter Bachrach, and then balance them with the more skeptical and harder-hitting "realism" of E. J. Dionne, and Thomas Byrne Edsall and Mary D. Edsall—perceptive journalists with a keen eye for strategy as well as analysis. I ask: What are the ideas and programs that a strategy for greater participation and democratic reform can be built around? What kinds of strategies flow from what kinds of ideas?

Transitions

By the 1980s, Robert Dahl loosened his commitment to classic pluralism, as he searched for ways to augment popular rule and especially to reduce persistent political inequalities. He works these out in his 1985 book, *A Preface to Economic Democracy*, in a way that breaks his former cast of republican liberalism.

Peter Bachrach makes an analogous journey, but for him it is a move from the plain democratic school of explaining nonparticipation directly into the radical democratic school. Especially in his 1992 *Power and Empowerment* with Aryeh Botwinick, his recent theme, like Dahl's, is of economic democracy. Now coming to what appear to be similar conclusions, these historic adversaries actually recast their creative tension. In so doing, they raise important ideas for a strategy to overcome apathy and nonparticipation.

Economic Democracy

In his 1989 *Democracy and Its Critics*, Dahl again promotes ways to enhance the quality of "polyarchy," here by narrowing the distance between policy elites and citizens.[1] He has for a long time been concerned with the size of polyarchies, the scale of decision making, and political equality,[2] and now concludes that increasing international scale may actually require invigoration of democratic institutions at the national and local level more than the development of new international institutions. As part of a possible future "third democratic transformation," there may develop: change in the total number of polyarchies (based on changing conditions within nations); a change in the scale of political life, especially as important decisions are increasingly influenced by international political and economic pressures, weakening the autonomy of the democratic state; and change in "structures and consciousness" within existing polyarchies:

> A more democratic society might result, for example, from a far greater equalization of political resources and capacities among citizens or from an extension of the democratic process to important institutions previously governed by a nondemocratic process.[3]

It is in his 1985 A *Preface to Economic Democracy*, however, that Dahl gives his most systematic treatment as to how domestic democratization needs to proceed, setting his sight (as he had in a preliminary way in *After the Revolution?*[4]) on corporations. His argument is that more democracy within industry is morally defensible, will not hurt economic efficiency, and will enhance democracy by ensuring greater political equality and more political interest.

Dahl's rhetorical strategy is to engage Alexis de Tocqueville to develop a philosophical justification for a more democratic economy. Understanding the importance of equality for democracy, Dahl writes, Tocqueville asked to what degree is equality detrimental to liberty? Is there a trade-off, then, between democracy and liberty? Dahl answers: If self-governing through democracy is itself a fundamental inalienable right, and if equality of condition is necessary to political equality, which itself is basic to the idea of democratic process, then if there is a conflict it is one "between fundamental liberties people . . . enjoy by virtue of governing themselves through the democratic process, and other liberties of a different kind," such as economic liberty and the right to property. While economic liberties were important then to the independence necessary for free republican government, today they are transmuted illicitly to the political economy of corporate capitalism, allowing "undemocratic governments" to "intrude deeply into the lives of many people."

> Thus a system of government Americans view as intolerable in governing the state has come to be accepted as desirable in governing economic enterprises.[5]

The core to a rational belief in democracy, Dahl claims, is that people in certain "kind[s] of association[s] possess a *right*, an inalienable right to govern themselves by the democratic process." Democratic associations are characterized by seven "assumptions": (1) "a need to reach at least some collective decisions that will be binding on all the members"; (2) an agenda setting, and final decision stage in making decisions that are then binding; (3) "binding collective decisions [that] ought to be made only by persons who are subject to the decisions"; (4) a "weak principle of equality: The good of each person is entitled to equal consideration"; (5) a "principle of liberty" in which each person "in the association is entitled to be the final judge of his or her own interests," with the burden of proof always resting on others to demonstrate exceptions to this principle; (6) a "strong principle of equality: With respect to all matters, all the adult members of the association (the citizens of a government) are roughly equally well qualified to decide which matters do or do not require binding collective decisions"; (7) an "elementary principle of fairness: In general, scarce and valued things should be fairly allocated."[6] In order not to violate these assumptions, five procedural criteria must be met: (1) equal votes; (2) effective participation; (3) enlightened understanding; (4) final control of the agenda by the demos; and (5) inclusiveness.[7] These criteria, Dahl argues, fully specify the democratic process and political equality, and both bureaucratic socialism and corporate capitalism fail to meet their requirements.

Dahl demonstrates that the trade-off between liberty and equality—and by extension, democracy—is problematic, for three reasons. Not only is there more than one kind of liberty, and not only do certain forms of what has been called "economic liberty" undermine genuine political and economic liberty, but the solution to the real modern threat to liberty—economic inequality—is based on a right more fundamental than that of economic liberty. It is based on the right to self-government. "Like a state," he writes, "a firm can also be viewed as a political system in which relations of power exist between governments and the governed. If so, is it not appropriate to insist that the relationship between governors and governed should satisfy the criteria of the democratic process—as we properly insist in the domain of the state?" If it is valid to employ democracy to govern the state, it "must *also* be justified in governing economic enterprises," for such are also political systems "in which relations of power exist between governments and the governed."[8] The real trade-off is between economic inequality (masquerading as economic liberty) and genuine political and economic liberty, equality, and democracy.

Traditional arguments against this view fail, Dahl says, especially because free citizens and free labor (important moral bases, respectively, of liberalism and capitalism) are constrained by the application of power both by states and firms, especially when the firms are powerful modern corporations. It is proper to apply a "strong principle of equality" to corporations even in technological society because it implies only that people have the responsibility to decide how to decide critical issues that will be mutually binding, including when to allow experts to decide. On practical issues, he reports, the experiences of other countries indicate that worker participation in decision making either has no effect on or actually increases efficiency,[9] and capital can be generated in ways other than from private stockholders.

Defending large-scale private property insulated from democratic accountability also fails the more important test of morality. How does even a right to economic liberty translate into a claim to private property, or especially to private control over massive corporations? And even if there is a fundamental right to private property, how can one demonstrate that it is superior to the right to self-government? Dahl concludes: "I am not aware of any reasoned justification for private property and a specification of its scope that would also justify a claim to private ownership of enterprises in existing corporate form."[10]

Even the argument that liberty requires independent resources would "at most" justify economic liberty, not private property or private ownership of economic enterprises, and certainly not private control over corporations. Where it could justify "access to a minimum supply of resources—the minimum required for the exercise of democratic rights, for example—[it could not justify] the right to acquire an indefinitely large supply of resources."[11] Private property, he concludes, is not a right "comparable to the fundamental right to self-government." Consequently, the people "are entitled to decide by means of the democratic process how economic enterprises should be owned and controlled" in order to achieve "democracy, fairness, efficiency, the cultivation of desirable human qualities," and "such minimal personal resources as may be necessary to a good life."[12]

Dahl asks, "What kind of economic order would best achieve the values of democracy, political equality, and liberty . . . ?" One that would "help to generate a distribution of political resources favorable to the goals of voting equality, effective participation, enlightened understanding, and final control of the political agenda by all adults subject to the laws."[13] But it would meet four other goals as well: justice, including "economic fairness"; efficiency; improved virtue and intelligence of the people; and the personal economic resources necessary to facilitate a good life. Boldly he claims,

> We therefore see no convincing reasons why we should not exercise our right to the democratic process in the government of enterprises, just as we have already done in the government of the state. And we intend to exercise that right.[14]

Dahl favors cooperative ownership of self-governing enterprises, which from one perspective "would look something like capitalism; viewed from another, it would look like decentralized socialism."[15] He opts for a model, drawn from European experience, requiring legislatures "to bring a steady transition" including establishing a bank, setting aside "a percentage of revenues, profits, or payrolls," and using income and inheritance taxes to disperse "the residual concentration of wealth." Widely distributed authority and resources, and political and economic stability, could then "provide an appropriate social and economic foundation for a democratic order."[16] He wonders whether Americans, torn between the ideals of democracy, political equality, liberty, and "unrestricted liberty to acquire unlimited wealth,"

> possess the firmness of purpose and the clarity of vision to assert the priority of democracy, political equality, and the political rights necessary to self-government over established property rights, economic inequality, and undemocratic authority within corporate enterprises.[17]

Theoretical Changes

Dahl's recent work is the culmination of a transition that has been developing for years, embedded in which are important methodological and conceptual changes as well. Dahl now incorporates into his view of power the two- and even at times a modified version of the three-dimensional view, loosens his behavioral methodology, and broadens his notion of interests. He also develops broader definitions of what should be considered political, what is democracy, what is the real nature of political inequality, and what we can reasonably expect from people as political actors and citizens. These are a major redrawing of his classic distinction between *homo civicus* and *homo politicus*, and reflect new expectations of how much political participation we should expect and apathy we should tolerate.

There is little doubt, for example, that now A exercises power over B not only when A gets B to do what he or she wants but also when A (corporate capitalists or bureaucratic socialists) enjoys the fruits of his or her power to get B (workers in large organizations) to follow the current rules of the enterprise without A having to do anything, including being aware that A has or is exercising power. Dahl must be accepting that power can operate in the absence of observable decisions, because he is here engaged in trying to bring to awareness those rules and the hidden agenda and why we should change them. Indeed, Dahl advances here an elite theory of power that just as surely would fail the same "test" he had conceived for C. Wright Mills's "power elite" thesis as had, in Dahl's judgment, Mills's theory almost thirty years before.[18]

His concept of interests transmutes accordingly when he suggests that it is "in the final analysis" that citizens determine their own interests, acknowledging that real interests may be different from current preferences. Here is Dahl's theory of false consciousness: The present economic order, which routinely spins out economic and political inequality,

> acquired legitimacy, at least in part, by clothing itself in the recut garments of an outmoded ideology in which private ownership was justified on the ground that a wide diffusion of property would support political equality. As

a consequence, Americans have never asked themselves steadily or in large numbers whether an alternative to corporate capitalism might be more consistent with their commitment to democracy.[19]

By including corporations within the orbit of what should be considered political, and by broadening his view both of what constitutes political inequality and what its "private" sources may be, he expands the scope and depth of political participation that he thinks possible and desirable. Political apathy becomes more problematic and less natural. He also loosens his formal behavioral methodology, for instance, setting up a hypothetical contrast model through which to argue that the actual experience of worker-controlled firms may not be definitive, because most often these have been efforts to rescue financially troubled businesses. Breaking in practice with the logical positivist *cum* behavioral quest to develop neutral operational explications for central political concepts, Dahl now sees "contested concepts" (liberty, for example), implying that his brand of real democracy has trailing along with it a coterie of concepts whose meanings have been drawn closely to match his rendering of it.

Neo-Pluralism

David Held characterizes the views in Dahl's *Preface to Economic Democracy* as "neo-pluralist" and a significant break with his early writings. According to Held,

> In stark contrast to A *Preface to Democratic Theory* (1956), Dahl now concludes . . . that modern "corporate capitalism" tends "to produce inequalities in social and economic resource so great as to bring about severe violations of political equality and hence of the democratic process."[20]

Formerly believed by neo-pluralists like Dahl and Charles Lindblom to be merely economic, these inequalities are now viewed as constraining the "very capacity of governments to act in ways that interest groups may desire." Neo-pluralists see a "system of private investment" and property that "creates objective exigencies that must be met if economic growth and stable development are to be sustained," creating a political agenda that must be at least "biased towards, the development of the system of private enterprise and corporate power."[21]

Contrary to the classical pluralist formulation, Dahl and Lindblom have given up on the idea both that analytically all interest groups can be treated equally and that the government serves as a neutral arbiter in interest group disputes. They remain neo-*pluralists*, Held suggests, however, because they "do not claim to present a settled or complete picture of the forces and relations underpinning contemporary democratic politics."[22] Instead, they con-

tinue to believe that liberal democracy "generates a variety of pressure groups
. . . an ultimately indeterminate array of political possibilities," and "affirm"
the institutions of liberal democracy as "crucial" obstacles "to the development of a monolithic unresponsive state."[23]

Held is right to claim that Dahl has broken with classical pluralism and
the label neo-pluralist seems an apt one. He stretches the point a bit, however, when he seems to suggest that Dahl's analysis is informed by a developed
concept of structural constraints. I take as evidence Dahl's briefly and very
weakly argued discussion of "transitions" to economic democracy in which
self-governing enterprises are somehow legislated without even a hint of the
kind of political strategy that could bring about such momentous changes.

Could the formidable obstacles to his program be overcome? Yes, and
Dahl makes a very persuasive case as to why they should be. Without a deeper
understanding of how political economies cast their net of power, however,
he remains at a disadvantage in designing a strategy to temper constraints
sufficiently in order to gain power within them.[24]

Better Democracy Through Class Struggle?

Peter Bachrach and his co-author, Aryeh Botwinick, in their 1992 book,
Power and Empowerment, also tackle the problem of how the economic system
of corporate capitalism limits political democracy. Their conclusion is that
"class struggle" is necessary today to revivify democracy.

With Botwinick, Bachrach poses an argument that is very close to being
based upon Lukes's third dimension of power, and self-consciously so.[25] He
defines what he now calls "the structural mobilization of bias" as "a set of
structures including norms, beliefs, rituals, institutions, organizations, and
procedures ('rules of the game') that operate systematically to benefit certain
groups and persons at the expense of others."[26] Beginning with his 1982 article "Class Struggle and Democracy," he also revises his earlier views on the
"developmental" value of participation and consequently participatory democracy, and their relation to grievances and class. Following George Kateb,
he now sees that workers' participation "separated from power" may have
merely therapeutic benefits and actually constitute "repressive participation."

> Carole Pateman, for example, does not consider whether participation, in
> its various forms, can elicit recognition of an incongruity *between feelings of
> well-being and a loss of individual autonomy*; a sense of well-being might serve
> to mask the subordinate status of the participant and, in fact, might abet it.
> By participating, the individual may reinforce his or her own repression.[27]

This critique of Pateman, by extension, is also a critique of his own earlier work on the developmental role of participation as such. Now he suggests
participation enhances the ability of the worker to know his or her interests

and increase autonomy *only if* it increases the worker's freedom and power. "Feelings" are no longer, as earlier in his career, the ultimate grounds for judging whether a person is freely pursuing his or her interests. Now he argues that in "relatively nonparticipatory, class-dominated society such as the United States," "genuine" participation by workers exists when their "demands and actions challenge the power structure of the corporation and thus produce the conditions for *raising workers' consciousness*."[28] The social scientist, then, cannot avoid bringing standards to bear that go beyond the thoughts or feelings or grievances of nonparticipants in order to tell when real participation exists, and not its cooptative analog.

Bachrach concluded in his 1982 article that workplace democracy is necessary to revive democracy, and that a kind of "class struggle" is necessary to achieve workplace democracy. Mainstream social science not only doesn't see the democratic vitality of such struggle, however, but usually perceives it "as a threat to the stability, if not the survival, of democracy."[29] "Given the magnitude of the democratic crisis which we now face," he asked social scientists, "does any alternative exist?"[30]

By 1992, Bachrach and Botwinick develop this argument into a full-blown theory about the causes of nonparticipation, as well as political strategy to overcome alienation. They call on workers and their allies "to engage in a class struggle for participatory rights," especially at the workplace; to use workplace democracy as leverage to redraw the terms of political debate, realign the political parties, and challenge the corporate elite for power; and thereby to restore the health of American democracy. Now unambiguously focusing on the third dimension of power, they explain the "strong correlation between socioeconomic status and political participation."

> Since it is largely the lower classes who lack participatory structures to afford them an opportunity to help them determine who they are and what they want, it is not surprising that they primarily constitute the growing nonparticipatory party in American politics.[31]

Where then does political apathy come from?

> It is not only that workers have been manipulated by a cultural hegemony and therefore embrace establishment values. Although this is partly so, their passivity stems primarily from their lack of an alternative philosophy and program that makes sense to them in terms of their actual experience.[32]

Workers are "multi-conscious," Bachrach and Botwinick claim, often holding contradictory dominant values fostering acceptance of their roles in life *and* deviant values formulated, however imperfectly, in class terms. Workers feel powerless to change their lives, however, because their "fractured" value system leaves them without alternatives with which to break out of their complacency and passivity.

Bachrach and Botwinick focus less on resource redistribution[33] and more on an essential political "right to participate in the workplace,"[34] one that is not simply a right with which to protect oneself, but a *participatory* right[35] with which to exercise power, and develop interests *and* motivation for real participation. For them this entails both "stripping the legal veil of the private away from large corporations" in order to make these "autocratically managed institutions" democratic, and limiting "the expansion of the [definition of] public to relatively large corporations," preserving the private sector as "an essential haven for contemplation and experimentation free from governmental interference."[36]

The link between a strategy of participatory rights and the present understanding of working people is democratic *leadership*, and more forthrightness by democratic theorists. No longer willing to dismiss the role of leadership, as earlier participatory theorists too often had done, they require it to be clearly democratic: "close and regular dialogue and interaction between leaders and followers in the choice and formulation of public issues and in the shaping of public policies become the mark of democratic leadership."[37]

They conclude that the "legitimation of working-class struggle as a democratic strategy" is "the only effective means toward achieving a democratic transformation of industry." It also could "generate a transformation of national politics in which class politics become the norm—a politics in which single-issue, fragmented interests are overshadowed by national issues raised by class-oriented parties." James Madison's own class theory of politics led to his solution of "fragmented interest politics and minimum citizen participation," and this solution to the reality of class conflict, they insist, is both "the root of our problem" and an important "clue" to its solution:

> To persist in ignoring Madison's approach—as though the phrase "class struggle" has been bewitched by a Marxian goblin—is to divorce democratic theory from the active concerns of a large proportion of the citizenry.

Like Madison, they favor pluralism. They suggest, however, that "*democratic* pluralism has the best chance to survive and grow if it is grounded in class struggle," one that "activates subordinate groups" by enabling them to organize, create an identity, "and participate politically along class lines."[38] And they give four reasons in support of "class struggle" based on "participatory rights": Mass struggle has worked before; participatory rights can promote efficiency, replacing "rigid hierarchies with [flexible, decentralized] participation by professionals, technicians, and workers"; workers, labor leaders, and professional and technical workers may now listen due to "major anxiety if not trauma" over job insecurity growing ever more acute in the global economy; it can help bridge the gap between "worker and middle-class groups, including environmental, neighborhood, civil rights, and women's organizations."[39]

Democratic theorists who refuse to consider such a strategy, Bachrach and Botwinick argue, fail to see both the class structure of society and class struggle as "a way to revitalize our failing democratic polity, as a way to realign parties along class lines and thus generate expanded citizen participation and public consciousness of issues of national concern."[40] They harshly criticize *A Preface to Economic Democracy*, claiming that "Dahl has not fully exercised his responsibility as a democrat and as a political scientist" because he ignores "the power issue inherent in the implementation of his proposal." He neither deals with the necessity of class struggle to attain his goals nor acknowledges the role it has played in American history in bringing about reforms far more modest than economic democracy.[41] They accuse Dahl and "other like-minded theorists" of coming "up with barren strategies for change," and they pose a paradox that results from such defaults: "As workplace democracy becomes more accepted as an essential democratic goal, it simultaneously becomes more elusive, unattainable, and utopian."[42]

Cultural Hegemony or Political Identity?

Dahl fails to explain how a change in values will come about if practices shaped by system demands in turn encourage values that make sense for the exercise of those practices. Unfortunately, Bachrach and Botwinick's solution also sounds removed. Understanding to a degree not evident in Dahl just what their reforms are up against, they develop a strategy acutely sensitive to the need to gain power while trying to implement it.

Like Dahl's theory, however, their strategy seems utopian. Having argued that self-perception of interests can be limited either by "cultural hegemony" or by the lack of an alternative philosophy that speaks to "experiences," in the practical matter of strategy they partially suppress the second insight—even though in theory they stress it—in favor of the first.[43] Class struggle remains foreign today to the lexicon of all but the most "class conscious" of working people, not simply because of abstract "cultural hegemony," but because, as a direction, it doesn't speak to their experiences or their needs, and *therefore* is inconsistent with the political identities to which they are committed. Some reasons may be that it makes it difficult to distinguish between personal, private, and large-scale corporate property (even though Bachrach and Botwinick themselves clearly do), it seems to want to abolish property itself, it casts a pall of antidemocratic uniformity in which the individual is subsumed in a tangible organic creature over which he or she can have no control, it elicits a vision of history on a path beyond human intervention, and it implies the destruction of people unlucky enough to be immoral enough not to be part of the right class—and so on. There is, then, a kind of "Marxian goblin" properly identified with the way the idea of "class struggle" has been used, and there are good reasons people believing in democracy would be skeptical. On practical grounds, moreover, most workers would not be far off the mark in not believing such a strategy could work. On prudential grounds (and perhaps grounds of pride), most don't want to see the world divided into capitalist against laborer, and they would agree with Bachrach and Botwinick that they want their polity to have a democratic, pluralistic character. These are real concerns that, I believe, are profoundly misunderstood simply as "cultural hegemony."

Yet Bachrach and Botwinick are also right. There is a class character to both the American economy and American politics, and these are intimately related. They are also correct that dominant political culture makes it difficult to talk about issues of social class, and in this specific sense their argument about cultural hegemony is right. And they do insist that "the very idea of class struggle would itself be democratically contestable."[44] Yet they are at once too optimistic and too pessimistic.

People are "multi-conscious," as they suggest, simultaneously holding "deviant" and dominant values, and are not locked into an "ideological monolith." They conclude from this that "militancy and radicalism can be nurtured and developed within the existing hegemonic order." There needs to be "an alternative vision which effectively connects the concrete concerns, needs, and anxieties of working-class people with what they would consider to be their democratic right to share equally, as individuals, in decision making on all levels of the enterprises in which they work."[45]

Subordinate ideologies may exist, however, that are different from dominant so-called "hegemonic" ideology, without either being oppositional or *being translatable* into oppositional points of view. Contemporary cynicism is of that style: "The world is corrupt, the rich get richer, the poor get Medicaid, and I get nothing."

On the other hand, what is it within how people see themselves that—for good reason—should be preserved and even encouraged? One question I think particularly useful is, why do we more often see ourselves as "working people" rather than members of "a working class"? Is it only because we are rampant individualists? Would deconstruction of these terms explain an essential "conflict" Bachrach and Botwinick, from a class-struggle model, believe they find when most workers consider themselves to be "conservative or moderate politically" *and* agree with the statement "America needs a new political party built around the interests of working people"?

A central problem is their notion of cultural hegemony[46] itself, which seems to imply a manipulation of consciousness rather than a dialectic of interpendent power relations, structural roles, and conscious subject identity formation. What kind of work life, what model of progress, what sort of leisure is conceivable in contemporary society? Jobs can be resented *and* seen as necessary to progress. Jobs can be resented as demeaning *and* seen as an essential source of identity and power, among the options in these arenas ever likely to present themselves in a working person's life. In what sense are these complex aspirations, gripes, and choices captured by the notion of cultural hegemony? And so even when Bachrach and Botwinick talk about the experiences of workers, they need to see them less as masses of similarly situated people, and more as individuals who individually arrive at often similar conclusions. Their model of ideational development needs to refocus on the beliefs and experiences of individuals in order to find out how common commitments sometimes form to impede the freedom of common people.

Dilemma of Relevant Theory

The dilemma both Dahl and Bachrach founder on is this: In order for a political theory of social change to be plausible, it must uncover relations of power in society, while at the same time discover within those relations a way toward change. Those who probe deeply tend to understand power relations in a way that makes them seem intractable. Those who probe less, who often appear more practical-minded, or believe themselves to be, tend to lose sight of what they are really up against. Where Dahl doesn't fully suggest how pervasive power is, his call for change is rendered utopian. Where Bachrach and Botwinick somewhat too quickly dismiss the reasons people may not want to pursue their brand of new and "more democratic forms," they at once overdetermine how power relations shape consciousness, and undervalue experiences of people in coming to their conclusions. Dahl's theory of power has not mastered the third dimension. Bachrach and Botwinick overdraw from it, not fully capturing the force of the commitment to the political identities that Americans have not only been socialized into but that they create, adopt, and call their own.

Dahl deserves credit for broadening his analysis and raising fundamental internal questions about the beliefs of Americans, but as he reaches for legitimacy, his depth of analysis slips and his strategy seems naïve. Bachrach deserves credit for challenging democratic theorists and practitioners alike with fundamental questions: Are you willing to do what it takes to achieve democracy? Are you willing to confront the social class character that today limits democratic aspirations? In reaching to analyze political power, his touch slips on the political identity of the Americans he is trying to empower.

In the end, neither fully succeeds, but once again we are in their debt as they ask from each's perspective some of the most important questions that now need asking. The new creative tension between them, and within each of them, helps us all better understand the dilemma democrats face today.

Democratic Realism?

The perfect antidote to the idealism of democratic theorists trying to revive democracy may be the realism of seasoned political journalists trying to do the same.

Washington Post reporter E. J. Dionne argues that Americans "hate politics" because liberal and conservative elites, from the 1960s and 1980s respectively, have captured political dialogue, which no longer addresses the concerns of most Americans. For much of the public, where liberal welfare and racial policies impugned their values of individual responsibility and merit and undermined support for the beneficiaries, conservative economic policy hurt their interests by relieving taxes on the capital and income of the wealthy in the name of tax relief. With all the shouting about the religious right, racial quotas, the death penalty, whether government or private enterprise creates efficiency, and "the meaning of the Vietnam War," real problems were ignored.

Solving real problems faced by the average American would require an "individualism . . . tempered by civic obligation and [recognition] that the preservation of personal liberty is an ineluctably cooperative enterprise," as well as a return to loyalty and service based on personal trust and commitment. He writes,

> Americans hate politics because that trust and commitment have eroded, and with them the ideals of democratic citizenship.[47]

To reverse this trend, Dionne argues, we need to create a "new political center" that speaks to all citizens about "the civic interest," as neoconservative Mark Lilla claims Franklin Roosevelt did; or as liberal Robert Reich suggests, also about the New Deal, "one not of altruism so much as 'enlightened self-interest' in the outcome of . . . ineluctably *social* endeavors." While talking about "citizenship and civic virtue sounds utopian," Dionne claims it to be "the essence of practical politics." "Only by restoring our sense of common citizenship," he writes, "can we hope to deal with the most profound—and practical—issues before us": how to balance rights and responsibilities; how to create a compassionate welfare state that understands personal accountability; "how to pay for the size of government we want; how to restore dialogue and friendship among the races; how to promote strong families while respecting the rights of those who live outside traditional family structures"; how to use government effectively "to restore America's competitiveness."[48]

Just as during the Cold War, the "democratic idea" today needs to recognize "both political *and* social rights," and that progress needs the "the capitalist's insistence on individual initiative and the communitarian's insistence on the broadest possible definition of citizenship and the most inclusive view of the national community."[49] In order to "end America's hatred of politics," Dionne suggests, we need "an organizing idea" that accepts both "the efficiencies of markets and the importance of a vigorous public life." That idea, he believes, is "republicanism," in which "politics is not simply a grubby confrontation of competing interests but an arena in which citizens can learn from each other and discover an 'enlightened self-interest' in common." But a "democratic civic culture" requires an end to the "either/or approaches" to political disagreement; it needs to recognize that "democracy is built on a constant struggle among competing goods, not on an absolute certainty about which goods are paramount." "A nation that hates politics," Dionne concludes, "will not long survive as a democracy."[50]

Dionne is right to try to build on what is best in American culture. The enlightened self-interest he seeks, however, may require more fundamental changes than he yet endorses. He seems to want a kind of liberal glasnost without tackling perestroika, the tougher problem of restructuring.

Thomas Edsall and Mary Edsall share Dionne's view that liberalism has lost touch with its core constituency, and while they also want to see the kind of republic Dionne seeks emerge from the ashes of the New Deal, their analysis has a tougher edge, an even sharper political eye. In their view, the conservative political coalition, particularly at the presidential level, is made possible by the way liberals have dealt with the issues of race, rights, values, and taxes. Like Dionne, they believe liberals must be willing to engage in policy discussions and value debates that they have tried to avoid.

In particular, Democrats "failed to understand the *political* need to couple newly granted rights and preferences with a persuasive and visible message of reciprocal obligation."[51] Policies to achieve equity through racial preference "are claimed as a 'right' by one side and denounced as a fundamental violation of democratic principle by the other," creating profound "conflict that overrides shared interests."[52] Today this is reinforced by "urban racial conflict" and "urban squalor, danger, deviance, and decay" that are "resented and disapproved of" by whites living both in city and suburb, at a time when fully half the population now lives in the twenty largest metropolitan areas.

More clearly than Dionne, Edsall and Edsall argue that the way for Democrats to fight out of this trap is to create a bottom-up coalition, regardless of race, based largely on economic and social positioning that itself is to "an extraordinary degree determined by political power." Yet

> the political power of those on the bottom rungs of the ladder has, for the past two decades, been fractured by the dynamic interaction of race, the rights revolution, the rise of a Democratic middle-class reform elite, and the intensifying battle over taxes.
>
> This fracturing has permitted the moral, social, and economic ascendance of the affluent in a nation with a strong egalitarian tradition,

and has permitted a diminution of economic reward and social regard for those who simply work for a living, black and white.[53]

"The real tragedy" is that liberalism, the past engine of progressive change, "has lost the capacity to mobilize a majority of the electorate" and "liberal values, policies, and allegiances have become the source of bitter conflict between groups that were once mutual beneficiaries of the progressive state." Yet, as public funds become scarce, they warn, "the incentive to assault liberal orthodoxies—many strongly tied to race—will intensify," and with it the potential for intraparty civil war, as those within the party targeted for attack by the right may become more unyielding, even forced into a "bloody competition with each other."

Conservatism will then be free, as it has been in much of this century, to be "the political and philosophical arm of the affluent. Entrusting the economic interests of the poor and of the working class," the Edsalls claim, "to such a philosophy risks serious damage to both groups."[54] As global competition gets more intense, the debate is likely to grow harsher. It will leave "little or no room for traditional liberal Democratic policies sheltering the disadvantaged," as it generates "increasingly brutal pressure on America's economic and political systems, and on policies offering special protection, preference, or subsidy to groups within the population—whether they be ethnic or racial minorities, unskilled workers, prisoners, elected officials, the elderly, the disabled, AIDs victims, or single mothers." At stake are the American social order, our sense of national morality, and

> the American experiment itself, endangered by a rising tide of political cynicism and alienation, and by basic uncertainties as to whether or not we are capable of transmitting a sense of inclusion and shared citizenship across an immense and diverse population—whether or not we can uphold our traditional commitment to the possibilities for justice and equality expressed in our founding documents and embedded in our most valued democratic institutions.[55]

This is what is at risk unless liberals and Democrats—"intellectually fearful, reluctant to engage in the values debate, debilitated by a reformist agenda that has effectively disenfranchised core constituents, driven less by principle than by a desperate need to protect past gains"—are able to build a bottom-up coalition based on economic populism and mutual obligation that cannot as easily be flanked on the right.

Both E. J. Dionne and Thomas and Mary Edsall develop cogent analyses of the strengths and weaknesses of American liberalism, conservatism, and political discourse and practices over the last thirty years. They correctly point to deficiencies in liberal strategies, hypocrisies by elite liberals who want justice so long as they are not inconvenienced, and the way, intentionally or not, costs of reforms were shifted onto others less able to pay for them than their elite liberal champions. They are right that liberals and conservatives have gotten stuck in orthodoxies that do not well serve public debate, the American republic, civility, or democracy, and that this is a reason many have grown to hate politics. The Edsalls are clearer than Dionne in their regard for the social class character of an effective repoliticizing strategy, but it is unclear how the strategy, even if initially politically successful, would be able to correct the social inequity that propels it.

To the extent a bottom-up coalition was united by redistributive proposals, for example, would these not run into the buzz saw of limited public funds the Edsalls themselves describe, and be fatal to its success and ultimately its political sustainability?

Dionne offers a highly principled way to re-establish a political center of gravity for democracy, but his quest also may prove elusive. For quite some time a number of centrist and conservative Democrats have suggested workfare as a way to help build support for a principle of *mutual obligation* within society of the kind Dionne (and the Edsalls) seek. If seriously based upon a principle of mutuality, however, workfare suggests this rule: People who need welfare and who can work should both *have to* and *be able to* earn their place in the safety net.[56]

There are two main possibilities. The far more likely is that some version of workfare will be adopted that cannot fully sustain the rule or, in the case in strictly punitive workfare, that cannot sustain it at all. The other is that a strong version of workfare consistent with it will be adopted, but would generate other problems precisely because of its fresh support and thoroughgoing nature. There is little reason to hope, for example, that work engaged in through workfare would be very productive economically, or that workfare graduates would become much better prepared than before for the increasingly competitive job market and be better able to contribute to future productivity. If these prove true, workfare—available to all who meet the requirements of the rule—will drain capital, actually undermine productivity and employment, and perhaps even increase the need for workfare. Paradoxically, firmly grounded in moral principle, the strong version of workfare might aggravate the welfare problem, cause confusion, and ultimately increase the level of cynicism as to whether such problems have remedies, at all—precisely what we are trying to overcome.

There are more hopeful possibilities. These unintended consequences of workfare might get us to think more deeply about what is interfering with the principle of mutuality. Or simply discussing the problems a plan might create, without implementing one, might encourage us to ask if there are better ways to achieve the principle of mutual obligation, perhaps ways that make the economy at once more productive *and* more equitable.

In the real world, it seems unlikely that policy makers (perhaps quietly aware of some of these possibilities) would support a strong version of the workfare rule. The danger is that a type of workfare will be advanced—legitimated through the principle of mutuality, but unable fully to sustain it—that will further obscure the real obstacles to genuine mutuality, civic motivation and trust, and thereby to democratic politics of better quality.

Invigorating and sustaining a morally coherent political center may require a thorough rethinking of the terms of core issues—workfare is just one example—that currently dominate the political debate. For this achievement, so necessary to the life of democracy, Dahl and Bachrach's views balance those of Dionne and the Edsalls, with realism of another kind.

The Paradox

Dahl, Bachrach, Dionne, and the Edsalls are victims of a paradox. So are we all. If we make proposals that seem acceptable in contemporary political discourse, we tend to miss that they are acceptable because important relations of power, made opaque by that discourse, are not challenged by our proposals. Those who develop strategies seeking to fully uncover those relations tend to make proposals that overfly the real power. They crash especially hard when they overexplain powerlessness, or forget that some power is enabling and some is actually better understood as authority, given legitimacy through the grounded experiences of the society's members.

Dionne especially, but the Edsalls as well, trips on the front side of the paradox, Bachrach on the rear, and Dahl on both sides as he suggests little strategy for his ideas—mainly the security of his convincing proofs that they can be derived from American ideals—rendering them, at once, charming and politically aloof.[57] How, then, can we employ the instinct for realism of Dionne and the Edsalls, the orderly logic of Dahl, and the desire to uncover hidden power—and hunt for empowerment through participation—of Bachrach, to break free of the paradox?

⊟ Conclusion

Real Political Equality

> To a stranger all the domestic controversies of the Americans at first appear to be incomprehensible or puerile, and he is at a loss whether to pity people who take such arrogant trifles in good earnest or to envy that happiness which enables a community to discuss them. But when he comes to study the secret propensities that govern the factions of America, he easily perceives that the greater part of them are more or less connected with one or the other of those two great divisions which always existed in free communities. *The deeper we penetrate into the inmost thought of these parties, the more we perceive that the object of the one is to limit and that of the other to extend the authority of the people.*[1]
>
> —Alexis de Tocqueville, *Democracy in America*, vol. 1

Explanation as Strategic Craft

Explanations of political phenomena imply suggestions of what, if anything, should be done, and suggestions have in their breeding tacit explanations of the object of suggestion. Standing behind both explanation and suggestion are more philosophical notions about what can and should be done in the world as it is and can be. Seeing how theory, explanation, and strategy overlap deepens our self-awareness as political thinkers and actors. Theories have expectations; good explanations are the pillars of theories. All explanations imply political practices and strategies. For explanations to be powerful and theory to help understanding, however, they must imply political practices and strategies that, read historically, can plausibly be said to have had a good chance to make the expectations come true.[2]

Explanations of nonparticipation, therefore, imply an answer to the questions as to whether nonparticipation is a problem requiring remedy, and what kind of remedy is appropriate. Conversely, proposals and even strategies have hidden within them notions of theory and explanation that help render them more or less reasonable guides to solving particular problems—indeed, to identifying particular problems. Theorists and strategists may deny that their work has such implications, in which case they would be wrong; or they can

235

say that the suggestions of theory or practice implied were not the motivation for developing their ideas, in which case they may well be right. In either case, the suggestions remain.

If theory and strategic suggestions together are interwoven in the enterprise of political analysis, why not make both explicit? One could argue, as I have done earlier, that doing so for a social scientist would be the height of self-conscious and responsible inquiry.[3] Here I want to propose a corollary. Doing so allows theories and ostensible practices to put pressure on each other and serve the interest of *social scientific truth* as such. To suggest a theory that is pessimistic (hinting that little is likely to change for the better) without discounting, through reasoned analysis, alternative proposals for change raises questions about the theory or the imagination or both. To develop an optimistic theory without being able to stipulate ways it can come about also puts pressure on the theory's optimistic moments, perhaps revealing weakness in the theory or a failure of imagination of the theorist.

Real Political Equality

After the returns were in, analysts called the 1994 congressional election an "earthquake" in American electoral politics, but said little about the 61.2 *percent* of the electorate that didn't show up. In 1992 we heard reports about how much turnout had increased over the election four years before (the increase was, in fact, about 4 percent). Pundits, however, seemed unaware—or unconcerned—that the year of comparison—1988—had witnessed the *third lowest* turnout in this century; in 1992, the United States remained deep in nineteenth place among the twenty leading industrial democracies. Neither in 1992 nor in 1994 was there *any* discussion of the damage to political equality—perhaps the core ideal of American democracy—of such high rates of nonparticipation.[4]

Consider now the startling conclusions of Steven J. Rosenstone and John Mark Hansen in their 1993 *Mobilization, Participation and Democracy in America:*

> The thirty-year decline of citizen involvement in elections and the more recent decline of citizen involvement in government has yielded a politically engaged class that is not only growing smaller and smaller but also less representative of the American polity. In fact, *the economic inequalities . . . that prevail in the United States today are as large as the racial disparities in political participation that prevailed in the 1950s.* America's leaders today face few incentives to attend to the needs of the disadvantaged.[5]

"Class equality in participation was greatest," they report, "in the high-turnout elections of the 1960s and least in the low-turnout elections of the 1980s." If "increasing the scope of conflict decreases the class bias,"[6] as they say, then lower rates of participation in this century and especially decreases over the last thirty years indicate increased class and educational bias, and suggest pressures exist that foster *reduced* political equality. Today the problem of nonparticipation in politics simply cannot be addressed seriously unless we consider that however much formal and legal political equality may have been achieved, as a practical matter political inequalities may actually be increasing.

Political rights such as the legal enfranchisement of women, African-Americans, and poor whites are clearly established, but inequalities have grown that *diminish* the value and force of the rights. Arguably, all other things being equal, the right to vote of a working-class male in 1960 was of greater value than that today. Arguably, the power of a lower-middle-class black woman would be greater today *if* the class bias in the electoral system were at the same level as it was in 1960.

The question could then become, how can the scope of conflict be widened in order to decrease bias and increase political equality? I want to put it somewhat differently: How can the ideal of *real political equality* be used to widen the scope of conflict, increase political participation, and thereby create political institutions capable of protecting political equality through widened participation?

Raising the problem of real political equality as a central issue and political objective, and object of scholarly inquiry, tests democratic commitments, controls the quality of explanations of nonparticipation and apathy within democratic theory, and allows us to think through our design of democratic practices, to ask properly and answer satisfactorily the other questions of democratic life.

What does real political equality mean? First and most obviously, it is an ideal, it will never fully be attained, there will remain areas of sharp contestation even among its proponents as to what it really should mean. Yet it is an ideal with as strong a base in American lore as any likely to have any influence on the resources of power that shape modern American life.

The principle at the basis of this strategic and moral choice is simple: One person, one person's worth of power within the polity as defined by politically equal persons. Of course, each word is loaded, and coming to practical resolution of what this means will prove exceedingly difficult. Dahl's assumptions concerning and formal criteria for democratic associations discussed in the last chapter are a good place to start to fill out this vision.[7]

Next, specific reforms need to be developed to level the political playing field. In chapter 14, I reviewed a variety of arguments to do so, by Piven and Cloward, Burnham, Teixeira, and Ginsberg and Shefter. Each provides starting points for reform proposals. Throughout, I have argued that we need to fully explore the three dimensions of power identified by Lukes and deepened in the ways we have extended the analysis of power.[8] With regard to issues of political equality, power analysis comes into force in the following way. The first dimension of power is the most obvious, and calls for greater equality of political resources, whether money, television time, access to media, or others. The second is more elusive and focuses most particularly on the ability to set the political agenda, and especially the subtle ways in which issues are kept from arising, making it appear that they don't exist at all. Here of course political resources play a role; but more important is the organizational basis of politics itself. As a constituency broadens its base, it forces the political agenda to adjust to this new base and, as Rosenstone and Hansen show, gives leaders incentives to change mobilizing practices.[9] Without such incentives, they reason, "the pressures that political leaders face to use their own resources most efficiently build a class bias into their efforts to mobilize"; "class differences in mobilization [in America] typically aggravate rather than mitigate the effects of class differences in political resources."[10] To the extent we can achieve greater political equality, then we also give leaders an incentive to change the agenda, which further expands the base and protects political equality.

Finally, in the—most elusive—third dimension of power, we come up against the ways in which social structure and ideas, and how we perceive both, help guide, restrict, and enable our thought and action and our ability to act and see in new ways. Reform here is most difficult. Translating those private troubles that have political sources into public issues is the single best way people, regardless of differences, can escape the limits of their milieu and together create a more just and democratic society. One way to build a sense of grounded identity—indeed, a greater sense of common purpose and identity—that can make good use of the fate of self-consciousness is to give new life to or develop anew a public sphere (or spheres or associations) where democratic discussion and development can take place. But Jürgen Habermas cautions that

> a public sphere that functions politically requires more than the institutional guarantees of the constitutional state; it also needs the supportive spirit of cultural traditions and patterns of socialization, of the political culture, of a populace accustomed to freedom.[11]

It needs what Tocqueville called "habits of the heart." But how do we reinvigorate cultural traditions upon which to base a public sphere if the public sphere is needed to help nurture those traditions? One chance is by beginning with our own belief in political equality—that part of us as a people that is most "accustomed to freedom"—and building democratic renewal around that fundamental American democratic ideal.

Here then are some proposals and priorities for consideration. Each captures one or more of the faces of power identified by Lukes. The list is not original; indeed, some years ago Robert Dahl urged political scientists to "begin a serious and systematic reexamination of the constitutional system much beyond anything done up to now," including several of the recommendations below.[12] These proposals are preliminary. The dual test to apply to them or to additions or substitutes is whether they are likely to enhance political participation and *real* political equality.

1. A national campaign is needed among citizens for *real* political equality. From the point of view of real democracy, especially in the present context of national and international economic and political reorganization, current rates of nonparticipation are at crisis proportions and should become a public issue of the first order. The President and Congress would serve us well by establishing a Commission on Nonvoting to investigate its causes and consequences, and offer recommendations on how America can achieve turnout levels comparable to those in European democracies and our own best nineteenth-century standards, and 70 percent turnout by the year 2000.[13]

2. The American electorate needs to be remobilized and elections need to become *the* way the most important political decisions are made—unless some other way is found with equal potential for popular decision making that meets strong criteria of political equality. In this regard, some of the "big-fix" reforms Teixeira rejects certainly seem worthy of serious consideration—in particular, proportional representation, elimination of the electoral college, and, especially, universal automatic registration of all eligible voters. Why not give substantial minority views a chance to be represented, or ethnic minorities and women to more fairly choose representatives, through proportional representation,[14] unless we are afraid of finding out the nature of our consensus? The "permanent campaign," as Burnham suggests, will have to be ended, as will Ginsberg and Shefter's "politics by other means," so that we will be able to come in from the "political state of nature."[15] Some of the reforms and concerns outlined here will help accomplish this goal.

3. Political parties need to be reinvigorated—unless some other institutions or practices can be developed to replace the aggregating, educational, and mobilizing functions attributed to them. At their best, political parties can offset individual economic and social inequality through the power of organization. Political equality also requires that political campaigns, issues, and messages be more defined with differences more clearly spelled out. Invigorated parties or replacement institutions could help service these needs.[16]

4. Political equality requires that education be considered a *fundamental* right under the Constitution. It is possible that strong congressional legislation can achieve a comparable objective, but this may require either new Supreme Court rulings or a constitutional amendment.[17] The rationale is clear. With the decline of mass institutions of mobilization, especially in a more complex era, individuals have fewer reference points as to where their interests lie, and less hope they will be met. Educational skills become that

much more critical, especially if we are fated to remain individuals in a political "state of nature." Indeed, the correlation between low levels of education and nonvoting is even stronger than that between nonvoting and low socioeconomic status. Finally, as education becomes increasingly necessary even for many entry levels jobs, a poor education becomes an even more formidable obstacle to economic achievement and, therefore, to political resources and political equality.

5. Private wealth must be *eliminated* from politics. A thorough investigation of how this principle is violated needs to be undertaken. We need to adopt either *very* low limits on individual campaign contributions or a fair system of public financing of elections. As long as people can pay for political influence, political equality is impossible. There is no reason why it should have *any* influence on the political process, notwithstanding the 1976 ruling of the Supreme Court in *Buckley v. Valeo* and the beliefs of some civil libertarians, or the possible need for a constitutional amendment. Political action committees should be eliminated; bundling of campaign contributions and other ways even current law is circumvented need to be ended.

6. A principle of fairness for political access is needed, based on the idea that each citizen counts equally—one person, one person's worth of political access. Such a principle should be applied to financing elections, access to media, and perhaps even for financing political organizations themselves, and other politically relevant distribution of resources. It's an old-fashioned idea, but the number of signatures of support that can be gained by volunteers is not a bad model from which to begin.

7. Public issues must become more comprehensible.[18] While the reforms discussed here will help make the political agenda more democratic and the lines of issues more clearly drawn, modern complexity also mandates special focus on clarity. While complexity is often overdrawn to limit feelings of efficacy or to restrict access, modern life *is* more complex, and this issue should be addressed independently. Real complexity, however, makes removing obfuscation and artifice even more critical, because complexity and lack of comprehensibility today have an aura of legitimacy about them. Political equality requires that the public understand, for example, the critically important role and composition of, and selection process for, the Federal Reserve Board and other major national, regional, and local governing institutions set up to be insulated from democratic accountability. Without such knowledge, the public will never know what kinds of *political* decisions are permissible under the present relationship of the government to the economy or be able to make judgments on those parameters. While Teixeira's voluntary media reforms would help, a more comprehensive approach is needed, including the development of more equitable access to the media. Perhaps a new type of professional is also needed, a combination educator-journalist whose job it would be to clarify the policy process and even to help explain why the policy

agenda has been assembled as it has and what the consequences of various choices are.[19]

8. All reforms should have simplicity as one goal, to prevent further discouraging those from participating who begin with the biggest disadvantages. In fact, the present confusing systems of governmental authority need to be simplified, clarified, and made more democratic. The unnecessary complexity of representative government should be simplified, especially the confusing array of office-holders, each with different district lines, often elected in different years. Few know who any of their elected officials are or what they do. Does anyone really believe in this day and age that bicameral legislatures in state governments prevent tyranny? Real political equality implies a far more intelligible political universe than we have today.

9. All important mediating institutions need to be studied for reform, including but not limited to the media, political parties, educational institutions, and interest groups and voluntary associations. Indeed, Tocqueville's model of voluntary associational activity provides a useful frame through which to scrutinize today's group activity. Voluntary associations foster and rely on participation in associational activity, and, as Tocqueville believed, their members could thereby develop a political and social identity through which to counter isolation and achieve understanding.[20] Political equality is impossible without more political coherence than we now have.

10. Political equality in the United States will become more difficult in an era of a more fully global market unless there is greater political equality *in all the nations* with which we trade. To the extent persons in other nations are inhibited from making demands on their society—for example, for working conditions, health-care benefits, environmental protection, equal status for women or ethnic minorities—international economic pressures on our society will increase, becoming a constraint on political equality here.

Democratic Realism

Political equality by itself is an insufficient strategy, for two reasons. First, it is a strong idea, with serious implications for the kind of social and economic as well as political relations we will have in the future. If seriously pursued, it will be taken seriously by those who prefer political oligarchy. Second, ironically, it is unlikely to provide sufficient motivation to draw and hold together a coalition of sufficient strength to support it, not appreciated fully enough by those it would benefit, seeming too abstract, remote, or difficult to achieve. In some sense, it is all these, so it must be tied to a broader strategy and program that requires raising issues that address fundamental political needs, as they now exist, of a majority constituency.

A new American coalition for greater democracy can be formed around programs to minimize political inequality, mitigate economic and social inequality, and address quality of life concerns that affect virtually all. These could begin with the best in American culture, the ideal of free individuals, reach into the best of market economics, the resourcefulness and initiative and right to be rewarded for hard work of that individual, but reject greed, manipulation of needs, and the obsession to produce for the sake of production rather than for that of the consumer's real wants and necessities.

Distributive issues will be important both in their own terms—that is, because and to the extent they are needed for survival and are just—and because those who would benefit most from them also are part of the constituency for greater political equality. These issues, however, as Dionne and the Edsalls both suggest, need to be based primarily on universal principles.

To say this is to open an extremely controversial subject, yet I believe it is one that must be discussed freely in order to achieve significant long-term increases in political participation. The practical goal is to make it more difficult to turn issues of race especially, but also ethnicity and gender, into wedge issues that have prevented and will continue to prevent long-term development of the kind of constituency needed to achieve greater real political equality and greater participation, and therefore greater equity. The moral goal is to include those who have been unfairly passed over in recent redistributive efforts. Programs like affirmative action, for example, can play a useful role in a reconstituted political agenda to extend political participation, but the focus of the agenda must be on universal approaches to disadvantages,[21] which should also include social, educational, and economic inequalities, beyond gender or race or other easily identified ascriptive characteristics.

One way to begin reconciliation of these needs is to recognize the legitimacy of the problems of all groups of people who have faced unfair disadvantages, whatever the ethnic background or gender. To this end, I propose a thought experiment. Why not base some affirmative action programs on an individual's history of economic and educational disadvantages regardless of race, ethnicity, and gender? I believe asking and trying to answer questions like this is always worthwhile; it is likely to reveal quite a lot about our own political disposition, as well as what we believe can be accomplished in American society today should the principle of equal opportunity be taken very seriously.[22] However, what if we answer this question in the negative? Then a strategy that actually will benefit those who most *need and deserve* special programs—that is, the most disadvantaged within disadvantaged classes of persons—will never succeed unless these programs are on the political periphery of a broader program based upon universally applicable principles of fair distribution of opportunities and rights.

A program focused on universal principles has the best chance of redefining the political agenda in ways that may spark new political interest, perhaps stretching our normal ideas about what is appropriate for political contestation itself. It also has the best chance of developing the kind of broad support that could politically sustain important changes.

Here are questions to consider about two programs that have some of the criteria of universality that I believe necessary. First, what happened to the goal of full employment, specifically to the principles of the Full Employment Act that was passed into law in 1946? The answer to this question I think would tell us a lot about our recent history. Are there comparable principles that should be part of the political agenda today?

Second, could government be used to leverage a more democratic form of capitalism—in which workers would gain an enhanced decision-making role in the production process, and firms would receive, in turn, preferential access to capital from such sources as municipal and union pension funds? In *Democracy by Other Means*, John Buell argues that reforms such as these could create the conditions for a "democratic entrepreneurialism" that would appeal to our reform tradition, while also fostering good jobs, better community-business relationships, and greater social equity.[23]

One last question, which I think should be considered in *any* future political agenda, of the right, left, or middle—just for reasons of decency: What do we believe our attitude as a society should be to those people simply unable to compete effectively regardless of race or gender or other disadvantage—who have, in other words, the extra burden of failing in what for them at least was a thoroughly fair race?

Exclusively distributional programs themselves, however, are also problematic on practical and moral grounds. Practically, it is questionable that a strategy to increase democratic participation can be built solely on this basis. Morally, there are other issues of legitimate political concern, issues such as crime, the environment, quality of life, and civility itself.[24] These issues too have very important distributive justice aspects to them but, at the same time, they also have an impact on everyone, and go right to the fabric of what it means for members of a society to live together—indeed, what it means to have a society. People who place them higher than straight distributive issues on their agenda have a perfect right to have them included.

I do not here try to stipulate fully all issues. I don't know what they all are—though finding out is an important area of inquiry for democratic theory, as well as strategic practice for democracy today. One enlightening aspect of democratizing America would be to watch unforeseen issues be raised by people who were thought to be apathetic.

In order to develop strategies for democratic renewal, we will first need to break the lockjaw of the second face of apathy, and the lockstep in the march of political resentment of the last thirty-five years. A *program that focuses on real political equality, universal programs of social equity, fair distribution, real liberty for all individuals, and general quality of life is practically and morally necessary to achieve such an end.* Without such a program, issues that will keep the political agenda too restricted will prosper, and interpretations of political identity will proliferate that displace those capable of bringing the party of nonvoters back into the political arena.

The New Ideology of Apathy

In a recent issue of *Foreign Affairs,* Peter F. Drucker writes that what the United States needs

> is a deliberate and active—indeed, aggressive—policy that gives the demands, opportunities and dynamics of the external economy priority over domestic policy demands and problems. . . . will a *proposed domestic move* advance American competitiveness and participation in the world economy? The answer to this question *determines* what are the right domestic economic policy and business decisions. The lessons of the last 40 years teach us that integration is the only basis for an international trade policy that can work, the only way to rapidly revive a domestic economy in turbulence and chronic recession.[25]

Drucker here is developing a rationale strikingly similar to the one given by Huntington in the early 1980s, calling for modulating the demands of democracy in order to maintain American economic standing, protect American citizens, and ultimately preserve American democracy itself. Except now the political and military threats of Communism are replaced by the demands of the global market.

Like Huntington's, Drucker's rationale can slip into a justification for depoliticization. In his desire to integrate us effectively as a national unit in the new internationalism, for our own sakes, he proposes an austere course for many Americans, in effect asking them not to press political demands, asking us not to listen if they do. One question that remains unresolved is what kinds of disciplines, what kinds of legitimations will bind Americans to such depoliticization.

Drucker seems to fall back on the elite technocratic rationale familiar to us from Huntington's work, which still founders on the truth of Huntington's intuition that elite technocracy provides thin grounding for rationalizing depoliticization.[26] Stronger legitimacy requires a more subtle strategy, one cognizant of a more complex human subject than presumed—for example, by Herbert Marcuse's strong one-dimensionality thesis—and role models more binding than technocratic ones provide.[27]

Huntington's guide is still the most plausible starting point: Encourage abstract belief in democracy; carefully modulate democratic ideals in cadence with acceptable reality; actually adhere to technocratic roles now increasingly prescribed by the global market. Democracy will still be cut with distilled republican liberalism, thin technocracy, a generous splash of tolerance for old-fashioned political apathy. Only now the new ideology of apathy will increasingly underscore potent global free market values, and the need to obey private economic decision makers and, sometimes, the nation-state as the best hope against chaos in the dangerous, too quickly becoming post–new-world-order world, its advocates eating their nationalism and internationalism cakes and having them too. Leave the state and market leaders alone to protect us in the new world. Support them when they explain that experts have decided what is most efficient and productive in the international marketplace of technology, goods, and services. But oppose the state when what they will call "special interests" gain footholds there and try to interfere in the global economy. Don't let groups use the state (don't *you* use the state) for narrow interests. Don't use the one major political arena to engage in politics, in order words, except to oppose someone else who is trying to do so.

There is one other fresh ingredient. Today, the idea and not just the fact of political alienation will contribute to further depoliticization. Popular talk reflects increased feelings of cynicism, alienation, and indifference. Ruy Teixeira's analysis of political disconnection supports this assessment. Yet, explanations of nonparticipation that focus on subjective alienation without successfully locating structural, ideational, and practical sources actually can engender complacency toward it, a kind of analytic resignation to leave well enough alone. Or provide the underpinnings for minimalist strategies for change that will disappoint, reinforcing the feelings of disconnection and leaving the world as unintelligible as before. The message becomes, "It's all too complex in the complex new world circumstances. Reforms really don't do much good. A political life as morally demanding as democracy can't work in the real world. My withdrawal from politics is in part my fault, I really should care, but my fault is realistically grounded—it probably wouldn't do much good if I did." Political apathy now rooted in feelings of alienation becomes a realistic attitude of mature democrats.

All of these point to the future importance of issues of political participation and political apathy, and how we understand these. For as politics becomes more confusing, the ideology of the market more ambitious, the role of the state more ambiguous, the contours of its zone of operation more difficult to discern, the "enemy" less obvious to behold, both more political space for genuinely new ideas *and* new constraints on politics arise. And with all of these, a new problem. The ability of the political economy—and the sociocultural world it reflects, elicits, and enlists—to remain apolitical under the new circumstances may require even greater political passivity from those who are not being well served, whether materially or morally. The problem facing elites wishing to restrict participation in democracies will remain what it always has been. Political legitimacy is based on the principle of political equality. Through the vote and other forms of participation, in principle, political affairs can be altered by public decision in a way impermissible in civil society. Yet the public will have new reasons to intervene in economic, social, and political affairs, and perhaps develop, especially with the death of Communism, new ways of thinking about democratic intervention. But it may now be even more necessary than before for major private institutions and for government to act unimpeded by democracy.

The public will itself be bravely adrift in a confusing world of ideas, claims, facts, counterclaims, some innovative technocratic notions, older philosophical ideas about a free market, and the sheer weight of what seems like endless information, new facts, and reports of experts about the environment, national and ethnic rivalries, new enemies now to replace departed Communism, and more crime down the street—a world that seems increasingly immune to democratic or, perhaps, any other kind of control. Politically immobilizing uncertainty.

As we have seen, for years political scientists have been casting visions on the role of political participation in democracy, while compiling evidence about how democracy works in the real world. So much evidence, in fact, some decided they had to save the ideal from itself, reshape it, make it modern. Wittingly or not, some used undemocratic modern circumstances as modern democracy's new mold. They explained nonparticipation in ways that allowed the political priority of depoliticization to proceed with little challenge from students of democracy. Expect little from the people. Encourage them to expect little from democracy.

Beating the plowshare of democracy into a sword of political apathy, they severed the democratic wish from its root—popular rule. They sliced democratic aspirations in half. They invented *demi-democracy*.

In describing the kind of people who seem not to want to participate in politics, and explaining why they don't, theorists of the future also will ineluctably create a vision of the political landscape and what role American citizens should have in determining its contours. To the extent they articulate their views successfully, these become ways the American public comes to understand the new political world it inhabits, the new international context, the confusion of ideas and facts, and where—as citizens—they fit in.

Theories of social science become files of political ideas that help set future political agendas for good or ill, for fuller democracy or further depoliticization. Political scientists are already politically implicated. The successful ones become politically engaged.

Epilogue

A Time for Democracy

Americans are a democratic people in undemocratic circumstances.[1] But undemocratic circumstances should be unacceptable to a democratic people otherwise willing to defend their rights. Such circumstances should also be unacceptable to theorists of democracy. Yet as Americans, as democratic theorists, and each as a democratic thinker, we accept them too easily. Maybe following some professional students of politics, we have limited our democratic aspirations, quietly tailored them to the world. But that world does not seem more stable, and tempering our ideals has not allowed practical solutions to emerge. Modern reality still bites, it seems, ever more deeply into our core ideals.

Today our expectations of ourselves as democratic citizens and our explanations of why we act as we do should be as important as at any time in our history. Consider the dramatic interfacing of political, economic, and social change American democrats face today.

International Communism is extinct but the United States is engaged in a new world of increasing competition and less-clear order. The needs of Americans for social well-being, of some for survival, are increasing, but so are financial strains on government as the private sector scrambles to isolate, accumulate, and invest capital. Domestic push to reindustrialize—indeed, postindustrialize—continues, enhancing profitability, laying off workers, trimming benefits, reorganizing jobs and their rewards, driven hard by intense international competition. The standard of living has not risen in a quarter century. Quality of life is down, that's what many people say.[2]

Economic reordering increases the need to protect position, compete effectively, understand the new circumstances. But it inhibits government's ability to find the resources to help meet these challenges or coherently to explain the disarray. And so today we ask what unites us as a nation, what keeps the state our representative, what ties American corporations to us—as President Bush might say, what is our mission? We are not sure what we can do for our nation. We wonder what our nation-state really can do for us.

Americans vote in record low numbers. American political parties less and less aggregate interests or imagine the public interest. They appear engaged in prolonged contests of gamesmanship, jockeying for political advantage, currying public favor, ignoring the public's real needs. The media focus on dissolution and corruption, not their sources. We often listen to sermons, but rarely can we set our moral compass by the star of good works.

Today as much as at any time in history, Americans need to understand the *common* political, economic, and social forces that guide, and quietly establish boundaries for daily life. But organizations they inhabit and depend on, and leaders they no longer believe they can count on, seem poised to miscue on the break of political change.

But there is change. The advance of democracy in the Eastern Bloc nations *has* altered world history, and can help change *our* history, taking the bit out of the mouth of democracy here at home. We have lived for so long fearing that every assertion of popular rights might be—or be portrayed as—a covert operation run from some foreign shore, based on some foreign idea. With the passing of murderers and tyrants like Joseph Stalin and Leonid Brezhnev, totalitarianism should no longer be available to be portrayed as if it were the only contrast model to elite domination of our own society. The death of Communism could also kill the Red straw man—and open politics in unpredictable new ways.

Instead of democratic fulfillment,[3] however, we find this turning point leads in a direction very different from the one we expected. At just that time that we could subject critical issues of policy to real democratic deliberation and resolution, the ground under us has shifted—again. Now a "new" force sweeps aside our democratic aspirations, as the global economy becomes freer and more competitive, and constrains the ability of the nation-state to respond to its own people. Global marketeers, trading in capital, resources, products and services, in their ideological and practical thrust to make more efficient the international division of labor, insist: "International trade is an issue of market economics, not democratic politics." By reasserting the old market idea of just exchange, now to obscure transnational relations of power, they spray a new coat of private authority on their powers over the public. They hide them from the democratic eye. They *re*-depoliticize them. *This* is the new world order for which we are being asked—again—to sacrifice democratic fulfillment.

Yet, in liberal political theory and American public philosophy, the nation-state is the premiere locus of politics. If, in order to support reindustrialization, postindustrialization, and globalization of the economy, the government reorders past commitments it has made, in order to favor more clearly special interests over the public's welfare, and even over the nation's stability, the political terms of elite dominance may still become clear. Elected officials do have power and will not entirely escape a democratic settling of accounts. To the extent the public extracts meaning from the confusion, defies the uncertainty, engages in discussion, tries out new ideas, asks which relations of power are properly seen as political, renders transparent through hindsight power relations opaque to democratic foresight—participation may again becomes central to the making of history.

Re-politicization then may allow us to ask some critical questions for a fuller democracy, too often neglected in today's discourse: Which arenas beside government, what vehicles different from parties and interest groups, and which forums, other than the one-way communication characteristic of mass media, should be the sites—through which we define the substance—of this new politics of participation? What should be appropriately considered political and subject to democratic contestation and discussion, and which are the areas of life in modern communities that should resolutely be kept—and which should become—private?

Effective participation to revivify democracy, however, will not be easy to come by. In the emerging economy, meritocratic success and educational status will become ever more important to life chances,[4] politically weakening those who work with their hands, while splitting them apart from more educated allies. Differences between races, ethnicities, genders, sexual preferences make less likely mutual understanding and support for those troubles that may actually have common sources, make more likely future cycles of depoliticization. And increasingly the races are divided in beliefs about the sources of current problems and the role of government in their proper solution.[5]

Tensions between people with differences, however, also increase because the short-run market in distinctive identities is bloated. The question— "What is the difference between important identity differences and different styles of creating identities in market culture?"—too often goes unasked. Given the demands on self-worth, under the pressures of extreme competition, there is a tendency to over-define identity, exaggerate differences, push away palpable allies, define positioning in a way that isolates political position. The more insistent you become that the system fails you only because of *who* you are, the more the constitutional irony deepens, for your implicit claim is that if only the system of government, laws, economic institutions, and society treated you as it did those who succeed, you too would succeed. You may be right, but you endorse the competitive scramble if you question *only* the unfair race.

If the modernity of Enlightenment is at endgame, requiring of us more realistic understandings of rationality and progress—and of the modern notion that future human goodness is built primarily upon them—so much the better. Democracy, at its best, is well suited to easing these pains of late modern realism, and maybe, as well, of healing the wounds of life together in a pluralist society. At its best it asks individuals and groups to engage in a kind of therapy—in the way the Greeks meant it, clarification of the self, or in the way C. Wright Mills did, locating the political sources of private troubles.

Perhaps it is well suited for fallible humans because it asks—sometimes forces—us to deal with imperfections of our own and others, including our need to exclude. Maybe it can open hidden closets, allowing practical expression to that stored rage—and those shelved hopes—appropriate to politics. Political grace of this sort, however, is very special, and rare in human history. Its best chance is through democratic fulfillment—and this requires *real* political equality.

There is another side to democracy, of course, in which it doesn't give so much as take, asking everyone to be responsible, which is another way of saying impose more disciplines on the self. It too creates identities and "others"; even the ideal of participation suggests a vision of the "normal" person, the right kind of social order, the wrong type of people. Therefore, while democracy can offer opportunities to reveal, and through revelation to heal, it also intrudes, forcing illicit entry into private chambers. In this way democracy also becomes a form of discipline we impose on others[6] and on ourselves.

Fuller democracy will have two valences, then, allowing greater expression, greater release, more satisfaction, better protection of self-interest, while demanding more social responsibility, more self-discipline. Today the self is already micro-managed by modern public and private institutions, and supervises itself closely in the marketplace of self-worth. People need relief. If there is a decline of leisure, however, this relief is denied in the one place it should be safe[7]—especially if some forms of "leisure" have become still another kind of discipline. If unsublimated aggression rises in the late modern era, as dislocations add up and frustrations mount, renewed democratic opportunities and responsibilities will be under pressure to produce a more satisfying life, ultimately freer from impositions. Or they can add to the anger, and burn democracy out from within.

Democracy is hard work. We will enjoy and defend it more, labor harder at it, and work better through it, if it becomes more of a craft—a craft whose limits we know—one that is its own reward but that also produces *useful* things.

Here is where responsible inquiry faces a future challenge. For democracy to become a craft we need the techniques of success, in the form of sound explanations of nonparticipation, and smart strategies to invigorate democracy, and the self-confidence that they bring. But something more is needed: a strong, yet temperate, faith in the democratic idea. Whether we demonstrate that faith—over the years—will become critical evidence testing just how sound and smart our explanations and strategies were. Right now, however, there is an early test, because first we have to choose.

How much do we really believe democracy can work today? Do we value it enough—do we have the desire and the will—to see it through to fulfillment? As American democrats, how much do we really want to see democracy below the socioeconomic borders of the middle classes, and beyond our geographic borders—past Europe and Japan—into parts of the world where more democracy may mean the release of suppressed desires?[8]

In the long run, increasing democratic participation may require structural changes that go beyond the proposals offered here, for there is an inherent depoliticizing tendency when overwhelming public or private power is arrayed against even the best efforts of citizens to cast their votes or to participate in other ways. My own prior commitment is to democracy itself, however, and the explanation and strategic suggestions I have proposed presume both that we are capable of beginning the process of choosing, and clarifying what we want, *and* that in the beginning, as well as in the end, it is up to us to choose to engage in that greater democratic debate.

Once we have chosen, democracy in America becomes the first political issue. How can we become *full* participants, so that we can best ask, and fairly and smartly resolve, all the other questions that need answering today? Which is where this work began.

Democracy is a process, a goal, a way of life. It is a challenge and a commitment. It is a challenge many Americans took up, believed in, an ideal they suffered in war to defend. Conservative scholars are right to remind us that the founders set up a republic, not a democracy. They are wrong to say, today, that alone is good enough. Democracy is a commitment we never fully made. It's time.

Notes

Introduction

1. Bernard R. Berelson, Paul F. Lazarsfeld, and William N. McPhee, *Voting: A Study of Opinion Formation in a Presidential Campaign* (Chicago: Univ. of Chicago Press, 1954), 314.
2. Samuel P. Huntington, "The United States," in *The Crisis of Democracy*, ed. Michel J. Crozier, Samuel P. Huntington, and Joji Watanuki (New York: NYU Press, 1975), 114.
3. George Will, "In Defense of Nonvoting," *Newsweek* (October 10, 1983):96.
4. Charles Krauthammer, "In Praise of Low Voter Turnout," *Time* (May 21, 1990):88.
5. Ibid.
6. Thomas R. Dye and Harmon Zeigler, *The Irony of Democracy: An Uncommon Introduction to American Politics*, 9th ed. (Belmont, Calif.: Wadsworth, 1993), 2.
7. Ibid., 407–408, 410–411.
8. Everett Carll Ladd, *The American Polity*, 5th ed. (New York: W. W. Norton, 1993), 386. See also Ladd's *Where Have All the Voters Gone*, 2nd ed. (New York: W. W. Norton, 1982).
9. Ladd, *American Polity*, 375.
10. Ibid., 382.
11. Ibid., 386.
12. Sidney Verba and Gary R. Orren, *Equality in America: The View from the Top* (Cambridge, Mass.: Harvard Univ. Press, 1985), 9.
13. Kevin Phillips, *The Politics of Rich and Poor: Wealth and the American Electorate in the Reagan Aftermath* (New York: Random House, 1990), 8–23.
14. Verba and Orren, *Equality in America*, 9–17.
15. Ruy A. Teixeira, *The Disappearing American Voter* (Washington, D.C.: Brookings Institute, 1992), 7–9.
16. M. Margaret Conway reports that while people between thirty and sixty-five vote at higher rates than others, when other social characteristics are controlled for, "voter turnout increases with age"; from *Political Participation in the United States*, 2nd ed. (Washington, D.C.: CQ Press, 1991), 17.
17. Teixeira, *Disappearing American Voter*, 62, 66, 70.
18. Indeed, Bobo and Gilliam suggest this is a change from the late 1950s into the 1960s, when blacks actually "were more active than whites at any given level of

socioeconomic status"; from Lawrence Bobo and Franklin D. Gilliam Jr., "Race, Sociopolitial Participation, and Black Empowerment," *American Political Science Review*, 84 (June 1990): 387–388; Conway, *Political Participation*, 30.

19. Norman R. Luttbeg and Michael M. Gant, *American Electoral Behavior 1952–1992*, 2nd ed. (Itasca, Ill.: F. E. Peacock Publishers, Inc., 1995) 112–113; Conway, *Political Participation*, 31–35.

20. Frances Fox Piven and Richard A. Cloward, *Why Americans Don't Vote* (New York: Pantheon, 1989), 119. My emphasis.

21. Bobo and Gilliam, "Race, Sociopolitical Participation," 380–381.

22. Steven J. Rosenstone and John Mark Hansen report that "blacks and women encounter an 'ascriptive barrier' to communication with predominantly white, male, public officials," psychologically doubting white male politicians will be sympathetic. "African-Americans are less likely to be central to the electoral coalitions of white politicians, and office holders are therefore less likely to mobilize them to express their opinons"; from *Mobilization, Participation, and Democracy in America* (New York: Macmillan, 1993), 75–79. Conway reports, "[i]ncreases in all forms of political participation among women can be expected," with changes in educational level, employment, role expectations, and attitudes (theirs and the publics); from *Political Participation*, 35.

23. Teixeira, *Disappearing American Voter*, 3–4.

24. Philip Green, "A Review Essay of Robert A. Dahl, *Democracy and Its Critics*," *Social Theory and Practice* 16 (Summer 1990): 217, 235, 234.

25. W. B. Gallie, "Essentially Contested Concepts," in *Proceedings of the Aristotelian Society*, 56 (London, 1955–1956), reprinted in *The Importance of Language*, ed. Max Black (Englewood Cliffs, N.J.: Prentice-Hall, 1962), 121–146.

26. William E. Connolly, *The Terms of Political Discourse*, 3rd ed. (Princeton, N.J.: Princeton Univ. Press, 1993), 200.

27. Steven Lukes, *Power: A Radical View* (London: Macmillan, 1974), 15.

28. Ibid., 20.

29. Ibid., 24–25.

30. See, for example, Jeffrey Isaac, "Beyond the Three Faces of Power: A Realist Critique"; Terence Ball, "New Faces of Power"; and Nancy Harstock, "Gender and Sexuality: Masculinity, Violence, and Domination," in *Rethinking Power*, ed. Thomas E. Wartenberg (Albany, N.Y.: SUNY Press, 1992). Isaac and Ball discuss Lukes, whom I analyze further in chapter 12.

Chapter 1

1. David Held, *Models of Democracy* (Stanford, Calif.: Stanford Univ. Press, 1987), 41–42. In this chapter, I draw heavily on Held's excellent account of the liberal and republican traditions.

2. Ibid., 54.

3. Anthony Arblaster, *Democracy* (Minneapolis: Minnesota Univ. Press), 23, 22.

4. M. I. Finley, *Democracy, Ancient and Modern*, 2nd ed. (New Brunswick, N.J.: Rutgers Univ. Press, 1988), 13.

5. See Bruce Johansen, *The Forgotten Founders: How the American Indians Helped Shape Democracy*. (Boston: Harvard Common Press, 1987). For assessments of

views that some African tribes had practices that included democratic elements, see Walter O. Oyugi et al., eds., *Democratic Theory and Practice in Africa* (Portsmouth, N.H.: Heinemann, 1988).

6. Arblaster, *Democracy*, 43. Arblaster suggests: "Plato can reasonably be thought of as the most radically and implacably antidemocratic of all political philosophers," and that Aristophanes "mocked popular rule and its leaders time and time again." See 16, 20–21.

7. C. B. Macpherson, *The Real World of Democracy* (New York: Oxford Univ. Press, 1972), 1–2.

8. For a discussion of how a "science of virtue" affected the founding, see Russell Hanson, *The Democratic Imagination in America: Conversations with Our Past* (Princeton, N.J.: Princeton Univ. Press, 1985), 72–75. I am indebted to Hanson in chapters 1, 2, and 3 in this volume for his fine analysis of American ideological and political development.

9. Hanson suggests that the emphasis of Madison and the Federalists on design did not mean they abandoned "virtue as the foundation of republican politics," talking "both as if virtue were to be restored, and as if it were to be replaced by a more reliable basis for understanding human action." Both Federalists and Antifederalists were skeptical about people's virtue, but following Machiavelli's move away from the virtues of "the prince," "the Federalists were more confident than their opponents that virtue could be incorporated as a *systemic* feature of republican politics"; from *Democratic Imagination*, 71–72.

10. Indeed, Madison was a very strong civil libertarian trying and failing to broaden First Amendment protection against encroachments by the national government on free speech and press, and also failing at getting an additional amendment directly applicable to the states.

11. James Madison, *Federalist* No. 10, in *The Federalist Papers*, ed. Isaac Kramnick (London, Eng.: Penguin, 1987), 123–127. Hanson argues that Adair "demonstrates that Madison borrowed this argument on the extended republic from Hume, who believed that Montesquieu's arguments were much more applicable to the founding of an extended republic than to its preservation. Madison, of course, turned this on its head and made the extended republic the bulwark of preservation for republican politics" (Hanson, *Democratic Imagination*, 68, note 15). See Douglass Adair, " 'That Politics May be Reduced to a Science': David Hume, James Madison and the Tenth Federalist," *Huntington Library Quarterly* 20 (August 1957): 343–360.

12. Madison, *Federalist* No. 51, 322.

13. Madison, *Federalist* No. 10, 125.

14. Quoted in Held, *Models of Democracy*, 57, from *The Spirit of Laws*.

15. Quoted in Arblaster, *Democracy*, 40.

16. Madison, *Federalist* No. 51, 321.

17. Ibid., 318–320.

18. Richard Henry Lee, "Letter from the Federal Farmer," in *The Case Against the Constitution: From the Antifederalists to the Present*, ed. John F. Manley and Kenneth M. Dolbeare (Armonk, N.Y.: M. E. Sharpe, 1987), 94.

19. Quoted in Hanson, *Democratic Imagination*, 66, 67. See *The Antifederalists*, ed. Cecelia Kenyon (Indianapolis: Bobbs-Merrill, 1966).

20. Quoted in Hanson, *Democratic Imagination*, 69–70. See Kenyon, *The Antifederalists*.
21. Lee, "Letter from the Federal Farmer," 97. My emphasis.
22. Quoted in *The Federalist Papers*, ed. Kramnick, 63; from J. Q. Adams, *Life in a New England Town 1787–1788* (Boston, 1903), 46.
23. Herbert J. Storing, *What the Anti-Federalists Were For*, ed. Murray Dry (Chicago: Univ. of Chicago Press, 1981).
24. Madison, *Federalist* No. 10, 128.
25. For a discussion in this point, see Kenneth M. Dolbeare and Linda Medcalf, "The Dark Side of the Constitution" in *The Case Against the Constitution*, ed. John F. Manley and Kenneth M. Dolbeare (Armonk, N.Y.: M. E. Sharpe, 1987).
26. Hanson, *Democratic Imagination*, 88.
27. Ibid., 76.
28. Ibid.

Chapter 2

1. James Madison, *Federalist* No. 10, in *The Federalist Papers*, ed. Isaac Kramnick (London, Eng.: Penguin, 1987), 124.
2. Ibid., 128.
3. Ibid., 126.
4. Quoted in John F. Manley, "Class and Pluralism in America," in *The Case Against the Constitution: From the Antifederalists to the Present*, ed. John F. Manley and Kenneth M. Dolbeare (Armonk, N.Y.: M. E. Sharpe, 1987), 111.
5. "Abigail Adams to John Adams," in Kenneth M. Dolbeare, *American Political Thought*, 2nd ed. (Chatham, N.Y.: Chatham House, 1989), 81.
6. Ibid., 81–82.
7. Robert N. Bellah, Richard Madsen, William M. Sullivan, Ann Swidler, and Steven M. Tipton, *The Good Society* (New York: Random House, 1992), 99.
8. Tocqueville actually feared concentration of power more in the states than in the federal government.
9. Alexis de Tocqueville, *Democracy in America*, vol. 2, ed. J. P. Mayer and Max Lerner (New York:, Harper & Row, 1966), 666–667. See Robert Dahl, *A Preface to Economic Democracy* (Berkeley: Univ. of Calif. Press, 1985), ch. 1.
10. Dahl, *Preface to Economic Democracy*, 44–51.
11. On this point, see Seymour Martin Lipset, *Political Man* (Baltimore: Johns Hopkins Univ. Press, 1981), 7–8.
12. Quoted in Robert N. Bellah, Richard Madsen, William M. Sullivan, Ann Swidler, and Steven M. Tipton, *Habits of the Heart* (New York: Harper & Row, 1985), 36–38.
13. William Graham Sumner, *What Social Classes Owe to Each Other* (New York: Harper Brothers, 1884); excerpt in Dolbeare, *American Political Thought*, 353.
14. Quoted in Dolbeare, *American Political Thought*, 354.
15. Louis Hartz, *The Liberal Tradition in America* (New York: Harcourt, Brace & World, 1955), ch. 6.
16. E. E. Schattschneider, *The Semi-Sovereign People* (New York: Holt, Rinehart and Winston, 1960), 35.

Chapter 3

1. See Madison, *Federalist* No. 42, in *The Federalist Papers*, ed. Isaac Kramnick (London, Eng.: Penguin, 1987), 273–279.
2. David O'Brien, *Constitutional Law and Politics: Struggles for Power and Government Accountability*, 2nd ed. (New York: W. W. Norton, 1991), 444.
3. Alexander Hamilton, *Federalist* No. 78, in *The Federalist Papers*, 436–442.
4. Two formative "liberty of contract" cases were *Allgeyer v. Louisiana* (1897) and, of course, *Lochner v. New York* (1905). The Court weakened the Fourteenth Amendment's equal protection clause not only in the famous *Plessy v. Ferguson* case of 1896, declaring segregation constitutional under the "separate but equal" doctrine, but also in the 1883 Civil Rights Cases, declaring the Fourteenth Amendment not to be applicable to discrimination in public accommodations by private parties. (In the 1873 Slaughterhouse Cases—unrelated to race—it had already emasculated the privileges and immunities clause, although in this pre-*Lochner* era case it did so within its rationale to allow state protection of public health against claims of ownership. Justice Bradley's dissent in this case prefigures the Court's subsequent "liberty of contract" doctrine.)

    Thus we have a tragic irony in American constitutional history. At the very time the Court was strengthening the protection of private property through the "liberty of contract" interpretation of the due process clause, it was weakening litigants' ability to use any part of the Fourteenth Amendment to prevent racial mistreatment. However, the Court was hardly alone in this post-Reconstruction era in contributing to the transition not from slavery to equality, but from slavery to Jim Crow apartheid.

    See note 5 below for a discussion of the Court's complex attitude toward how free enterprise should develop in an emerging corporate economy.
5. I describe here only the overall long-term trend of the Court's involvement on one specific issue constellation—liberty of contract. My purpose here is only to provide a quick sketch. A fuller analysis of the role of the Court, other institutions of government, private and public actors, and political ideologies and legal doctrines might begin with the following.

    Although in 1895 in *United States v. E. C. Knight Company* the Court clearly narrowed the scope of the commerce clause with its view that production (distinguishing it from distribution) did not constitute commerce, Martin Sklar argues the Court's attitude toward the federal role in commerce, and toward the economy, is more complicated than this alone indicates. From 1897 until 1911 the Court understood the Sherman Anti-Trust Act to outlaw all restraints of trade, not just unreasonable restrictions of competition as was the case under the common law, and under the Court's reading of the Sherman Anti-Trust Act from its passage in 1890 until 1897. This effectively expanded what constituted illegal commercial activity. So while the Court was developing the "liberty of contract" doctrine, and simultaneously restricting what would count as interstate or foreign commerce, it was also making it plain that within what did count as interstate trade only the federal government, and not private parties (such as corporations) would be allowed to regulate. In effect it determined during a volatile period that, under the Sherman Act, only Congress could regulate and that Congress's regulatory choice was to allow unfettered competition. Sklar believes this reading of "restraint of trade" was an opening to use the federal regulatory power granted by Congress under the Sherman Act far more aggressively than any of the presidents, including "trust-buster" Theodore Roosevelt, chose to.

More important, Sklar claims: "The Sherman Act as construed by the Court took regulatory authority out of the market, where one-dollar-one-vote ruled, and placed it in the political arena, where (theoretically) one-person-one-vote ruled." By 1914, the result of this intensely political struggle was to depoliticize the market, both through new legislation (the Federal Trade Commission Act of 1914), and reassertion by the Court (in its 1911 *Standard Oil* decision promulgating the Rule of Reason) of the less restrictive common law meaning of restraint of trade. Where the earlier Court's very restrictive view was more sympathetic to the older style of entrepreneurial free enterprise, allowing only government regulation, now private actors subject to judicial review were able to take primary roles in regulating the market, while the executive and legislative powers of the federal government were relegated a secondary role. This important shift indicates that the Court was ambivalent as to where it stood between aging entrepreneurial free enterprise, and the emerging corporate form and its need for greater private regulation of the market.

The Rule of Reason decision and the FTC Act, Sklar concludes, adapted "the legal order to corporate capitalism [and] was an integral phase of the corporate reconstruction of American capitalism in general. It stands as a signal achievement of the Progressive Era." And it served the "pro-corporate" goal of getting the trust question out of politics. Sklar emphasizes, however, that "neither in its realization nor in its form was the adaptation a foregone conclusion. It was an outcome of political contention stretching over twenty-five years (and beyond), a contention that saw the rise of significant populist and socialist-party politics, the temporary splitting apart of both major parties (the Democrats in the 1890s, the Republicans in 1910–1914), and more lasting political realignments. It was, finally, an outcome of a great social movement for corporate capitalism that rejected a statist for a liberal form." For a very insightful account of the Populist and Progressive eras, and the relation of law to politics and economics, see Martin J. Sklar, *The Corporate Reconstruction of American Capitalism, 1890–1916: The Market, the Law and Politics* (Cambridge, Eng.: Cambridge Univ. Press, 1988). See especially 166–175.

6. This era has been commented upon by many scholars as indicated below, but is far from alone in importance. As note 5 suggests, another is the Progressive era that shortly follows it, as Martin Sklar's work cited there shows. Undoubtedly these eras are best understood as on a continuum.

7. Ruy A. Teixeira, *The Disappearing American Voter* (Washington, D.C.: Brookings Institute, 1992), 8–9.

8. E. E. Schattschneider, *The Semi-Sovereign People* (New York: Holt, Rinehart and Winston, 1960), 67–72.

9. Ibid., 4–6.

10. Kevin Phillips, *The Politics of Rich and Poor: Wealth and the American Electorate in the Reagan Aftermath* (New York: Random House, 1990), 56–58.

11. Quoted in Frances Fox Piven and Richard A. Cloward, *Why Americans Don't Vote* (New York: Pantheon, 1989), 28.
12. Schattschneider, *Semi-Sovereign People*, 79.
13. Piven and Cloward, *Why Americans Don't Vote*, 53.
14. Ibid., 26–54.
15. Schattschneider, *Semi-Sovereign People*, 79–82
16. Herbert Croly, *The Promise of American Life* (Hamden, Conn.: Archon, 1963), 196.
17. Ibid., 214.
18. Kenneth M. Dolbeare, *American Political Thought*, 2nd ed. (Chatham, N.Y.: Chatham House, 1989), 390.
19. Walter Dean Burnham, *Critical Elections and the Mainsprings of American Politics* (New York: W. W. Norton, 1970), 74.
20. See Teixeira, *Disappearing American Voter*, 8–9, for a summary of "Turnout in U.S. Presidential Elections, 1824–1988."
21. For example, the New Deal really made no move on civil rights until after its legislative program was finished, and then what it did was minimal.
22. This phrase is taken from Russell Hanson, *The Democratic Imagination in America* (Princeton, N.J.: Princeton Univ. Press, 1985), 257–292.
23. Hanson recalls the history of the Socialist party as "a series of factional disputes and purges, beginning with its formation in 1901. . . . By 1937 the left in America was hopelessly splintered"; from *Democratic Imagination*, 284, fn. 11.
24. Ibid., 283, 291.
25. See Walter Dean Burnham, "The Eclipse of the Democratic Party," *Democracy* (July 1982), 7–8.
26. For the 1988 estimate, see Ruy Teixeira, *Disappearing American Voter*, 9. Luttbeg and Gant, estimate a 4 percent increase in turnout, from approximately 51 percent in 1988 to 55 percent in 1992. They use different methodology from Teixeira, basing their estimates upon all persons of voting age, while Teixeira bases his estimate on legally eligible voters. See Norman R. Luttbeg and Michael M. Gant, *American Electoral Behavior 1952–1992*. 2nd ed. (Itasca, Ill.: F. E. Peacock Publishers, 1995), 91–95.

Chapter 4

1. See in this volume, ch. 1, 31–32.
2. See in this volume, ch. 1, 24–29, and note 9.
3. C. B. Macpherson, *The Life and Times of Liberal Democracy* (Oxford, Eng.: Oxford Univ. Press, 1977), 43.
4. Heinz Eulau, *The Behavioral Persuasion in Politics* (New York: Random House, 1963). Eulau argues in this classic statement of behavioralism: "Political institutions are never more or less different from the patterns of behavior of the people who create them or the regularities of their actions . . . institutions can and must be analyzed in terms of the behavior of their *molecular units*, the individuals whose relations to each other and behavior towards each other are more or less rigidly structured" (my emphasis, 15). The great advantage, however, of the physical scientist over the behaviorist, he writes, is the former's "objects of study": "Atoms,

neutrons or electrons do not care how they are defined"—"they do not talk back" (5). In his commentary, Eulau displays a richer understanding of human motivation and interaction than the methodology he promotes can sustain. Contrast, for example, his discussion of meaning, motive, behavior, and explanation on page 6 and his radically inductive view of a "science of politics," pages 9–10. See also "macro-micro dilemmas," 123–127.

5. Anthony Downs, *An Economic Theory of Democracy* (New York: Harper & Row, 1957), 5.

6. The positivist orientation is itself so important to the explanations of nonparticipation I explore in chapters 5 through 7, indeed, to aspects of some of the others as well, that at the end of chapter 7 I will draw out some of its philosophical assumptions and political implications. An argument could be made that all the writers considered throughout this work, with the exception of Marcuse, are empiricists of some sort. But from chapter 7 onward, they all believe the study of politics is essential to improve political life, and all are much more sensitive to the possibility that the most important political phenomena are the most difficult to observe.

7. Bentley studied groups not to praise them, as later behavioralists and pluralists would, but to develop a scientific category in order to uncover how power operates and society changes. The purpose of political science, for him, was to gather information objectively and then put it in the service of democracy. Raymond Seidelman, with Edward J. Harpham, *Disenchanted Realists: Political Science and the American Crisis, 1884–1984* (Albany, N.Y.: SUNY Press, 1985), 67–81.

8. Quoted in David Held, *Models of Democracy* (Stanford, Calif.: Stanford Univ. Press, 1987), 152, taken from Max Weber, *Economy and Society*, vol. 2 (Berkeley: Univ. of Calif. Press, 1978), 971. Held's discussions of Max Weber and of Joseph Schumpeter have been very helpful, and I have leaned heavily on them.

9. Quoted in Held, *Models of Democracy*, 156, taken from "Politics as a Vocation," *From Max Weber*, ed. Hans Gerth and C. Wright Mills (New York: Oxford Univ. Press, 1972).

10. Quoted in Held, 153, taken from Weber, *Economy and Society*, 971.

11. Joseph A. Schumpeter, *Capitalism, Socialism, and Democracy*, 3rd ed. (New York: Harper & Row, 1962), 264, 284–285.

12. Held, *Models of Democracy*, 174.

13. Ibid., 183.

14. Albert Somit and Joseph Tanenhaus, *The Development of American Political Science* (New York: Irvington Publishers, 1967), 176–180. See also note 4 above.

15. Seidelman, *Disenchanted Realists*, 150, 152–153.

16. Russell Hanson, *The Democratic Imagination in America: Conversations with Our Past* (Princeton, N.J.: Princeton Univ. Press, 1985), 427.

17. J. G. A. Pocock, *The Machiavellian Moment: Florentine Political Thought and the Atlantic Republican Tradition* (Princeton, N.J.: Princeton Univ. Press, 1975).

Chapter 5

1. Bernard R. Berelson, Paul F. Lazarsfeld, and William N. McPhee, *Voting: A Study of Opinion Formation in a Presidential Campaign* (Chicago: Univ. of Chicago Press, 1954), 312.

2. Ibid., 323.
3. Ibid., 320.
4. Ibid., 321.
5. Ibid., 322.
6. In *Voting*, Berelson, Lazarsfeld, and McPhee claim that it is a "mistake to give purely political explanations for nonparticipation" such as considering "failure to vote a politically motivated 'choice' or 'protest,' " suggesting that nonvoting is related to social conditions (32). But if there are social forces at work predisposing certain types of people to not vote, this fact alone serves to undermine their conclusion that the *system* of democracy prospers, so they must mean that nonvoting reflects lack of interest that is the responsibility of the individual in spite of these conditions. And contentment, while not mentioned, is necessary to sustain their view of "harmonious community interest" (320). Otherwise, they would then have to show how high levels of apathy (now based on indifference even to one's own contentment) are compatible with consensus critical to a modern democratic polity. Lester Milbrath is more explicit: "As long as public officials perform their tasks well, most citizens seem content not to become involved in politics"; from *Political Participation* (Chicago: Rand McNally, 1965), 143.
7. Unlike most works of this period, *Voting* discusses in some depth the political roles of women. Helene Silverberg suggests, "In one of the most important theoretical innovations of this [survey research] literature, *Voting* systematically examined women's behavior in a variety of political roles (e.g., as voters, party activists, and union members)"; from Helene Silverberg, "Gender Studies and Political Science: The History of the 'Behavioralist Compromise,' " in *Discipline and History*, ed. James Farr and Raymond Seidelman (Ann Arbor, Mich.: Univ. of Michigan Press, 1993), 366–367. See Berelson et al., *Voting*, 102.
8. Carole Pateman, *Participation and Democratic Theory* (London, Eng.: Cambridge Univ. Press, 1970), 7. My emphasis.
9. Berelson, Lazarsfeld, and McPhee, *Voting*, 316.
10. Paul F. Lazarsfeld, Bernard Berelson, and Hazel Gaudet, *The People's Choice*, 1st ed. (New York: Duell, Sloan & Pearce, 1944). Although Berelson et al.'s data in *Voting* correlated voting preference with socioeconomic characteristics, they systematically considered neither groups, race, or class in the range of X, nor issues, in the range of Y, in explaining nonparticipation. On social equality, see Sidney Verba, Norman H. Nie, and Jae-on Kim, *Participation and Political Equality* (Cambridge, Eng.: Cambridge Univ. Press, 1978), 307. The latter report that while social class is not an important ingredient of political competition, with neither strong working-class consciousness nor parties organized specifically along class lines, "At the same time the class basis of political activity is very strong— the participant population is heavily biased in the direction of those who are more affluent and better educated—more so than in other nations. . . . the very absence of class organizational sense meant that class would play a key role in relation to individual political activity. In the absence of *explicit* contestation on the basis of social class the haves in society come to play an inordinate role in political life." See also Sidney Verba and Norman H. Nie, *Participation in America—Social Equality and Political Democracy* (New York: Harper & Row, 1972).

11. Berelson, Lazarsfeld, and McPhee, *Voting*, 32.
12. See pages 5–6 in the Introduction of this volume. See also Frances Fox Piven and Richard A. Cloward, *Why Americans Don't Vote* (New York: Pantheon, 1989), 115.
13. Samuel P. Huntington, "The United States," in *The Crisis of Democracy*, ed. Michel Crozier, Samuel P. Huntington, and Joji Watanuki (New York: NYU Press, 1975), 114–115.
14. Ibid., 113–115.
15. Samuel P. Huntington, *American Politics: The Promise of Disharmony* (Cambridge, Mass.: Belknap, 1981), 41.
16. Ibid., 69.
17. Ibid., 129.
18. Ibid.
19. Ibid., 222.
20. Ibid., 228–229.
21. Ibid., 231–232.
22. Ibid., 261.
23. Ibid., 85.
24. Huntington, "The United States," 114.

Chapter 6

1. Philip Green, "A Review Essay of Robert A. Dahl, *Democracy and Its Critics*," *Social Theory and Practice* 16 (Summer 1990):221.
2. Robert A. Dahl, *Who Governs?* (New Haven, Conn.: Yale Univ. Press, 1961), 1.
3. Robert A. Dahl, *A Preface to Democratic Theory* (Chicago: Univ. of Chicago Press, 1956), 71, 128, 132, 145–46.
4. Ibid., 31, 133–134.
5. Ibid., 132.
6. Ibid.
7. Robert A. Dahl, *After the Revolution? Authority in a Good Society* (New Haven, Conn.: Yale Univ. Press, 1970), 105–106.
8. Ibid., 140–141.
9. Ibid., 103.
10. Ibid., 110.
11. Robert A. Dahl, *Democracy in the United States: Promise and Performance*, 3rd ed. (Chicago: Rand McNally, 1976), 37, 104.
12. Dahl, *After the Revolution?*, 110.
13. Robert A. Dahl, *Modern Political Analysis*, 2nd ed. (Englewood Cliffs, N.J.: Prentice-Hall, 1970), 80.
14. Robert A. Dahl, "On Removing Certain Impediments to Democracy in the United States," *Dissent* (Summer 1978), 318–319. Reprinted from *Political Science Quarterly* 92 (Spring 1977), 1–20.
15. George Von der Muhll, "Robert Dahl and the Study of Contemporary Democracy: A Review Essay," *American Political Science Review* 71 (1977):1095.
16. Dahl, *Modern Political Analysis*, 77–78.
17. Dahl, *Democracy in the United States*, 104.

18. Dahl, *After the Revolution?*, 142–143. My emphasis.
19. Robert A. Dahl, *Who Governs?*, 279. For a related discussion of the "moral stance" of Robert Dahl, see John Buell's doctoral dissertation, *The Critique of Abstract Individualism* (Univ. of Massachusetts at Amherst, 1974), 30.
20. Peter Bachrach, "Interests, Participation, and Democratic Theory," manuscript prepared for delivery before the American Society for Political and Legal Philosophy, New York City, December 29, 1971, 10, 17.
21. Von der Muhll, "Robert Dahl," 1093.
22. Robert A. Dahl, *Dilemmas of Pluralist Democracy: Autonomy vs. Control* (New Haven, Conn.: Yale Univ. Press, 1982), 188.
23. Correspondence from John Buell, January 1994.
24. Nelson W. Polsby, *Community Power and Political Theory* (New Haven, Conn.: Yale Univ. Press, 1963), 113.
25. Philip Green and Robert Dahl, "What Is Political Equality?," *Dissent* 26 (Summer 1979):352. Also see Dahl, "On Removing Certain Impediments to Democracy," 351.
26. Ibid., 356.
27. Peter Bachrach, "Interests, Participation, and Democratic Theory," 15.
28. See Dahl, "On Removing Certain Impediments to Democracy," 322–323, and 238–241 in this volume.
29. See ch. 15 of this volume for development of this idea.
30. Bachrach, "Interests, Participation, and Democratic Theory," 20.

Chapter 7

1. I have modified this from the formula developed by William H. Riker and Peter C. Ordeshook, *An Introduction to Positive Political Theory* (Englewood Cliffs, N.J.: Prentice Hall, 1973), 62–63. For a good brief overview of rational choice theory, see M. Margaret Conway, *Political Participation in the United States*, 2nd ed. (Washington, D.C.: CQ Press, 1991), especially 130–131.
2. Carole Jean Uhlaner, "Political Participation, Rational Actors, and Rationality: A New Approach," *Political Psychology* 7 (1986):556.
3. See William H. Riker and Peter C. Ordeshook, "A Theory of the Calculus of Voting," *American Political Science Review* 62 (1968):25–42, especially 28. Brian Barry argues, "But whereas Riker leaves the phenomenon unexplained, Downs boldly tries to cover it from within his economic model. . . . According to Downs, the citizens in a democracy always consider that they benefit heavily from the continuance of the system, as against its replacement by some other; but the system must collapse if too few people vote"; from Brian Barry, *Sociologists, Economists and Democracy* (Chicago: Univ. of Chicago Press, 1978), 19.
4. Uhlaner, "Political Participation," 556–557. Riker says of Downs, "it is certainly no explanation to assign a part of politics to the mysterious and inexplicable world of the irrational." Brian Barry accuses Riker of criticizing Downs "as if this were his last word on the subject." Barry argues that the "amendment" that Riker puts forward "is in essence the same as one put forward by Downs himself, though Downs describes it as a factor increasing the reward of voting and Riker counts it as a reduction of the cost"; from Barry, *Sociologists, Economists and Democracy*, 15.

5. William H. Riker, *Liberalism Against Populism: A Confrontation Between the Theory of Democracy and the Theory of Social Choice* (Prospect Heights, Ill.: Waveland, 1982), 1.
6. Ibid., 9.
7. Ibid., 1–2.
8. Ibid., 234–238.
9. Ibid., 244.
10. Jane J. Mansbridge, *Beyond Adversary Democracy* (New York: Basic Books, 1980), 3 and throughout.
11. Jon Elster, "The Possibility of Rational Politics," in *Political Theory Today*, ed. David Held (Stanford, Calif.: Stanford Univ. Press, 1991), 137.
12. Mansbridge, *Beyond Adversary Democracy*, ch. 1 & 2.
13. Riker, *Liberalism Against Populism*, 244.
14. While disseminating the findings of social choice theory "is a desirable additional defense" against populism, he admits it is an "arcane theory" (it took Riker himself "a score of years of reflection on Black's and Arrow's discoveries to reject the populism I had initially espoused") and believes this would be "a task for generations"; from Riker, *Liberalism Against Populism*, 252.
15. Frank C. Zagare, "Liberalism Against Populism: A Confrontation Between the Theory of Democracy and the Theory of Social Choice, by William H. Riker," Book Reviews: *Empirical Theory and Methodology*, 77 (1983):844–845.
16. Riker, *Liberalism Against Populism*, 199–200.
17. Zagare, "Liberalism Again Populism," 845.
18. Riker, *Liberalism Against Populism*, 239.
19. Ibid., 241.
20. Uhlaner, "Political Participation," 559–560.
21. Ibid., 561–565.
22. Ibid., 567, 566.
23. Ibid., 571. Uhlaner extends the same lines of analysis in " 'Relational Goods' and Participation: Incorporating Sociability into a Theory of Rational Action," *Public Choice* 62 (1988):253–285; and "Rational Turnout: The Neglected Role of Groups," *American Journal of Political Science* 33 (1989):390–422. She continues to try to rectify the inability of rational choice to explain why a Downsian voter "would not just stay home," and to reconcile its basic idea of people as utility maximizers with the fact "groups play an important role in the political process": "I argue that individuals do not behave atomistically within the political sphere but rather are joined with others in groups with shared interests." Such affiliations create not only consumption benefits for the individual but the possibility of group political support that group leaders can use to negotiate with candidates, bringing support for group-favored policies back to the group (another group incentive to vote) in return for votes; from "Rational Turnout," 420, 419.
24. Elster, "The Possibility of Rational Politics," 120.
25. Barry, *Sociologists, Economists and Democracy*, 15.
26. Ibid., 20.
27. Elster, "The Possibility of Rational Politics," 116, 117.
28. Barry argues that the "power of the 'economic' method is that, in appropriate

kinds of situations, it enables us, operating with simple premises concerning rational behaviour, to deduce by logic and mathematics interesting conclusions about what will happen. Whether a situation is 'appropriate' or not depends on the extent to which other factors can safely be ignored"; from *Sociologists, Economists and Democracy*, 15–16.

29. Heinz Eulau, "Liberalism Against Populism: A Confrontation Between the Theory of Democracy and the Theory of Social Choice, by William H. Riker," a review essay, *Journal of Economic Literature* 21 (June 1983):562.

30. For Eulau, see ch. 4, note 4 in this volume.

31. Brian Fay, *Social Theory and Political Practice* (New York: Holmes and Meier, 1976), 47, 46. Fay's short work is excellent. See especially ch. 1 on positivist social science and on science itself.

32. Alisdair MacIntyre, *After Virtue.* 2nd ed. (Notre Dame, Ind.: Univ. of Notre Dame Press, 1984), 96.

33. Perhaps not so ironically, in our modern life, dominated by cost-benefit calculations of game theoretic competitions between economistic self-interested participants, positivist social science matures and its special branch of game theory develops, both seeking (lost?) predictability.

34. MacIntyre, *After Virtue*, 93–103. Jon Elster argues against "the feasibility of large-scale social engineering," that "no theories exist that allow us to predict the long-term equilibrium effects of large-scale social reforms. . . . Consequently, political choices are made under conditions of radical cognitive indeterminacy"; from Elster, "The Possibility of Rational Politics," 122.

35. MacIntyre, *After Virtue*, 103–104.

36. Ibid., 104.

37. Michael H. Best and William E. Connolly, *The Politicized Economy* (Lexington, Mass.: D. C. Heath, 1976), 127–131. Best and Connolly report a dramatic reversal at a Vauxhall auto plant in England. Just as sociologist John Goldthorpe's findings about satisfaction at work and "lack of class consciousness" were going to press, as the London *Times* reported: "Wild rioting has broken out at the Vauxhall car factories in Luton. Thousands of workers streamed out of the shops." Apparently as they discussed together the interviews they had been subjects of, they began to reconsider their answers, discovering they really had been 'resigned' to their fates rather than contented with them. The more they discussed, the more "their collective sense of discontent increased."

38. Best and Connolly, *The Politicized Economy*, 155, note 13.

39. One terrible way it has been done is through Stalin's notions of science, and a science of history.

40. William E. Connolly, *Appearance and Reality in Politics* (New York: Cambridge Univ. Press, 1981), 33–34.

Chapter 8

1. E. E. Schattschneider, *The Semi-Sovereign People* (New York: Holt, Rinehart and Winston, 1960), 68.

2. Ibid., 71.

3. Ibid., 39, 35.

4. Ibid., 105.
5. Ibid., 107.
6. Ibid., 110–111.
7. Ibid., 105.
8. Lewis Lipsitz, "On Political Belief: The Grievances of the Poor," in *Power and Community*, ed. Philip Green and Sandford Levinson (New York: Pantheon, 1969), 188.
9. Peter Bachrach and Morton S. Baratz, "The Two Faces of Power," *American Political Science Review* 61 (December 1962):949. Earlier the authors ask, "can a sound concept of power be predicated on the assumption that power is totally embodied and fully reflected in 'concrete decisions' or in activity bearing directly upon their making?" The answer: "We think not. Of course power is exercised when A participates in the making of decisions that affect B. But power is also exercised when A devotes his energies to creating or reinforcing social and political values and institutional practices that limit the scope of the political process to public consideration of only those issues which are comparatively innocuous to A. To the extent that A succeeds in doing this, B is prevented, for all practical purposes, from bringing to the fore any issues that might in their resolution be seriously detrimental to A's set of preferences." Ibid., 948.
10. See Bachrach and Baratz, "Two Faces of Power," and Peter Bachrach, "Interest, Participation, and Democratic Theory," manuscript prepared for the American Society for Political and Legal Philosophy, New York City, December 29, 1971. Same title appears in *Participation in Politics* (New York: Lieber-Atherton, 1975), J. Roland Pennock and John W. Chapman, eds., 39–55.
11. Peter Bachrach and Morton S. Baratz, *Power and Poverty: Theory and Practice* (New York: Oxford Univ. Press, 1970), 48–49. They say about covert grievances: They "are covert in the sense that they have not been recognized as 'worthy' of public attention and controversy, but they are overt in that they are observable in their aborted form to the investigator."
12. Ibid., 46.
13. Ibid., 49. My emphasis.
14. Ibid., 53.
15. For an early view on ideology, see ibid., 92–94, 55–57.
16. Ibid., 36.
17. Ibid., 49. My emphasis.
18. Bachrach, "Interest, Participation, and Democratic Theory," 2, 5. My emphasis.
19. Peter Bachrach, "Corporate Authority," 267, in *Political Theory and Social Change*, ed. David Spitz (New York: Atherton, 1967).
20. Peter Bachrach, *The Theory of Democratic Elitism* (Boston: Little, Brown, 1967). My emphasis. Note that "feelings" are no longer sufficient. Now they must be "justifiable" in order to be a true gauge of whether one's interests are being met. The legitimacy of the feeling is itself now contestable.
21. Bachrach, "Interest, Participation, and Democratic Theory," 5.
22. For example, he accepts that Robert Lane's conclusions in "The Fear of Equality" (*American Political Science Review* 53 [1959]:35–81) might be correct that the rational self-interest of workers may be in accord with the status quo: "the worker . . . is reasonably content with the system." He continues, however: "Nonetheless

on strictly political grounds I contend there is a *prima facie* justification in doubting whether workers' articulated preferences reflect their real interests." See Bachrach, "Interest, Participation, and Democratic Theory," 12–13.

23. Steven Lukes, *Power: A Radical View* (London, Eng: Macmillan, 1974), 23–24.

24. In some respects, Bachrach's view of interests has some of the problems of "need" theorists, generally. See William E. Connolly, *The Terms of Political Discourse*, lst ed. (Lexington, Mass.: D.C. Heath, 1974), 45–83.

25. Bachrach, "Interest, Participation, and Democratic Theory," 2. My emphasis.

26. Ibid., 6. My emphasis.

27. Ibid., 8–9.

28. Bachrach and Baratz, *Power and Poverty*, 44–45.

29. Bachrach concedes that workers are uninterested in national politics, arguing that they are more likely to be interested in work life issues. Yet people may reject "national" politics, as Bachrach is well aware, because the issues as drawn don't represent their present concerns. While he understands that elites can unconsciously work in their own interests, he underplays the extent to which nonelites can unconsciously work *against* their own: "For purposes of analysis, a power struggle exists, overtly or covertly, either when both sets of contestants are aware of its existence or when only the less powerful party is aware of it"; from Bachrach and Baratz, *Power and Poverty*, 50. Finally, he argues both that "It is doubtful . . . that in those political exercises in which they do participate that their articulated preferences actually reflect their more deep-seated concerns"; *and* that there is "no basis to presume that alienation significantly impairs their ability to make rational political choices." This reflects the deeper tension in his work at this stage between acknowledgment that workers and the "underclass" are not fully conversant with their interests and his desire to avoid elitism and charges of not following proper methodology. See "Interest, Participation, and Democratic Theory," 12–15.

Chapter 9

1. James Miller, *Democracy Is in the Streets* (New York: Simon & Schuster, 1987), ch. 4. Miller calls Mills's *The Power Elite* "a book that was closely studied by virtually every early leader of SDS," 85.

2. Ronald Aronson writes about Marcuse's influence on the New Left: "In the 1960's Marcuse legitimized us. . . . *One-Dimensional Man* expressed how negative, how oppressive was this society that seemed so positive. It broke with the American end-of-ideology smugness intellectually as the Civil Rights movement broke with it politically. Marcuse gave philosophical and historical validation to our inarticulate yet explosive demand for a totally different vision." Quoted in Douglas Kellner, *Herbert Marcuse and the Crisis of Marxism* (Berkeley: Univ. of Calif. Press, 1984), 376.

3. C. Wright Mills, *The Causes of World War Three* (New York: Simon & Schuster, 1958), 21.

4. Ibid., 22–23. My emphasis.

5. C. Wright Mills, *The Power Elite* (London, Eng.: Oxford Univ. Press, 1956), 314–315.

6. Ibid., 311.
7. Ibid., 319.
8. Ibid., 307.
9. Ibid., 312. My emphasis.
10. Irving Louis Horowitz, ed., *Power, Politics and People* (New York: Oxford Univ. Press, 1967), "Introduction," 19, 20. My emphasis. In 1983, Horowitz wrote a biography of Mills in which he is more equivocal in his praise: C. *Wright Mills: An American Utopian* (New York: The Free Press, 1983). Calling Horowitz's biography of Mills "a sure guide to Mills's main writings," Steven Lukes says Horowitz seems "oddly unsure of their lasting value. Was he, as Mr. Horowitz once wrote, 'the greatest sociologist the United States has ever produced'? Or did he, as Mr. Horowitz now says, 'organize and clarify the obvious,' offering insights that are 'easy to underestimate'?"; from Steven Lukes, "Scholar and Pamphleteer: C. *Wright Mills: An American Utopian* by Irving Louis Horowitz," *The New York Times Book Review* 13 November 1983): BR 11.
11. Mills, "Culture and Politics," in *Power, Politics and People*, 245.
12. For an excellent guide to Mills's life and career, see Horowitz, C. *Wright Mills*.
13. C. Wright Mills, *The New Men of Power* (New York: Harcourt, Brace, 1948), 260.
14. Ibid., 291.
15. Ibid., 267–268.
16. Ibid., 268.
17. Ibid., 280, 279.
18. Ibid., 271.
19. Ibid., 270. My emphasis.
20. Ibid., 269–270.
21. Ibid., 270.
22. Ibid., 274.
23. Ibid., 273–274.
24. Peter Clecak, *Radical Paradoxes* (New York: Harper & Row, 1973), 36–37.
25. C. Wright Mills, *White Collar: The American Middle Classes* (New York: Oxford Univ. Press, 1951), 230. However, wage earners are more alienated and vote less (331–332).
26. Mills, *White Collar*, xvi.
27. Mills, *White Collar*, 59. The "rhetoric of competition" provided business with ideological cover to legitimize rationalization of the market. For small businesses, it became the rallying cry with which their political leaders could mobilize and exploit anxieties. As public belief it emphasized both a largely defunct free market and the idea of merit as determining economic advantage, thereby obscuring the role of political bargaining and struggle. As private dream, it blurred the differences between democratic and class property.
28. Ibid., 65.
29. Ibid., 66.
30. Ibid., 234–235.
31. Ibid., 285.
32. Ibid., 240.
33. Ibid., 254.
34. Ibid., 252.

35. Ibid., 256, 255.
36. Ibid., 257.
37. Robert A. Dahl, "A Critique of the Ruling Elite Model," in C. *Wright Mills and the Power Elite*, ed. G. William Domhoff and Hoyt B. Ballard (Boston: Beacon, 1968), 35. Dahl's "test" is: "The hypothesis of the existence of a ruling elite can be strictly tested only if: 1. The hypothetical ruling elite is a well-defined group. 2. There is a fair sample of cases involving key political decisions in which the preferences of the hypothetical ruling elite run counter to those of any other likely group that might be suggested. 3. In such cases, the preferences of the elite regularly prevail" (31). He repeats this criticism, although in somewhat muted form, in *Democracy and Its Critics* (New Haven, Conn.: Yale Univ. Press, 1989), 367, note 15. See the discussion of Dahl in ch. 15, 221, and note 18, of this volume, where I suggest he may himself now be a candidate for this test and may fail it.
38. See the Introduction of this volume, 12–14, for a review of Lukes's analysis of power.
39. Horowitz, C. *Wright Mills*, 277. Horowitz suggests that Dahl also misses Mills's point, which was not that there did not exist some pluralism at the middle levels of power, in middle-sized towns like New Haven, Connecticut, but that such power distribution was of secondary importance to that of the national structure of elite power.
40. Clecak, *Radical Paradoxes*, 64.
41. Mills, *White Collar*, 106.
42. Ibid., 77.
43. For Mills, bureaucracy could be a source of authority as well as manipulation, and rational bureaucracy could be "the most efficient type of social organization yet devised."
44. Mills, "The Conservative Mood," in *Power, Politics and People*, 208. My emphasis.
45. Mills, *White Collar*, 300.
46. Mills, *Power Elite*, 318–319.
47. Mills, *White Collar*, 353–354.
48. C. Wright Mills, *The Sociological Imagination* (London, Eng.: Oxford Univ. Press, 1966), 172–173. My emphasis.
49. Mills, *Sociological Imagination*, 171.
50. Quoted in Clecak, *Radical Paradoxes*, 54.
51. Ibid.
52. Mills, "The New Left," in *Power, Politics and People*, 259.
53. Horowitz suggests that toward the end of his life, "Mills became the writer seeking world historic vindication, and he tried to achieve it by violating nearly every canon of the sociological imagination he had urged upon others. . . . Mills the political ideologist ultimately betrayed Mills the social scientist"; from C. *Wright Mills*, 300–302. Yet, he concludes that in his "final and personally agonizing years, Mills addressed himself to the open secrets of society." Saying publicly the things known to everyone secretly requires the most courage: "Mills had that sort of courage." Horowitz concludes he is best characterized "in terms of seriousness: the achievement of enlightenment through the classic tradition in social science" (328–330).

54. Mills, *Power Elite*, 24–25.
55. Mills, *Sociological Imagination*, 194.
56. Robert Bohlke and Kenneth Winetrout, *Bureaucrats and Intellectuals* (Amherst, Mass.: Univ. of Mass.), 6. But see in *White Collar*, 173–175, 309–313.
57. C. Wright Mills, "Situated Actions and Vocabularies of Motive," in *Power, Politics and People*, 440–441.
58. Ibid., 440.
59. Ibid., 440, and note 3.
60. Ibid., 452.
61. Mills, "The Unity of Work and Leisure," in *Power, Politics and People*, 347–352.
62. See 138 this volume. In *White Collar*, he suggests, sometimes, "political indifference" is "reasoned cynicism," and " 'political apathy' " is "horse sense" (327, 347).
63. While gender issues are not central for Mills, see his "Women: The Darling Little Slaves," in *Power, Politics and People*, 339–346; and 172–178 in *White Collar*.
64. Mills, *Sociological Imagination*, 171.

Chapter 10

1. Seyla Benhabib, *Critique, Norm, and Utopia: A Study of the Foundations of Critical Theory* (New York: Columbia Univ. Press, 1986), 176.
2. John Fry, *Marcuse—Dilemma and Liberation: A Critical Analysis* (Stockholm: Almqvist & Wiksell International, 1974), 45.
3. Herbert Marcuse, "Obsolescence of the Freudian Concept of Man," in *Five Lectures: Psychoanalysis, Politics, and Utopia*, trans. Jeremy J. Shapiro and Shierry M. Weber (Boston: Beacon, 1970), 47.
4. Herbert Marcuse, *One-Dimensional Man: Studies in the Ideology of Advanced Industrial Society* (Boston: Beacon, 1964), 18.
5. Jürgen Habermas, "Technology and Science as 'Ideology,' " in *Toward a Rational Society*, trans. Jeremy J. Shapiro (Boston: Beacon, 1968), 84.
6. Herbert Marcuse, "Industrialism and Capitalism in the Work of Max Weber," in *Negations: Essays in Critical Theory*, trans. Jeremy J. Shapiro (Boston: Beacon, 1968), 223–224.
7. Marcuse, *One-Dimensional Man*, 166.
8. Herbert Marcuse, "Repressive Tolerance," in *A Critique of Pure Tolerance* by Robert Paul Wolff, Barrington Moore, Jr., and Herbert Marcuse (Boston: Beacon Press, 1969), 106; and Herbert Marcuse, *An Essay on Liberation* (Boston: Beacon, 1969), 65.
9. See Robert Paul Wolff, "Marcuse's Theory of Toleration," *Polity*, 6 (Summer 1974). Wolff explains Marcuse's theory of toleration this way: "Tolerance, for Marcuse, is liberating when it is the established order's grudging acceptance of negative or oppositional expressions which seek to tap the unconscious as a way of attacking surplus repression. Tolerance is repressive when it is, as in our present society, an easy acceptance of the surface manifestations of the negativity in such a manner as to rob it of its transcending capability and leaves surplus repression untouched" (476).
10. Marcuse, "Repressive Tolerance," 106–110.
11. Marcuse, *One-Dimensional Man*, 6. Marcuse's theory of toleration was extremely controversial. Alisdair MacIntyre sharply criticizes him for not realizing that the

"*telos* of tolerance is not truth but rationality," and rationality requires toleration of alternative ideas. Douglas Kellner suggests that Marcuse backed off his harsher version of confronting pseudo-tolerance with intolerance in his later writings. In "Repressive Tolerance," Marcuse claims that "the alternative to the established semi-democratic process is *not* a dictatorship or elite, no matter how intellectual and intelligent, but the struggle for real democracy. Part of this struggle is the fight against an ideology of tolerance which, in reality, favors and fortifies the conservation of the status quo of inequality and discrimination. For this struggle, I proposed the practice of discriminating tolerance." Herbert Marcuse, "Postscript 1968" to "Repressive Tolerance," in A *Critique of Pure Tolerance*, 122–123.

12. Marcuse, *One-Dimensional Man*, 79.

13. Ibid., 11. My emphasis.

14. Douglas Kellner, *Herbert Marcuse and the Crisis of Marxism* (Berkeley: Univ. of Calif. Press, 1984), 234, 235. Kellner is right not to view *One-Dimensional Man* "simply as the epic of total domination." But I do believe that Marcuse sometimes puts forth a theory of total domination. What else could it mean for alienation "to become *entirely objective*"?

15. For Kellner's full argument against this point, see *Herbert Marcuse and the Crisis of Marxism*, 234–240.

16. See Marcuse, *Counterrevolution and Revolt* (Boston: Beacon, 1972) and *Essay on Liberation*.

17. Kellner is also correct when he says that Marcuse believed that "the system of advanced capitalism itself plays a structuring role in helping to produce science and technology, which it shapes and uses for specific social purposes," although Marcuse also suggests in *One-Dimensional Man* that capitalism was being transformed into something new: advanced industrial society. Kellner, *Herbert Marcuse*, 263.

18. MacIntyre sharply criticizes Marcuse, saying that only "self-education" truly liberates. Making people "objects of liberation by others is to assist in making them passive instruments; it is to cast them for the role of inert matter to be molded into forms chosen by the elite." In his account, Marcuse's impoverished subject illicitly justifies elite domination of the majority and fosters apathy. See Alisdair MacIntyre, *Herbert Marcuse: An Exposition and a Polemic* (New York: Viking, 1970), 105–106.

19. She continues, "Yet they never abandon it altogether; even when the historical process seems to destroy all hope in the *revolutionary* subject, the search for *a subject* whose needs and interests might represent those of humanity as such continues"; from Benhabib, *Critique, Norm, and Utopia*, 143.

20. *One-Dimensional Man*, even with its many faults, is superior to these later works in that it lays out a serious theory. The later works may accomplish better reportage of by then more obvious conflicts, but they do little to improve the basic theory.

21. For this reason, John Fry asserts that libido as a "material substratum" allows Marcuse to "have his idealist cake and eat it too," while Schoolman accuses him of behaviorism and MacIntyre calls him a "pre-Marxist" thinker. Benhabib writes of Marcuse: "On the one hand, in order to anchor the possibility of revolt in some

domain that could escape the ravages of the administered world, Marcuse had to turn to the resistant and immutable core of human instincts; on the other hand, faced with the utter malleability of conscious needs and the formation of false ones, he had to draw a distinction between true and false needs. . . . it is partly the authoritarianism of such a project which has led Habermas to emphasize the merits and significance of bourgeois democratic-liberal traditions"; from Benhabib, *Critique, Norm, and Utopia,* 336–337.

22. Morton Schoolman, *The Imaginary Witness: The Critical Theory of Herbert Marcuse* (New York: NYU Press, 1984), 257–259.

23. Jürgen Habermas, "Psychic Thermidor and the Rebirth of Rebellious Subjectivity," in *Habermas and Modernity,* ed. Richard J. Bernstein (Cambridge, Mass.: MIT Press, 1985), 74–77. Habermas suggests that *Eros and Civilization* is Marcuse's "most Marcusean one." Yet, in spite of the role instincts played in Marcuse's theories, shortly before his death, referring to the normative basis of critical theory (and whether it was grounded in natural law), he said to Habermas: "Look, I know wherein our most basic value judgments are rooted—in compassion, in our sense for the suffering of others" (77).

24. See for example, Marcuse, *Essay on Liberation,* 9–10.

25. Kenneth Kenniston, *Young Radicals* (New York: Harcourt, Brace & World, 1968), 127.

26. For an excellent account of the SDS, see James Miller, *Democracy Is in the Streets* (New York: Simon & Schuster, 1987).

27. Schoolman, *Imaginary Witness,* 211.

28. Ibid., 210.

29. Thomas Fitzgerald, "Why Motivation Theory Doesn't Work," *Harvard Business Review* (July/August 1971):42.

30. Ibid., 43.

31. See MacIntyre's critique of positivist social science in ch. 7, 114–116, this volume.

32. Alisdair MacIntyre, *After Virtue,* 2nd ed. (Notre Dame, Ind.: Univ. of Notre Dame Press, 1984), 100.

33. Wolff, "Marcuse's Theory," 476.

34. MacIntyre, *After Virtue,* 105–106. My emphasis.

35. Habermas, "Technology and Science," 112.

36. Daniel Bell, *The Cultural Contradictions of Capitalism* (New York: Basic Books, 1976), 220–282.

37. Stuart Hampshire, *Morality and Pessimism* (Cambridge, Eng.: Cambridge Univ. Press, 1972), 31.

38. Ibid., 12.

39. See Stuart Hampshire's discussion of action and self-consciousness in *Thought and Action* (New York: Viking, 1959), 169–222.

Chapter 11

1. Huntington bases his conclusion that we can afford to temper democratic ideals on this point. See ch. 5, 82, this volume.

2. In part, this shortfall is explained by the times during which some of these authors

wrote, and some did show sensitivity. Mills wrote about the ways in which women were treated as "darling little slaves"; Marcuse believed there was liberating potential in feminism (see Douglas Kellner, *Herbert Marcuse and the Crisis of Marxism* [Berkeley: Univ. of Calif. Press, 1984], 340) and in African-American subculture, and indeed within women; and Dahl at times has been clear about the victimization of African-Americans. Nevertheless, issues of gender and racial disadvantages were either at the periphery, inadequately developed, or absent in the theorists reviewed, some of whom set the terms of the debate within democratic theory.

3. Steven J. Rosenstone and John Mark Hansen, *Mobilization, Participation, and Democracy in America* (New York: Macmillan, 1993), 204.

4. Lawrence Bobo and Franklin D. Gilliam Jr., "Race, Sociopolitical Participation, and Black Empowerment," *American Political Science Review* 84 (June 1990):377, 388. Their review, recounted here, is based on the work of William J. Wilson; John W. Moore; Eddie N. Williams and Milton D. Morris; Rufus Browning, Dale Rogers Marshall and David H. Tabb; James Jennings; Reynolds Farley and Walter Allen; Michael C. Dawson and Ronald E. Brown; Kenny J. Whitby; Melvin Thomas and Michael Hughes.

5. Rosenstone and Hansen, *Mobilization, Participation, and Democracy*, 59, 200–203.

6. Charles Green and Basil Wilson, *The Struggle for Black Empowerment in New York City* (New York: McGraw-Hill, 1992), 40–41.

7. Rosenstone and Hansen, *Mobilization, Participation, and Democracy*, 223–224.

8. This subject will be pursued further in chapter 15 in a discussion of the work of journalists E. J. Dionne and Thomas and Mary Edsall.

9. See the discussion on the relation of socioeconomic class and voting turnout in the Introduction, this volume, 4–6.

10. Green and Wilson, *Struggle for Black Empowerment*, 163–164.

11. Carole Pateman, *The Disorder of Women* (Stanford, Calif.: Stanford Univ. Press, 1989), 220–221.

12. Susan Moller Okin, "Gender, the Public and the Private," in *Political Theory Today*, ed. David Held (Stanford, Calif.: Stanford Univ. Press, 1991), 69.

13. Ibid., 70.

14. Ibid., 78.

Chapter 12

1. Richard Sennett and Jonathan Cobb, *The Hidden Injuries of Class* (New York: Vintage Books, 1972), 98.

2. Ibid., 75.

3. Jean Baker Miller, "Women and Power," in *Rethinking Power*, ed. Thomas E. Wartenberg (Albany, N.Y.: SUNY Press, 1992), 242.

4. Ibid., 242.

5. Ibid., 243.

6. Ibid., 243–244.

7. Ibid., 244.

8. Ibid.

9. Ibid., 245.

10. Ibid., 246.

11. In playing down power as enablement, Lukes seems to miss the powers of women that Miller describes, a failing that may itself be male engendered.
12. Joan Cocks, *The Oppositional Imagination* (London, Eng.: Routledge, 1989), 182–183.
13. Ibid., 189.
14. Ibid., 190.
15. Ibid., 190–191.
16. Unfortunately, I have not been able to locate the citation in my records. I include it because of its unusual power.
17. Frank Parkin, *Class Inequality and Political Order* (New York: Praeger Publishers, 1972), 88.
18. Ibid., 92.
19. Nancy Fraser, *Unruly Practices* (Minneapolis: Univ. of Minnesota Press, 1989), 169.
20. William E. Connolly, *Appearances and Reality in Politics* (New York: Cambridge Univ. Press, 1981), 68.
21. Steven Lukes, *Power: A Radical View* (London, Eng.: Macmillan, 1974), 24–25.
22. Jeffrey Isaac, "Beyond the Three Faces of Power: A Realist Critique," in *Rethinking Power*, ed. Thomas E. Wartenberg (Albany, N.Y.: SUNY Press, 1992), 41.
23. Quoted in ibid., 44.
24. Ibid., 47.
25. Ibid., 46.
26. I say "in part" because it generally is also in part a relation of authority in which the teacher does not need to use power. Indeed, an unintended consequence of Isaac's tendency to reduce power relations to the locution "power to" as a derivative of structural roles may be to treat all authoritative role relations as power relations. While discussion of this is beyond the scope of this work, it makes sense, I think, not to treat authority simply as another form of power. For a discussion that bears on these issues, see "Authority and Legitimate Power," in William E. Connolly, *The Terms of Political Discourse*. 3rd ed. (Princeton, N.J.: Princeton Univ. Press, 1993), 107–116. Also see note 32 below.
27. Although I think it is fair to say that within Lukes's idea of "power over" is implied what one would be free to do ("power to," especially discover and pursue one's interests) were there no constraints of "power over" limiting one (however, see note 11 above).
28. Isaac argues Lukes's focus on the locution "power over" brings him close to the behavioralism he criticizes. Isaac wants a "realist" social science that investigates a world of "things" with essential properties and not merely "events" that result from actions. Yet people's essential powers may be hidden to themselves, or remain undeveloped (as well as hidden to the observer) until constraints are removed, or at least until definitions of reality are reshuffled. William Connolly proposes a "test" of "real interests" that bears on this question: "Policy x is more in A's real interest than policy y if A, were he to experience the *results* of both x and y, would *choose* x as the result he would rather have for himself"; from *Terms of Political Discourse*, 64. Connolly seems to want both to allow and *to prepare* or enable the agent by exposing him or her to a fuller range of alternatives and,

therefore, to act with more autonomy. This is similar to the "test" Lukes proposes at the end of his third dimension of power. Powers exist as properties "within" people both developed and revealed in practical activity. Nevertheless, Isaac is right that Lukes's notion of power is tied too closely to the idea of denying one's interests.

29. Ibid., 48–49. My emphasis. Isaac correctly suggests that C. Wright Mills had more of a realist and structural theory of power: In *The Power Elite*, "Mills insists throughout the book that the power of the elite is structurally determined, that they are a group 'in positions to make decisions having major consequences.' " (53). But Mills's hope, I think, was precisely that they were capable of exercising autonomy from the very structural roles that gave them power. Lukes, I think, also appreciates "social forces and institutional practices" in a way not as incompatible with the realist view of structural relations as Isaac claims.

30. This counterfactual becomes a theoretical "test" of whether interests have been harmed and therefore whether power is exercised, allowing Lukes to be both radical and empirical, and perhaps also allowing Isaac to charge him with being too empiricist *and* susceptible to attacks as "vanguardist."

31. Jürgen Habermas tries to establish that point of view through the idea that "legitimate power arises among those who form common convictions in communication free from coercion"; quoted in Terence Ball, "New Faces of Power," in *Rethinking Power*, 25. Even Michel Foucault tries explicitly to establish it toward the end of his life when he focuses on "those intentional and voluntary actions by which men not only set themselves rules of conduct but also seek to transform themselves . . . and to make their life into an *oeuvre*"; quoted in Thomas McCarthy, "The Critique of Impure Reason: Foucault and the Frankfurt School," in *Rethinking Power*, 147.

32. One responsibility the subject has is to be a primary judge of when he or she is following rules because they bear the good seal of genuine authority, or is doing so unfreely. If all power really is "power to" as a derivative of structural roles as "material causes," the ability to freely make this judgment seems denied the individual. Then, either the distinction between power and authority collapses, or it can be made only from Archimedean point somehow outside of roles and social structure or, as it actually will be made, by persons who will claim only *they* are free from such constraints. See note 26 above.

33. This itself begs the question as to whether this is truly an ontological question of humankind as such, or an historical question of late modernity. When I say "independent" here I do not mean separate from other factors, such as social structure, roles, ideologies, etc., but important as an "independent" source or cause of human activity. I am suggesting, in Isaac's terms, another "material cause of interaction."

34. Connolly raises an allied issue of import. In creating our own identities, at the same time we identify the "other" as different. I would extend his point to mean we attempt to achieve power over the "other" in our power to establish our own identities. Connolly's way of formulating this, it seems to me, calls into question the adequacy of the locutions *power over* and *power to*.

Chapter 13

1. Jürgen Habermas, *Legitimation Crisis* (Boston: Beacon, 1973). See William Connolly's discussion of Habermas in *Politics and Ambiguity* (Madison: Univ. of Wisconsin Press, 1987), ch. 5, especially 67–71.
2. Which is not to suggest at all that Habermas has given up on the possibility of democracy. Quite the contrary. He does, however, see formidable obstacles.
3. Michel Foucault, "Panopticism," in *The Foucault Reader*, ed. Paul Rabinow (New York: Pantheon, 1984), 206–207.
4. In spite of his effort to show the way in which Enlightenment concepts of the "normal" subject actually repress subjectivity, I would suggest he too must have in mind a range of what people are capable of and what is good for them.
5. Terence Ball, "New Faces of Power," in *Rethinking Power*, ed. Thomas E. Wartenberg (Albany, N.Y.: SUNY Press, 1992), 29.
6. Thomas McCarthy, "The Critique of Impure Reason: Foucault and the Frankfurt School," in *Rethinking Power*, 137.
7. Ibid. As McCarthy points out, though, Foucault's tendency to treat socialization as a process in which there is "an intrusion of disciplinary forces into bodies," or his idea of "docile bodies" where people simply act in compliance with sanctioned codes of behavior, fails to account for the agent's "understanding of social structures and their own reflexive use of cultural resources for making sense." Ibid., 133.
8. McCarthy, "Critique of Impure Reason," 147.
9. William E. Connolly, *Politics and Ambiguity*, 35.
10. Ibid., 68–69.
11. This is not to argue, at least on my part, that the idea of God is obsolete. It is enough for Connolly to establish that death today is more problematic because of less certainty in the existence of God.
12. William E. Connolly, *Identity/Difference: Democratic Negotiations of Political Paradox* (Ithaca, N.Y.: Cornell Univ. Press, 1991), 35.
13. Ibid., 77.
14. Ibid., 78.
15. Erving Goffman once described the way in which mental hospitals stunt the self-concept of inmates, and inmates adapt themselves to roles full of assaults on their dignity, respect, and self-worth as mortification of the self. He was describing a far more insidious situation. I am describing one, though, that I do take to be very important for students of democracy to consider. Erving Goffman, *Asylums* (New York: Anchor Books, 1961), 3–49, especially 14.
16. Indeed, today, there does seem to be a "normal" identity of disaffection, and forms of psychological "discipline" for those who refuse it.

Chapter 14

1. Ruy A. Teixeira, *The Disappearing American Voter* (Washington, D.C.: Brookings Institute, 1992), 1.
2. Some countries also do not vote on workdays, and some make voting compulsory,

making the "cost avoidance" of voting "technically a benefit"; from Teixeira, *Disappearing American Voter*, 14.

3. Ibid., 15–16. The two-party system is the one area in which he claims the United States has an advantage, on the theory that compromise, as required in multiparty coalition governments, dampens motivation. Bicameralism, however, also dampens turnout because compromise is necessary between each legislative house. His point on multiparty systems seems counterintuitive to the degree that citizens may feel they are offered a wider array of choices.

4. Ibid., 16–17.

5. Ibid., 104.

6. Nonvoting, he claims, has little impact on the actual outcomes of elections, as electoral results "are not likely to change through even highly implausible levels of nonvoter mobilization"; ibid. This has practical import because it means increasing voter participation can be supported by all political parties without fear that increased turnout would actually help one over another.

7. Ibid., 57.

8. Ibid., 146–147.

9. Ibid., 150–153.

10. Ibid., 154.

11. Ibid.

12. Ibid., 157.

13. Ibid., 161–162.

14. Ibid., 163–164.

15. Ibid., 164–175.

16. Ibid., 175.

17. Ibid., 177–178.

18. Ibid., 2–3. My emphasis.

19. Ibid., 181.

20. Frances Fox Piven and Richard A. Cloward, *Why Americans Don't Vote* (New York: Pantheon, 1989), 18–19.

21. Ibid., 20–21.

22. Douglas J. Amy, *Real Choices/New Voices: The Case for Proportional Representation Elections in the United States* (New York: Columbia Univ. Press, 1993), 221–223, chs. 5, 6, 7, 10. Recent Italian reforms may move that European democracy away from some of the features Amy supports and against this trend.

23. Teixeira, *Disappearing American Voter*, 156–157.

24. Walter Dean Burnham, "The Turnout Problem," in *Elections American Style*, ed. A. James Reichley (Washington, D.C.: Brookings Institute, 1987), 124–125. Recently, it is the Republican party, perhaps to break out of their historic minority Congressional status, that has tried hardest to define itself in cohesive party terms, especially through its House of Representatives candidates' "Contract with America" in the 1994 elections. Whether this will reinforce elite domination or force the Republicans in a more populist direction is as yet unknown. Clearly, House Speaker Newt Gingrich's leadership—at least as of January, 1995—is aimed at helping his supporters break out of the "state of nature."

25. Ibid., 132–133.

26. Piven and Cloward, *Why Americans Don't Vote*, 5, 19.
27. Ibid., 161–162. Mollenkopf finds in New York City that "black and Latino ADs [assembly districts] actually had slightly *higher* rates of registration than the white ADs despite their lower socioeconomic status. This finding goes squarely against the stereotype that minorities do not register. This stereotype is an artifact of the relative youth and lack of citizenship among New York's black and Latino residents"; from "Political Inequality," in *Dual City: Restructuring New York*, ed. John H. Mollenkopf and Manuel Castells (New York: Russell Sage Foundation, 1991), 341–342.
28. Walter Dean Burnham, *Critical Elections and the Mainsprings of American Politics* (New York: W. W. Norton, 1970), 187.
29. Ibid., 90.
30. Piven and Cloward, *Why Americans Don't Vote*, 21.
31. Ibid., 253–254.
32. Ibid., 254.
33. Burnham, "The Turnout Problem," 132; also see Burnham, "The Class Gap," *New Republic*, 9 May 1988, 30.
34. Burnham, "The Turnout Problem," 123. Burnham takes the phrase "permanent campaign" from Sidney Blumenthal, *The Permanent Campaign*, rev. ed. (New York: Simon & Schuster, 1983).
35. Burnham, "The Turnout Problem," 133.
36. Benjamin Ginsberg and Martin Shefter, *Politics by Other Means: The Declining Importance of Elections in American Politics* (New York: Basic Books, 1990), 1.
37. Ibid., 193–194.
38. Burnham, "The Turnout Problem," 133.
39. Burnham, *Critical Elections*, 188–189.

Chapter 15

1. Dahl argues that "Polyarchy III would result from the need to narrow the growing gap that separates policy elites from the demos." He believes telecommunications can play a central role, and that there will always be an "attentive public," not the whole public. Therefore, he also proposes what he calls the idea of "minipopuluses" "consisting of perhaps a thousand citizens randomly selected out of the entire demos," perhaps meeting with the aid of telecommunications to set agendas, deal with major issues, exist on any level of government. They might be aided by experts and they would complement, not replace, elected legislatures; from Robert Dahl, *Democracy and Its Critics* (New Haven, Conn.: Yale Univ. Press, 1989), 338–341. For a critique of Dahl's proposals, see Philip Green, "A Review Essay of Robert A. Dahl, *Democracy and Its Critics*," *Social Theory and Practice* 16 (Summer 1990), 217–241.
2. See Dahl's *After the Revolution?* (New Haven, Conn.: Yale Univ. Press, 1990), ch. 4; and ch. 6 especially, 90–91, this volume.
3. Dahl, *Democracy and Its Critics*, 312–313.
4. See the discussion of Dahl's *After the Revolution?* in this volume, ch. 6, 90, 93, and especially 94–95.

5. Robert A. Dahl, *A Preface to Economic Democracy* (Berkeley: Calif. Univ. Press, 1985), 161–162.
6. Ibid., 57–58.
7. See Robert Dahl, "On Removing Certain Impediments to Democracy in the United States," *Dissent* (Summer 1986), and ch. 6 this volume.
8. Dahl, *Preface to Economic Democracy*, 115, 111.
9. Ibid., 133.
10. Ibid., 76–77.
11. Ibid., 82.
12. Ibid., 82–83.
13. Ibid., 84–85.
14. Ibid., 135.
15. Ibid., 151.
16. Ibid., 160.
17. Ibid., 163.
18. In a footnote in *Democracy and Its Critics*, Dahl repeats earlier criticism of C. Wright Mills's "power elite" thesis; claiming that elite theorists do not "provide much evidence on the chain of control from these elites to the outcomes—for example, beliefs, agendas, or government decisions—over which they presumably dominate." Compare this with Dahl's "test" for Mills, reported in this volume ch. 9, note 37, in which the emphasis is on *decisions*. Here, he uses the looser language of "control" over agendas and beliefs, which raises quiet questions about Dahl's formal definition of power today.
19. Dahl, *Preface to Economic Democracy*, 73.
20. David Held, *Models of Democracy* (Stanford, Calif.: Stanford Univ. Press, 1987), 202.
21. Ibid.
22. Ibid., 205.
23. Ibid.
24. Philip Green, in "A Review Essay," is more critical of Dahl's work, although he too gives Dahl some credit for change: "Telecommunications, workers' control within the confines of existing patterns of ownership and ideologies of consumption, and the creation of 'minipopuluses,' will not revive democracy where it stagnates. Still . . . Dahl continues his attempt to move beyond the confines of his original conception of polyarchy" (240). However, Green sharply criticizes Dahl for not examining race or poverty, and in particular for being "oblivious to the problem that gender poses for political analysis." At various points in his work, however, Dahl does condemn racism, and inequality of economic resources as well (see Dahl, *After the Revolution?*, 111).
25. Peter Bachrach and Aryeh Botwinick, *Power and Empowerment: A Radical Theory of Participatory Democracy* (Philadelphia: Temple Univ. Press, 1992), 50–56. Criticizing the "liberal conception of power," Bachrach charges that "it fails to take into account the possibility that through processes of socialization and manipulation, people's interests can be shaped without their realizing it," and he broadens nondecision-making to include this. Therefore, "A exercises power over B when, in her own interest, she gets B to do something that is contrary to B's interests."

26. Ibid., 14.
27. Peter Bachrach, "Class Struggle and Democracy," *Democracy* 2 (Fall 1982):32. My emphasis.
28. Ibid. My emphasis.
29. Ibid., 33.
30. Ibid., 39.
31. Bachrach and Botwinick, *Power and Empowerment*, 11.
32. Ibid., 17.
33. Against those who seek solutions through redressing economic inequality, based on the idea the participatory structure is itself "class neutral," they claim "the participatory structure itself is class biased . . . is too often perceived by subordinate classes as a system with little meaning for them in their everyday lives"; from ibid., 71–72.
34. Ibid., 162–163.
35. Ibid., 168.
36. Ibid., 137–138.
37. Ibid., 41–42.
38. Ibid., 156–157.
39. Ibid., 163–167.
40. Ibid., 17.
41. Bachrach and Botwinick also criticize Benjamin Barber's *Strong Democracy* for ending "in a whimper," failing to offer any implementation strategy, relegating participatory democracy as did Dahl "to a utopian status"; from Bachrach and Botwinick, *Power and Empowerment*, 116–117.
42. Bachrach and Botwinick, *Power and Empowerment*, 115.
43. See p. 224, this volume.
44. Bachrach and Botwinick, *Power and Empowerment*, 155.
45. Ibid., 162–163.
46. I am thankful to John Buell for encouraging me to probe the notion of cultural hegemony.
47. E. J. Dionne, *Why Americans Hate Politics* (New York: Simon & Schuster, 1991), 334.
48. Ibid., 333–334.
49. Ibid., 354.
50. Ibid., 354–355.
51. Thomas Byrne Edsall with Mary D. Edsall, *Chain Reaction: The Impact of Race, Rights, and Taxes on American Politics* (New York: W. W. Norton, 1991), 282.
52. Ibid., 284.
53. Ibid.
54. Ibid., 286–287.
55. Ibid., 287–288.
56. For discussion of the issue of welfare and resentment, see 197–200 this volume.
57. Writing about Dahl's criteria for polyarchy in *Democracy and Its Critics* (criteria similar to the ones discussed here and in chapter 6 above), Green claims, "Aside from voting equality, none of this is remotely within the realm of possibility in polyarchies as presently constituted, and Dahl is aware of this"; from "A Review Essay," 222.

Conclusion

1. Quoted in Seymour Martin Lipset, *Political Man* (Baltimore: Johns Hopkins Univ. Press, 1981), 310.
2. In discussing what is distinctive about critical social theory as opposed to positivist or interpretive theory, Brian Fay suggests: "the theories of such a science will necessarily be composed of, among other things, an account of how such theories are translatable into action, and this means that the truth or falsity of these theories will be partially determined by whether they are in fact translated into action . . . and if, as a result of the account's not becoming known, the social order develops along lines other than the theory predicted, then the truth of the theory is indeterminate." I would suggest that while critical social theory tries to influence history, all theory that gets a hearing actually may do so and is subject to a partial test in the way Fay suggests. Brian Fay, *Social Theory and Political Practice* (New York: Holmes & Meier, 1976), 95, note 6.
3. See the Introduction to this work, 9–10.
4. Norman R. Luttbeg and Michael M. Gant estimate a 55 percent turnout of the voting age population (VAP) in 1992, up from 51 percent in 1988. See their *American Electoral Behavior 1952–1992*, 2nd edition (Itasca, Ill.: F. E. Peacock Publishers, 1995), 91–95; and note 26, chapter 3, this volume. The 1994 VAP figure is for highest state-wide office and was provided by Ruy Teixeira in a phone interview.
5. Steven J. Rosenstone and John Mark Hansen, *Mobilization, Participation, and Democracy in America* (New York: Macmillan, 1993), 248. My emphasis.
6. Ibid., 241.
7. I do not infer that Burnham or Piven and Cloward would support the way I appropriate their work, although they might (at least in part). It is clear that Teixeira would not in large part. Regarding Dahl's criteria, Philip Green argues that, with the exception of equal votes, they are impossible in the real world and that Dahl knows this (see ch. 15, note 57, in this volume). The question is, will these reforms make them more possible by helping equalize political power?
8. See the discussion in chapter 12, this volume, especially of Lukes, Isaac, and Cocks.
9. Rosenstone and Hansen argue: "Unequal distributions of political resources are not, however, the sole reason for the class inequalities among the politically involved. The class biases in political involvement derive as well from class biases in political mobilization." Stating the main thrust of their explanation of nonparticipation, they suggest that "the strategic choices of political leaders—their determinations of who and when to mobilize—determine the shape of political participation in America," and "Participation in American politics rises and falls with the incentives the system presents to its leaders"; from *Mobilization, Participation, and Democracy*, 238, 36, 229.
10. Ibid., 241.
11. Jürgen Habermas, "Further Reflections on the Public Sphere," in *Habermas and the Public Sphere*, ed. Craig Calhoun (Cambridge, Mass.: MIT Press, 1993), 453.
12. Dahl argued that political scientists "need to give serious and systematic attention to possibilities that may initially seem unrealistic, such as abolishing the presiden-

tial veto; creating a collegial chief executive; institutionalizing adversary processes in policy decisions; establishing an office of advocacy to represent interests not otherwise adequately represented in or before Congress and the administrative agencies, including future generations; creating randomly selected citizen assemblies parallel with the major standing committees of the Congress to analyze policy and make recommendations; creating a unicameral Congress; inaugurating proportional representation and a multiparty system in congressional elections; and many other possibilities"; from Dahl, "On Removing Certain Impediments to Democracy in the United States," *Dissent* (Summer 1978):322–323.

13. Seventy percent is Teixeira's "upper limit" but, he believes, practical goal. See 206 this volume.

14. For a thorough analysis of proportional representation, how it can be applied in the United States, what impact it could have on underrepresentation by race or gender, and what its prospects are here, see Douglas J. Amy, *Real Choices/New Voices: The Case for Proportional Representation Elections in the United States* (New York: Columbia Univ. Press, 1993).

15. See the discussion in this volume, 210–216.

16. The Republicans have already had some success here. In the 1994 election, Newt Gingrich and his allies were able to deliver a cohesive Republican message—their "Contract with America"—supported by party discipline among House Republican candidates. Now in power, they are earnestly following through on it. It will be important to students of political party development to see whether they will be able to effectively do so.

17. For a key Supreme Court decision, see *San Antonio Independent School District v. Rodriguez* 411 U.S. 1, 93 S.Ct. 1278 (1973).

18. See 334–344, this volume. A good argument could be made that the infamous failure of the Clinton health care proposal in 1994 was made possible by its lack of comprehensibility, which, in turn, both made public opinion more manipulable and discouraged potential supporters. Quite aside from the issue of the plan's merits and its ineffective sponsorship, the confusion—some intentionally generated by opponents—did not serve democracy well.

19. Good teachers know how to do this in the classroom, and checks could be built in to make sure various points of view are fairly represented. A model already exists in the Public Broadcasting System, *MacNeil/Lehrer Newshour*, when a panel of five journalists is interviewed to get a cross-section of opinions. However, I would emphasize debate much less than the interviewers do and focus on discussion by a panel of dedicated professionals committed to the pedagogical craft of clarification.

20. While equality created dangers of atomization, isolation, and uniformity, for Tocqueville, these could be countered by regional and local differentiated associations that could contribute to diversity as well as community responsibility.

21. Deborah Rhode suggests that instead of focusing on gender differences in developing strategy and law, we should focus on disadvantages. This is plausible but needs to be developed into a broader principle as to what it means today to be disadvantaged. See Deborah Rhode, *Justice and Gender* (Cambridge, Mass.: Harvard Univ. Press, 1989).

22. Dinesh D'Souza offers a similar suggestion with regard to educational admissions in his book *Illiberal Education: The Politics of Race and Sex on Campus* (New York: Vintage, 1992), 251–253. Perhaps this indicates that some common ground of the kind Dionne seeks between fair-minded liberals and conservatives is possible (although it might mean one of us hasn't fully thought out the implications of such a proposal).

23. John Webber Buell, *Democracy by Other Means: The Politics of Work, Leisure, and the Environment* (Champaign, Ill.: Univ. of Illinois Press, 1995), forthcoming.

24. The desire for a more civil urban existence, for example, is today a quality-of-life concern that almost all urban dwellers share even though the quality of the lives, especially the material quality, may differ radically.

25. Peter F. Drucker, "Trade Lessons from the World Economy," *Foreign Affairs* (Jan./ Feb. 1994), 108. My emphasis.

26. See the discussion of Huntington in chapter 5, especially 87, this volume.

27. See the discussion of Marcuse in chapter 10, 159–162, this volume.

Epilogue

1. On the "undemocratic circumstances" of Americans, see "Gap in Wealth in U.S. Called Widest in West," *New York Times*: April 17, 1995, A1.

2. See Kevin Phillips, *The Politics of Rich and Poor: Wealth and the American Electorate in the Reagan Aftermath* (New York: Random House, 1990) on standard of living. Phillips, Dionne, the Edsalls, and Teixeira all report on discontent with quality of life.

3. I am indebted to Peter Cocks for pressing me to clarify my thoughts on democratic fulfillment.

4. Bharat Trehan, senior economist at the Federal Reserve Bank of San Francisco, asks: "What, then, should one make of the widespread concern about the falling real wage? Our discussion suggests that such concern reflects what is happening to one particular segment of the workforce. . . . the wages of workers with relatively less education are down. . . . the decline seems to be concentrated in industries that were more unionized, that employed relatively more men, and that have been hit harder by foreign competition. . . . [But] [t]he data reveal that relatively high-skilled workers have continued to do well, and the returns to college education have gone up sharply." From *FRBSF Weekly Letter*, Number 91–41, November 22, 1991.

5. See Thomas Byrne Edsall with Mary D. Edsall, *Chain Reaction: The Impact of Race, Rights, and Taxes on American Politics* (New York: W. W. Norton, 1991), 258.

6. See William E. Connolly, *Identity/Difference* (Ithaca, N.Y.: Cornell Univ. Press, 1991), chs. 3 and 6.

7. See Juliet Schor, *The Overworked American: The Unexpected Decline in Leisure Time* (New York: BasicBooks, 1991).

8. Does this mean that democracy abroad will have an ambiguous effect on democracy here? On the one hand, as I suggested in the Conclusion, greater political equality abroad allows greater political freedom at home. On the other, it is likely

to generate a desire for a greater total share of world resources, some of which we now enjoy. This does put pressure on democracy here to the extent it remains tied to a system of endless growth of the production of exclusive goods, and to the extent developing nations see their futures in the same terms.

Index

Adair, Douglass, 255n. 11
Adams, Abigail, 36, 168
Adams, J. Q., 256n. 22
Adams, John, 28, 30, 36, 37, 168
Adorno, Theodor, 154
affirmative action, 167, 186, 199–200, 242
Africa, 23, 254–255n. 5
African Americans, 48, 49, 163–165, 182–
  185; civil society, changes, 167–168; and
  the Constitution, 37; employment, 165; political participation, 2–3, 5, 6, 163–164,
  278n. 27; political power, changes, 164,
  165, 166–167, 168
After the Revolution? (Dahl), 90, 93, 94, 96,
  218
age, and voting, 5, 253n. 16
agency: interpretation and, 186; power and,
  188–190. *See also* subjectivity
Agrippa, 29
Alien and Sedition Acts, 31
alienation, 1, 139, 140. *See also* political alien-
  ation; political apathy
Allgeyer v. Louisiana (1897), 257n. 4
American Federation of Labor, 50
American Politics: The Promise of Disharmony
  (Huntington), 83
American Polity, The (Ladd), 3
Amy, Douglas J., 209, 210, 282n. 14
Anthony, Susan B., 2, 3
Antifederalists, 25–26, 29, 30, 68, 255n. 9
Antifederalists, The (Kenyon, ed.), 256n. 19
apathy. *See* political apathy
Arblaster, Anthony, 254n. 3, 255n. 6
Aristophanes, 23
Aristotle, 22, 23, 59
Aronson, Ronald, 267n. 2
Arrow, Kenneth, 100
Articles of Confederation, 25, 32, 44
Asylums (Goffman), 276n. 15
Athens (Greece). *See* democracy
Australian ballot, 51
authoritarianism, 1, 57, 74
authority, 130, 274n. 26, 275n. 32. *See also*
  power

Bachrach, Peter, 10–11, 12, 14, 76, 96, 97,
  124–132, 170, 217, 223–226, 227, 228, 233;
  behavioralism in, 125–126, 127, 128, 131;
  class struggle, 223–226; class struggle and

Madison, 225; cultural hegemony, 224,
  226–228; Dahl, criticism of, 94, 96, 97, 226;
  democratic leadership, 225; grievances, 125,
  127; interests, 125, 224 (*see also* Bachrach,
  power); interests, real, and participation,
  126, 127, 128–129, 130–131; mobilization
  of bias, structural, 223; nondecision-making, 124–125, 126, 127; political apathy,
  126, 224; political apathy and choice, 128,
  129; political apathy as a condition, 128;
  political apathy, explicated and critiqued,
  127–132; political equality, 127; political
  participation, 126, 127, 223–224, 280n. 33
  (*see also* Bachrach, interests); political participation, and right to participate at work,
  126, 127, 224, 225; power, 124–126, 127,
  279n. 25; power, changes in, 224; transitional theorist, 127
Ball, Terence, 196, 197
Bank of the United States, 30
Baratz, Morton, 124, 125
Barber, Benjamin, 280n. 41
Barry, Brian, critique of rational choice,
  110–111
Beard, Charles, 61
Behavioral Persuasion in Politics, The (Eulau),
  259–260n. 4
behavioralism, 61, 66–69, 73, 75, 108, 112–
  113, 114, 207, 211; "behavioral creed," 66;
  pre-war and post-war difference, 67–68. *See
  also* Eulau
Bell, Daniel, "end of ideology," 57, 73, 160
Bellah, Robert, 37, 39
benefits, expressive, 203–204
Benhabib, Seyla, 149, 154
Bentham, Jeremy, 59, 60
Bentley, Arthur, 61, 260n. 7
Berelson, Bernard, 1, 2, 10, 11, 12, 17, 74, 75,
  77–82, 87, 94, 95, 108, 121, 133, 138, 193,
  261n. 6, 261n. 7; "classical" theory of democracy, 77; political apathy, explicated,
  78; political apathy, critiqued, 78–82
bias of conflict, 47, 122. *See also* conflict;
  Schattschneider
Bill of Rights, 29, 30, 45
binds, political/psychological, 183–187, 195,
  201
Black, Duncan, 100
Blumenthal, Sidney, 210

285